RACE AND WHITE IDENTITY IN
SOUTHERN FICTION

ALSO BY JOHN N. DUVALL

Don DeLillo's Underworld.

The Identifying Fictions of Toni Morrison: Modernist Authenticity and Postmodern Blackness.

Faulkner's Marginal Couple: Invisible, Outlaw, and Unspeakable Communities.

Approaches to Teaching DeLillo's White Noise, edited with Tim Engles.

Faulkner and Postmodernism, edited with Ann J. Abadie.

Productive Postmodernism: Consuming Histories and Cultural Studies, editor.

RACE AND WHITE IDENTITY IN SOUTHERN FICTION
FROM FAULKNER TO MORRISON

John N. Duvall

palgrave
macmillan

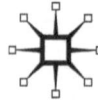

RACE AND WHITE IDENTITY IN SOUTHERN FICTION
Copyright © John N. Duvall, 2008.

Softcover reprint of the hardcover 1st edition 2008 978-1-4039-8387-9

First published in 2008 by
PALGRAVE MACMILLAN™
175 Fifth Avenue, New York, N.Y. 10010 and
Houndmills, Basingstoke, Hampshire, England RG21 6XS.
Companies and representatives throughout the world.

PALGRAVE MACMILLAN is the global academic imprint of the Palgrave Macmillan division of St. Martin's Press, LLC and of Palgrave Macmillan Ltd. Macmillan® is a registered trademark in the United States, United Kingdom and other countries. Palgrave is a registered trademark in the European Union and other countries.

ISBN 978-1-349-53936-9   ISBN 978-0-230-61182-5 (eBook)
DOI 10.1057/9780230611825

Library of Congress Cataloging-in-Publication Data

Duvall, John N. (John Noel), 1956-
   Race and white identity in southern fiction : from Faulkner to Morrison / by John N. Duvall.
     p. cm.
   Includes bibliographical references.
   1. American fiction—Southern States—History and criticism. 2. Whites in literature. 3. American fiction—20th century—History and criticism. 4. Stereotypes (Social psychology) in literature. 5. Ethnicity in literature. 6. Race relations in literature. 7. Literature and society—Southern States. 8. Southern States—Intellectual life—20th century. I. Title.

PS261.D88 2008
813'.509355—dc22   2007040929

A catalogue record of the book is available from the British Library.

Design by Scribe Inc.

First edition: May 2008

10 9 8 7 6 5 4 3 2 1

Transferred to Digital Printing 2009

CONTENTS

Acknowledgments   vii

Preface   White Face, Black Performance   ix

1   Artificial Negroes, White Homelessness,
          and Diaspora Consciousness   1

2   William Faulkner, Whiteface, and Black Identity   17

3   Flannery O'Connor, (G)race, and Colored Identity   63

4   John Barth, Blackface, and Invisible Identity   93

5   Dorothy Allison, "Nigger Trash,"
          and Miscegenated Identity   127

6   Black Writing and Whiteface   145

Notes   169

Works Cited   181

Index   189

Acknowledgments

This project grows out of insights of the many scholars working on whiteness and racial masquerade over the last two decades. When I was first mapping out this book's design, I co-edited a special issue of *Modern Fiction Studies* (Fall 2003) with Nancy Peterson titled "Racechange and the Fictions of Identity." My thanks to Nancy and to all the contributors (particularly Susan Gubar, who graciously added an afterword) for deepening my understanding of the nuances of racial performance.

Thanks also to everyone whose good questions pushed me toward greater clarity, particularly Theron Britt, Deborah Clarke, Anne Goodwyn Jones, Catherine Gunther Kodat, John T. Matthews, Deborah McDowell, Stacey Olster, and Judith Sensibar. My colleagues at Purdue were supportive listeners to my ideas, often recommending things for me to read. In this regard, thanks to Susan Curtis, Wendy Flory, Minrose Gwin, Bob Lamb, Dan Morris, Bill Mullen, Kip Robisch, and Ryan Schneider. In spring 2007, I taught a graduate course, "Moses and Modernism," with Sandor Goodhart that helped crystallize a number of issues regarding cultural appropriation. I'm grateful both to all the students from that course for their conversations about Faulkner, Hurston, and Reed, and to Sandy for his keen insights into the Mosaic tradition. A special thanks to Don Kartiganer for the opportunity to present some of my thinking at the 2007 Faulkner and Yoknapatawpha Conference, "Faulkner's Sexualities." But please don't blame any of these folks if you read something you don't like. I'm the sole proprietor of whatever shortcomings the reader finds in what follows.

My research and writing were aided by a Center for the Humanities Fellowship from the College of Liberal Arts during the fall of 2004, and a sabbatical during the spring of 2005. John Contreni, the Justin S. Morrill Dean of Liberal Arts, and Irwin Weiser, Head of the Department of English, provided additional funding to help me obtain permission to use two of William Faulkner's drawings that are reproduced in Chapter 2. I deeply appreciate all of the generous support from Purdue University.

For over twenty years, my wife, Kathy Schroth, has been, and remains, the reader who best helps me curb my tendency to produce sweaty prose. Her love and friendship make it all worthwhile. Our children—Patrick, Margaret, and John—continue to help me be a bit less full of myself than is my wont.

A portion of Chapter 1 appeared in the *Faulkner Journal* (Fall 2006/Spring 2007) as part of a special issue, "Faulkner and Whiteness," edited by Jay Watson, whose generous queries helped me hone a number of ideas that are in play throughout this study. Portions of Chapter 2 appeared in *A Companion to William Faulkner* (Oxford: Blackwell, 2007), edited by Richard C. Moreland, and in the "Misrecognition, Race, and the Real in Faulkner" issue of *Études Faulknérinnes* (4 [2004]: 39–51), edited by Michael Zeitlin, André Bleikasten, and Nicole Moulinoux. Many thanks to all of these editors and publishers for the opportunity to present my work and for permission to use it here.

PREFACE:
WHITE FACE, BLACK PERFORMANCE

In the latter half of the 1990s, two prominent African Americans from the world of arts and entertainment made startling and basically identical claims about the President of the United States. On the eve of the 1996 presidential election in which William Jefferson Clinton won a second term by defeating Bob Dole, comedian Chris Rock made the following observation on *Saturday Night Live*: "So we got a big election coming up. Who's gonna win? Bill or Bob? Bob or Bill? I like Clinton. Know why I like Clinton? Because he's got real problems. He don't got president problems. He got real problems like you and me, like running out of money, his wife's a pain in the ass, all his friends are going to jail. I know Bill Clinton. I *am* Bill Clinton!" Two years later, Nobel Prize winning author Toni Morrison, tongue in cheek, made explicit what Rock broadly implied:

> African-American men seemed to understand it right away. Years ago, in the middle of the Whitewater investigation, one heard the first murmurs: white skin notwithstanding, this is our first black President. Blacker than any actual black person who could ever be elected in our children's lifetime. After all, Clinton displays almost every trope of blackness: single-parent household, born poor, working-class, saxophone-playing, McDonald's-and-junk-food-loving boy from Arkansas. And when virtually all the African-American Clinton appointees began, one by one, to disappear, when the President's body, his privacy, his unpoliced sexuality became the focus of the persecution, when he was metaphorically seized and body-searched, who could gainsay these black men who knew whereof they spoke? ("Talk" 32)

In 2002, Rock and Morrison's shared conception of Clinton's blackness was institutionalized when Clinton became the first (and so far only) white inductee into the Arkansas Black Hall of Fame.[1]

This outing of Bill Clinton's "black" identity speaks directly to the kind of thinking about racial impersonation and figuration that this study explores. There are two ways of thinking about Clinton's relation to blackness. One could say, dismissively, that Clinton was engaged in a kind of cultural blackface. Such a claim, however, presumes that there is an authentic white southern identity lurking beneath a calculated performance of blackness by the man from Hope, Arkansas. However, such a claim overlooks the reality of Bill Clinton's upbringing. As a poor white who lived among poor blacks, Clinton could never engage in a metaphorical blackface minstrelsy because there was no conscious intent to parody or demean black culture. This leads us to the second way of thinking about Clinton's racial performance. Rather than blackface, Clinton's racial enactment was (and still is) a pastiche performed in whiteface. As president, Clinton projected a white face to America while performing cultural blackness. Or, perhaps more accurately, he performed the culture of impoverished rural Southerners, black and white, where his class difference as "white trash" meant that he was never truly a "white Southerner" in the first place. It is then this whiteface performance that fascinates me because of its potential to generate all sorts of cultural misrecognitions. It is precisely this liminal space of "Caucasian but not White" that is the focus of this study of southern fiction.

As I see it, Bill Clinton's relationship to blackness plays out in the full light of postmodern media culture the masked presence that William Faulkner almost obsessively developed in his modernist fiction from the 1920s to early 1940s. Derived from Faulkner's interest in the clownish figure from French pantomime, Pierrot, this masked presence is, as I will term it, the whiteface minstrel, a kind of artificial Negro who presents a white face to the world, even as he performs cultural blackness. (In the previous sentence, I use the pronoun "he" because, in Faulkner's fiction, this whiteface clown is almost always male.) The strength and power of Faulkner's creation of racially inverted white males create a type that several southern novelists who began publishing after World War II would redeploy in various guises. But, while the ends to which subsequent writers put their whiteface characters differ from those that Faulkner envisioned, both modernist and contemporary versions of whiteface challenge and complicate a southern worldview that, quite literally, would see the world in terms of black and white. I would, therefore, like to make a claim that, in light of Rock's and Morrison's comments, makes perfect sense: America's first black Nobel Laureate wasn't Toni Morrison—it was William Faulkner. Faulkner's blackness, however, is not the result of his embodying stereotypes of blackness. It emerges instead from his imagining a queer realm of white masculine performance that ultimately serves to detach blackness from the southern concept of the Negro.

The way I unpack this claim about Faulkner's blackness is, in part, through Toni Morrison's work on racial figuration in American literature, so that, although the subtitle of my study is "From William Faulkner to Toni Morrison," one could easily reverse the names. Read as printed, the subtitle suggests the historical sweep of my study, which takes up a number novels and short stories written from the 1920s to the 1990s. One might, however, reverse the order of the names ("From Toni Morrison to William Faulkner") to suggest something else—that applying Morrison's critical apparatus to Faulkner allows us to read, as it were, a never-delivered letter from Morrison to Faulkner, one that outlines how and to what extent the creator of Yoknapatapha County (as well as his successors who follow him in the performance of a whiteface minstrelsy) was not just playing *in* the dark, as Morrison has put it, but also playing *as* the dark.

Although I see Faulkner modeling the possibilities for figurative racial transformation for later southern writers in the twentieth century, he does have a notable nineteenth-century precursor in Mark Twain. *Puddn'head Wilson*, for example, stages the potential for whiteface to generate various kinds of social misrecognition. Published in 1894, Twain's satirical farce on southern racial politics takes place between 1830 and 1853, the very period that saw the rise of blackface minstrelsy. Fearing that her master may sell her son down river, the one-sixteenth black slave Roxy switches the white master's baby, Tom, for her one-thirty-second black son, Chambers; hence, the white child grows up a slave, while the "black" child (who is so light-skinned that he easily passes) is raised in the world of white privilege.

In the dizzying performance of race that ensues, the color line is crossed and recrossed innumerable times: the two white-appearing black characters, Roxy and the false Tom, in particular instances, actually don blackface in order to disguise themselves and pass as what they, in fact, are by southern racial law. But even as they blacken up, each engages in a different kind of performance: in chapter 18, Roxy follows Tom, disguised as a black man; in chapter 19, Tom, who has previously robbed various houses disguised as white woman, escapes after murdering his uncle disguised as a black woman. Here, Twain's novel literalizes the way crossings along one coordinate of identity (race) may be implicated in another type of crossing (gender).

But what is of most interest for my study is an exchange between Roxy and the white man who thinks he is her black son. Roxy, who has been freed when her master dies, returns to Dawson's Landing, Missouri, hoping for a small pension from her former master's son (who is really her son). Before she can meet with imposter Tom, the false Chambers informs Roxy that Tom has been disinherited for gambling. What ensues is a conversation in which Roxy and Chambers linguistically stand in for those stock blackface minstrels Tambo and Bones. Roxy begins:

> "Dissen*whiched* him?
> "Dissenhurrit him."
> "What's dat? What do it mean?"
> "Means he busted de will."
> "Bus—ted de will! He wouldn't *ever* treat him so! Take it back, you misable imitation nigger dat I bore in sorrow en tribbilation." (39)

As Eric Sundquist notes, at such moments, Twain is "implicated in the dangerous burden of minstrel humor" ("Mark Twain" 49). Twain, a devotee of the minstrel show, performs his own minstrel riff here, attempting to create humor, as the genre often does, from the malapropisms of his "black" characters. At the same time, Sunquist is also right that Twain "turns [minstrelsy] inside out" (48). False Chambers's response to Roxy's claim that he is an "imitation nigger" points to the reversal: "If I's imitation, what is you? Bofe of us is imitation *white*—dat's what we is—en powerful good imitation too. . . . [W]e don't 'mount to noth'n as imitation *niggers*" (39). For Sundquist, "Roxy, a black in whiteface, and Chambers, presumed to be a black in whiteface, play minstrel roles as 'imitation niggers,' Roxy by law and Chambers ironically by means of Roxy's act of rebellion" (48). But here, my use of the figure that I call "the artificial Negro" differs from Sundquist's. I reserve the term exclusively for racially white characters, such as Chambers, who perform cultural blackness. When it comes to the southern epistemology of race, the tragic (or in Twain's case, the farcical) mulatto finally is not the most subversive figure in the post-reconstruction, pre-civil rights South. Even if light enough to pass, the racially mixed figure still knows he or she is racially mixed, as well as the danger of exposure that attends passing. In other words, such white-appearing blacks still have internalized the oppressive binarism of southern racial politics.

At the conclusion of *Pudd'nhead Wilson*, once Roxy's deception has been discovered, the true Tom is restored to whiteness, but it is a whiteness that is alien and useless, creating an "embarrassing situation":

> He could neither read nor write and his speech was the basest dialect of the negro quarter. His gait, his attitudes, his gestures, his bearing, his laugh—

all were vulgar and uncouth; his manners were the manners of a slave. . . .
The poor fellow could not endure the terrors of the white man's parlor,
and felt at home and at peace nowhere but in the kitchen. The family pew
was a misery to him, yet he could nevermore enter into the solacing refuge
of the "nigger gallery"—that was closed to him for good and all. But we
cannot follow his curious fate further—that would be a long story. (121)

The authors in my study begin where *Pudd'nhead Wilson* ends. The long
story of the character who is racially white but culturally black must wait
for William Faulkner, who will shift the mode of the critical examination
of racial masquerade from farce to tragedy.

If, however, we follow Shelley Fisher Fishkin's sense of Twain's appropriation of the voice of "Sociable Jimmy," a ten-year-old African
American boy Twain met and wrote about in an 1874 essay, we are in fact
much closer to the kind of cultural terrain I see Faulkner and a number of
more contemporary southern novelists inhabiting. For Fishkin, Jimmy's
language forms the basis of Twain's representation of Huck Finn's voice,
"a voice with which Twain would change the shape of American literature" (15): "The cadences and rhythms of Jimmy's speech, his syntax and
diction, his topics of conversation, attitudes, limitations, and his ability to
hold our interest and our trust bear a striking resemblance to those qualities of speech and character that we have come to identify indelibly with
Huck. Both boys are naïve and open, engaging and bright. They are
unpretentious, uninhibited, easily impressed, and unusually loquacious.
They free-associate with remarkable energy and verve" (16).

Although Fishkin thinks that Twain's appropriation may well be
unconscious, Huck serves as an instance of the possibilities that form my
book's focus: the white who, wittingly or not, performs blackness. Huck,
though presented as white, grows out of Twain's encounter with black
culture. The difference between Huck and Chambers is simple:
Chambers, although racially white, believes he is black, is raised as if he
were black, and so enacts cultural blackness; Huck, who is a poor white,
never doubts his whiteness, is raised as a white racist, but performs linguistic blackness.

Despite his whiteface black performance, Huck does not occasion the
kind of social and personal misrecognition that characterizes such white
appropriations in twentieth-century southern fiction. While Huck does
come to experience his whiteness as a site of anxiety, he negotiates that
anxiety in ways that ultimately confirm his whiteness. In the famous passage in which Huck wrestles with his conscience about whether to send the
letter he has written to Miss Watson telling her where Jim, her runaway

slave, is, Huck ultimately decides to *"go* to hell" for the man whose humanity he recognizes:

> It was awful thoughts, and awful words, but they was said. And I let them stay said; and never thought no more about reforming. I shoved the whole thing out of my head; and said I would take up wickedness again, which was in my line, being brung up to it, and the other warn't. And for a starter, I would go to work and steal Jim out of slavery again; and if I could think up anything worse, I would do that, too; because as long as I was in, and in for good, I might as well go the whole hog. (271)

The stable irony that Twain deploys readily allows readers to recognize that, even though Huck can only articulate his ethically superior decision in terms of his failure to conform the his racist upbringing's "correct" sense of blackness, he has actually chosen better than his nurture. It is precisely Twain's stable irony that stabilizes Huck's racial identity, lifting this poor white out of his class background and granting him honorary "southern Whiteness." (Throughout this book, whenever "whiteness" strongly implies something more than simply racial identity [such as class or gender/sexual identity], I will capitalize the word to mark these extra— and typically subliminal—ideological valances.) Ultimately, Huck's mere presence does not cause discomfit in the body social; he is not marked as the abject or the other. At novel's end, Huck may not wish to go home to the white community (indeed he would rather "light out for the Territory" [362]), but it is a home to which he is always welcome. Such welcome is not always offered to those white characters linked to blackness in later southern fiction.

It is, then, to a historically grounded, yet wholly imaginary, sense of a white diaspora that I turn to in Chapter 1 in order to explore the profound sense of homelessness so often found in twentieth-century southern fiction. After detailing more fully the debt I own to previous scholarship on whiteness and ways of reading race as a figure, I turn to some specific class-based instances in "Barn Burning" and *Absalom, Absalom!* to clarify the ways in which Faulkner's whiteface minstrels perform as artificial Negroes.

Chapter 2 expands on my preliminary exploration of William Faulkner's use of blackness as a trope that complicates and often contests whiteness, even as that blackness helps constitute communal white identity. I begin with some explicit moments of self-portraiture in Faulkner's early work, particularly in his second novel, *Mosquitoes*, which addresses the matter of same-sex sexuality more directly than the author's subsequent fiction. I foreground an apparently minor character, a funny "little black man" named "Faulkner," since this character enables a discussion of the ways in which blackness in *Mosquitoes* points not to the otherness of the African American, but rather to contemporary notions of primitive sexuality. If *Mosquitoes* represents a benign version of the little "black" white man, *Sanctuary* imagines a far more sinister version of that figure— Popeye, the short, impotent gangster who rapes Temple Drake with a corncob. As with the character Faulkner, Popeye's nonnormative gender performance forges a link to blackness, which reflexively means that, for Faulkner's white characters, an association with blackness queers their white identity. Faulkner seemed to intuit the ways in which whiteness and heterosexuality served similar policing functions in the patriarchal southern community. His linking blackness to queer possibility becomes a way for his fiction to imagine ruptures in his culture's normative structures of identity.

The ways in which Faulkner's earlier writing explicitly deploys blackness as a form of authorial self-fashioning create a context for understanding how Faulkner uses whiteface in *The Sound and the Fury* and *Go Down, Moses*. Although there are many Faulkner narratives I might scrutinize for their constellation of blackness and the queer performance of white identity or of queer interracial desire, I wish to keep the focus exclusively on those characters who most fully create the deepest social misrecognitions. That is why, for example, I do not explore the racially mixed Charles Bon of *Absalom, Absalom!* and his homoerotic relationship with his half-brother, Henry Sutpen. Bon may be able to pass because of his white face and upbringing, but once those in the white community know he is passing, he can only be a Negro in their eyes.

My omission of a full discussion of the racially (and sexually) indeterminate Joe Christmas from *Light in August* may seem more puzzling. After all, Eric Sundquist has suggested that this novel is a kind of inverted passing narrative since it does not ask how "a black man [can] be a white man, but how . . . a white man [can] be a black man" (*Faulkner* 71). Since Christmas's performance of blackness helps better articulate what is at stake in my sense of the whiteface minstrel, I would like to explain a little more fully why Joe is not central. As I hope to have suggested already, white skin is insufficient to make a white Southerner. To the extent that in chapter 2 of *Light in August*, where the white community of Jefferson cannot initially categorize Joe when he arrives in town, he participates in the paradigm of whiteface inasmuch as he instantiates social misrecognition. But psychologically Joe is a different case. The one thing that Joe does not doubt is his doubt about his racial origin. For Joe to articulate that doubt is effectively to claim blackness. Over and above the one-drop rule of southern racial epistemology, doubt itself (at least about one's whiteness) is sufficient to constitute blackness as an accepted fact of blood. Once the larger community of Jefferson knows Joe's story (that he thinks he might have a parent who is part black), they have no doubt about what to call him. He becomes fixed as the "white nigger." At the moment the community can identify Joe in his "true" racial identity, all possibilities for a whiteface minstrelsy cease. It is only when the white face blocks the conscious recognition of a black performance that both the performer and the audience experience Faulkner's most uncanny exposure of racial politics. By breaking the proscenium arch, as it were, and announcing the information that he knows will cause the white community to pronounce him black, Joe in fact occludes the subversive potential of the whiteface minstrel. By outing himself and becoming the white Negro, Joe may implode the terms of the South's black-white binarism, but only two terms are in play. It is only when Faulkner's characters are unaware that they are performing blackness that this racial binarism explodes and reveals a proliferation of difference. What is subversive about the whiteface minstrel is, quite simply, that his disquieting— because unnamable—black performance occurs at the very heart of white community. Whatever his racial identity, Christmas certainly reveals that the experience of double consciousness is not a function of the amount of melanin in one's skin.

Instead of focusing on Joe Christmas, then, I turn in the remainder of Chapter 2 to Faulkner's racially inflected delineations of Quentin Compson and Isaac McCaslin. Quentin, a sensitive young man who agonizes over his virginity as a failure to enact "appropriate" (that is, heterosexual) masculinity, is the supremely displaced Southerner attending Harvard. On the final day of his life, Quentin is identified as someone who "talks like they do in minstrel shows," in other words, "like a colored man" (*Sound* 120). Quentin's southern accent oddly positions him in the North as a whiteface minstrel. If Faulkner's exploration of minstrel identity gains shades of complexity with Quentin, it in a sense culminates with Isaac McCaslin. Home is so problematic for Isaac McCaslin that he feels he must repudiate it and all his inheritance. However, since his inheritance is nothing less than white southern masculinity itself, Ike is left without a proper identity. This loss leads to his symbolic racial transformation into a black man, a transformation that is fundamentally misunderstood both by the white southern community and by Ike himself.

Taking the otherness of African Americans and mapping it onto the difference of nonheteronormative masculinity, Faulkner finds, in blackness, a central trope for his failed search for a usable white southern male

identity. Written prior to, and published shortly after, America's entry
into World War II, *Go Down, Moses* may be Faulkner's last great experiment with racechange, but the whitefaced artificial Negro persists in the
postwar period. In Flannery O'Connor's fiction, the subject of Chapter
3, the function of figurative blackness shifts from the sexual to the theological. Following this thread of blackness leads to a startling realization:
what O'Connor insists on in her fiction as moments of *grace* are also
always moments of *race*. In a range of O'Connor's stories—including
"Revelation," "Good Country People," and "The Displaced Person"—
dark imagery implies that the general condition of white salvation is
becoming artificially Negro. What one finds is a network of often black-
clad figures—from social misfits to priests—who stand in figurative relationship to the cultural abjection of the southern Negro. But the matter
is more complicated than a simple use of the African American as a figure
of spiritual possibility. As in Faulkner's fiction, O'Connor's presents a
series of portraits of individuals who, although Caucasian, lose their claim
to southern Whiteness in the very moment that their relation to race
becomes visible. At such moments (when these characters often literally
become colored), Whiteness is revealed as idolatry, a false faith that fails
those who believe in it. Central to this chapter are "The Artificial Nigger"
and *Wise Blood*, both of which allegorize the black migration from the
rural South. In the absence of actual African Americans, O'Connor suggests the ways that such poor whites as Mr. Head and Hazel Motes must
leap into the breach and fill the role of the serviceable other. Taken
together, these narratives suggest the interrelated nature of O'Connor's
tropes of the "artificial nigger" and the "new jesus."

Moving from O'Connor's use of artificial Negroes in the service of her
Catholic worldview, I turn in Chapter 4 to a very different kind of postwar writer, that high postmodernist John Barth, who deploys his artificial
Negroes to articulate a nihilist, existentially inflected project. Focusing on
Barth's Maryland trilogy, this chapter begins with *The Floating Opera* to
consider the centrality of the suicide of Todd Andrews's father to elements of masking and minstrelsy throughout Todd's inquiry. When he
discovers his father has hanged himself, Todd notes the way that death
has blackened his father's face and popped his eyes. What this means is
that, as the son of an "artificial Negro," Todd is always shadowed by a
metaphorical blackness that makes it impossible for him to contain minstrelsy within the novel's conclusion, which does authentically portray a
minstrel show. Todd's interactions with African Americans, though relatively minor in the overall narrative, reveal a network of meanings that

suggest Todd has already written himself into a minstrel performance long before he ever steps onto Captain Adam's showboat.

If Todd Andrews is unaware of the origins of his trauma—his secret black identity—Jacob Horner in *The End of the Road* uses that same secret black agency to ground contingent white identity. Todd's father may be figuratively black, but Jake's father figure is African American, the mysterious "Doctor" who orders Jake's treatment. It is from the Doctor that Jake learns mastery through the act of writing. In his second novel, then, Barth creates in Jake a novelist who reveals that the origins of his authority derive from his identification with his black master. If Todd is completely unconscious of his relation to blackness, Jake represents a movement toward consciousness of a black writerly interiority, a consciousness that simultaneously works to contain blackness. Chapter 4 concludes with a brief consideration of *The Sot-Weed Factor* to examine explicit moments of racial passing and misrecognition that circulate around the multiple identities of Henry Burlingame and his multiracial brothers. As mixed-race descendants of a white colonist, Burlingame and his brothers serve to illustrate that whiteness is always a socially conferred distinction, even as Barth works toward his ultimate accommodation with a contingent whiteness.

In Chapter 5, I examine a writer, Dorothy Allison, who manifests a strain of contemporary fiction that has been called "dirty realism."[2] The influences that Allison claims for her fictional practice are almost exclusively African American. Her appropriation of black aesthetics, I argue, anticipates the racechanging implications in her first novel, *Bastard out of Carolina*. Allison's intertextual engagement with Carson McCuller's *The Member of the Wedding* provides a critical purchase on issues of class in the earlier novel; however, Allison's figurative use of blackness encodes racial concerns in her attempt to recover a positive meaning for "white trash." Although this novel of impoverished whites and family violence is largely unconcerned with race, Allison blurs the boundary between "white trash" and "nigger" so that class cannot be thought of apart from race. Despite being the most self-consciously antiracist of the writers in this study, Allison nevertheless draws on a whiteface construction of the artificial Negro as a means of delineating her sexually abused protagonist, Bone Boatwright. Because Bone's birth certificate lists her father as "unknown," it cannot verify her whiteness. In this regard, Bone's metaphorical blackness resonates with Faulkner's racially indeterminate orphan, Joe Christmas.

In the concluding chapter, I shift the focus away from white southern writers and turn to Zora Neale Hurston's *Moses, Man of the Mountain* and Ishmael Reed's *Mumbo Jumbo* in order to consider how whiteface minstrels and artificial Negroes might function in African American fiction and, at the same time, how African American fiction complicates the notion of figurative racial transformation. Since both Hurston and Reed tell versions of the Moses story from Exodus, I triangulate my readings of their novels with one of modernism's most famous re-imaginings of Moses, Sigmund Freud's *Moses and Monotheism*, since it too has a racial subtext linked to Freud's Jewishness. For Hurston, the racechanging possibilities of Moses provide a way to de-essentialize racial categories. Like Freud's Moses, Hurston's is an Egyptian. But while Hurston opens up the Moses narrative to a pan-Africanist perspective, Reed travesties both Hurston and Freud. Hurston may imagine a Moses who is not really racially other coming to model masculinity for her African Americanized Hebrews, but Reed is deeply skeptical about any white performance of blackness being anything but a racist gesture. But even as Reed criticizes whites for appropriating blackness, I investigate what may be at stake in his own appropriation of other writers' words.

CHAPTER 1

ARTIFICIAL NEGROES, WHITE HOMELESSNESS, AND DIASPORA CONSCIOUSNESS

> Identity is always bounded and particular. . . . Nobody ever speaks of a human identity.
>
> Paul Gilroy, *Against Race*

THE RELATIONSHIP TO HOME FOR SO MANY CHARACTERS IN WHITE southern fiction of the twentieth century is deeply troubled. One way to think about their problem might be suggested by a negative inversion of an old saying: the heart is where home is not. These Southerners very sense of self becomes displaced because home becomes more of a concept (whether idealized or reviled) than a physical location. As a result, home repeatedly reveals itself as a dislocation in William Faulkner and Flannery O'Connor. With his sense of southern masculine identity in shambles, Quentin Compson commits suicide in Cambridge, Massachusetts, far from his north Mississippi home; Ike McCaslin flatly refuses to accept his inherited estate because of what he understands to be its history of miscegenation and incest. Perhaps the most supremely displaced person of the many who appear in O'Connor's fiction, Hazel Motes returns from World War II to find that his rural Tennessee home has literally vanished, which forces him to migrate to the city. But one can look beyond Faulkner and O'Connor. In John Barth's first novel, Todd Andrews has lost his family home during the Depression, and lives in a rundown hotel. More dramatically, Walker Percy's Lancelot burns down his restored southern mansion, killing his adulterous wife, and is confined to a mental institution. In Dorothy Allison's *Bastard out of Carolina*, "home" is never a fixed site for Bone Boatwright, since her family moves from house to house. Yet, home becomes that which must be escaped, since the only daddy she knows there repeatedly sexually molests her. All of these characters, in various ways, learn, as Thomas Wolfe's George Webber does, that you can't go home again. Although not immediately obvious, this problem of home and homelessness can be related to the politics of racial difference, which is grounded in a key piece of southern epistemology: whiteness knows itself in distinction to "the Negro."[1]

As white Southerners, all of these authors are aware of the problem of race in their region. Faulkner and O'Connor often feature racial conflict as the engine of their plots, and in the latter part of their careers, risk the position of public intellectual to comment on race in a moderately progressive fashion for whites of their time and place. Dorothy Allison has been an outspoken critic of racism in the white southern working class. But whether or not African Americans figure prominently in specific works, none of the writers in this study misses the figurative potential of blackness. In each of these writers' texts, one finds white characters specifically delineated in relation to blackness. *Race and White Identity in Southern Fiction* is not, then, primarily concerned with these authors' representations of African American characters. Rather, I wish to examine the ways in which these Southerners' most important white characters experience various largely subliminal processes of becoming black. What this study examines, then, is at once these writers' most daring and most problematic engagement with race. This book investigates the ways in which racial otherness constantly returns in southern fiction, even in the very moments when African Americans are barely visible or completely absent. Through figurative blackness, I argue, southern fiction explores a series of imbricated relationships between racial and other forms of otherness, particularly that of gender/sexuality and class. In white southern fiction, a whole range of issues surrounding otherness emerges, if we acknowledge the ways in which being Caucasian is a necessary, but finally insufficient, condition of southern Whiteness.

In Toni Morrison's terms, I examine the ways that white southern writers have been playing in the dark, using blackness to figure certain characters' (and perhaps their own) fantasized relation to otherness. For Morrison, white writers, in a fashion akin to minstrel entertainers, have been able to deploy images of blackness "in order to articulate and imaginatively act out the forbidden in American culture" (*Playing* 66). Morrison's sense of the minstrel possibilities of white writing has been engaged in broader cultural contexts by Eric Lott and Michael Rogin. Lott points out that prior to the Civil War, the Irish found a path to whiteness through blackface (*Love* 94–96), just as Rogin details the way Jewish entertainers in the 1920s, such as Al Jolson, were able to effect their assimilation into American culture—to become "white"—precisely by donning blackface (73–119). The southern writers I examine, however, seem quite different; that is, rather than a way to normalize themselves in white southern culture, they use central white characters (who may be minstrels, but minstrels in whiteface rather than blackface) to underscore the otherness and alienation that results from their fundamental inability to assimilate to the values of their white communities.

My study also draws on Susan Gubar's broad examination of racial impersonation in fiction, film, and poetry—from blackface minstrelsy to African American appropriations of whiteness. Gubar terms all forms of racial metamorphosis in art "racechange," and sees it emerging in the twentieth century as a "crucial trope of high and low, elite and popular culture, one that allowed artists from widely divergent ideological backgrounds to meditate on racial privilege and privation as well as on the disequilibrium of race" (5).

Although Morrison and Gubar have done groundbreaking work, their projects operate within certain boundaries: they almost always identify white writers' engagements with blackness as a problem or a failure. Morrison typically identifies a failure in aesthetic design,[2] while Gubar tends to see the failure in ethical terms. For Gubar, in the last instance, every white appropriation of blackness can only be a net loss in the search for a more ethical understanding of race. In speaking of John Howard Griffin's courageous *Black Like Me*, Gubar concludes, "even the most high-minded, idealistic motivations will not save white impersonators of blackness from violating, appropriating, or compromising black subjectivity in a way that will inevitably rebound against the ethical integrity of whites" (36). In the late 1950s, Griffin, who is implicated in Morrison's sense of blackface performance, took drugs to darken his skin so that he could go undercover to expose the racism of the deep South. His thinly fictionalized reportage of his experiences ranges from threats of violence by whites to his struggle with and acknowledgement of his own previously unrecognized racism. As a result of having written *Black Like Me*, Griffin was ostracized in his hometown and threatened with castration. Fearing for his family's safety, he finally left his home of Mansfield, Texas. Although he had merely been an impersonator passing along the color line, Griffin finds himself so marked by the experience that, willy-nilly, he reproduces the quintessential gesture of the Great Migration—like the African Americans from the rural South, Griffin too must leave home behind to avoid threats of violence.

One pragmatic concern arises from Gubar's position: it is but a small step from identifying certain texts as ethically compromised on racial matters to arguing that, on precisely those grounds, these same texts should be dropped from the curriculum and anthologies. If Gubar finds Griffin (whose commitment to directly confronting white racism is unquestioned) unredeemably compromised, how much more problematic are white southern writers, conflicted about race, whose texts often serve as canvases to work through issues of doubt, guilt, and identity? However useful a starting point Gubar undeniably provides, her broad characterizations of southern fiction's implication in racial masquerade often oversimplifies what is at stake in these writers' fictions. Far from being limited to an isolated moment at the end of *Go Down, Moses*, racechange is in play throughout this novel, to say nothing of Faulkner's work more generally. O'Connor's "The Artificial Nigger" and Barth's *The Floating Opera* might represent such things as racist statuary and blackface minstrelsy, but these are merely figures for a more profound engagement with whiteness that unfolds in the larger instances of racechange in these narratives.[3]

In part, of course, Morrison and Gubar are correct: there are aesthetic and ethical shortcomings to be identified in a white writer's appropriation of blackness. But they may be only half right, because there is also something potentially productive in such appropriations. When I claim that southern novelists' appropriations of blackness have a productive side, I do not mean at the level of mimesis. For the characters in this fiction, their relation to blackness is often confusing, painful, and occasionally fatal. White southern writers use of figurative blackness is literally productive because it allows them a way to map imbricated relations between racial otherness and other forms of otherness, such as gender, sexuality, and class. More importantly, figurative blackness enables readers to see that, whatever residual racism resides in these authors, their narratives negotiate racial struggle even when race seems absent from their field of vision; such narratives, in other words, are racialized in a way that enables a critical purchase on whiteness. And whiteness, it often turns out, is an unrecognized form of class privilege.

To identify those productive moments, I focus less on racism's impact on its victims than "on those who perpetuate it" (Morrison, *Playing* 11). The white southern writers in this study certainly present us with an array of white characters who perpetuate racism. Their means of perpetuating racism varies from unreflective belief in white supremacy to anxious attempts to confront their racialized thoughts. While their fiction often undercuts such racist characters, I am not claiming that these writers are free from racism. One can point to glaring lapses in which these writers validate claims to white southern identity through their statements about African Americans. Faulkner's infamous comment to an interviewer in 1956 about shooting Negroes in the street if it came to a second Civil War comes immediately to mind, as do some of O'Connor's sketches of stereotyped black behavior and racist jokes in her letters to Maryat Lee.[4] What Morrison has said of Faulkner could be as aptly applied to the other authors in this study. Speaking of his ability to gesture toward while simultaneously withholding racial information about his characters, Morrison concludes "I don't care if Faulkner was a racist; I personally don't care, but I am fascinated by what it means to write like this" ("Art" 101). It would be wrong to see these writers as race traitors who anticipated critical whiteness studies, and I proceed with the cautionary words of Mason Stokes regarding what recent studies of whiteness can and cannot do clearly in mind. The danger, he notes, is that too often in seeking a way out of whiteness such studies risk "insulting those who understand through experience the effect of skin color on one's ability to survive American racism" (183) and that the very desire to reinvent whiteness might "solidif[y], in a roundabout way, white privilege" (185).[5]

Nevertheless, I am fascinated by curious instances in white southern fiction of a recurring figurative strategy that complicates the black-white binary of southern racial thinking in the twentieth century. The blackness of the white characters I focus on is always related to their problematic relation to other categories of identity, such as sexuality or class, which helps to make visible the raced nature of their whiteness. Through their creation of in-between Caucasian characters that instantiate blackness, the white southern writers in this study might be said to participate in black culture by embodying it.

I make this assertion following E. Patrick Johnson's interrogation of what is at stake in, to invoke his book's title, "appropriating blackness." For Johnson, blackness is not an essence, but always involves performance. The questions he asks are germane to my study: "What happens when 'blackness' is embodied? What are the cultural, social, and political consequences of that embodiment in a racist society? What is at stake when race or blackness is theorized discursively, and the material reality of the 'black' subject is occluded? Indeed, what happens in those moments when blackness takes on corporeality? Or, alternatively, how are the stakes changed when a 'white' body performs blackness?" (2). For Johnson, "'blackness' does not belong to any one individual or group. Rather, individuals or groups *appropriate* this complex and nuanced racial signifier in order to circumscribe its boundaries or to exclude other individuals or groups"

(2–3). Johnson is fully aware of the dangers of stereotypes and fetishization that can accompany white appropriations of blackness, such as the linguistic appropriation of white rappers. What Johnson is willing to imagine (in ways that Gubar seems less able to) is that "cross-cultural appropriation of blackness" need not result only in "colonization and subjugation," and that it may, in fact, "provide fertile ground on which to formulate new epistemologies of self and Other" (6).[6]

It is in Johnson's spirit of inquiry that I pursue the figurative blackness of so many white characters in white southern fiction. White writers who appropriate blackness do so *not simply* as a fetishistic gesture ultimately in service of white hegemony. When I write "not simply," though, I mean it in a double-voiced sense as "not only or exclusively" and "not in a simple fashion." In other words, even to the extent that these writers may be implicated in fetishistic appropriation, both their constructions and their effects are complex, never simple.

I should be clear from the outset that not every whiteface act of passing in southern fiction disrupts the racial imaginary. In Harper Lee's *To Kill a Mockingbird*, for example, the performance of Dolphus Raymond merely confirms the racial binarism of the South. Raymond is a white man from a prominent family who has lost his claim to full southern Whiteness because he consorts with African Americans, lives with a black woman, and has fathered mixed raced children whom he acknowledges. He has disgraced himself racially, the white community presumes, because of his alcoholism, since he is always seen in public drinking from a bottle in a brown paper bag and walking unsteadily. In chapter 20, however, Raymond reveals to Dill and Scout that there's never anything in his bottle except soda. Raymond is trying to explain to Dill, a young boy upset with the prosecutor's treatment of the African American Tom Robinson during his trial, the force of southern racial prejudice. Raymond explains that he stages his performance of degenerate whiteness in order to give his white southern community a convenient narrative that allows it to explain away his behavior. Raymond essentially smoothes over any gap in the social fabric by his pretense; his act might allow him to lead the life he wants, but his association with black people in no way discomfits southern racial ideology. In other words, Raymond's whiteface performance does not make him figuratively black; he remains *Mr. Dolphus* to the children, this retaining the honorific unavailable to an African American male in the pre-civil rights South. The whiteface minstrels I am interested in are not masters of their theatricality as Raymond is, and their performances, in fact, open spaces in southern racial politics that leave the white community vaguely aware that there's something peculiar going on.

This figurative blackness that I am referring to I have already identified as whiteface minstrelsy, but we might also name it by borrowing from the title of one of Flannery O'Connor's well-known stories, "The Artificial Nigger," a narrative I will examine in Chapter 3. When I speak of "artificial Negroes," I mean Caucasian characters who have "blackened up," not in any physical sense, but rather in ways that are not immediately obvious, either to their white communities or to the characters (or perhaps even to the authors) themselves. The reason these racial crossings are opaque is because they are never as simple as the external transformation from white to black occasioned by blackface minstrelsy. In other words, there is no visible sign of their blackness. The white characters I examine do not parody, but rather internalize and perform blackness, almost always unconsciously and/or unwillingly. Despite varying degrees of individual and communal awareness, these white characters, as a result of their "blackness," often find themselves alienated from their white communities in ways that suggest that they reproduce elements of African American subjectivity. In other words, they're "black" but do not know it, or, if they suspect, they do not seem to comprehend fully what it means. I put "black" here in quotation marks because, clearly, these characters are represented as being unambiguously racially white. Their blackness, then, is not precisely race, but what came to be the twentieth-century's substitute for race—culture. Southern fiction is full of characters that are racially white, but culturally black. All of the multiple misrecognitions of the artificial Negroes in this study create something that is analogous to, yet distinct from, the experience of the racial passer. Like such Harlem Renaissance writers as James Weldon Johnson and Nella Larsen, the white writers I examine explore the matter of self-definition through the notion of hybridity inherent to passing characters.

Walter Benn Michaels has interrogated the paradoxical role of passing in instantiating racialized discourse. While Michaels is aware that "the concept of black or white blood has no biological currency," he is equally aware of its lingering social power as a metaphor: "since it is possible to pass only because that thing is already invisible (which is to say that no physical alteration is required for it to be concealed), then, on this account, passing is less a matter of hiding something than of refusing or failing to acknowledge something. . . . If, in other words, you are invisibly black, either you must find some way to represent your blackness or you must pass for white" (234–35). Even though Michaels is speaking of individuals who, by the southern one-drop rule, would be juridically black, his characterization of the matter speaks almost directly to the white characters examined in *Race and White Identity in Southern Fiction*. Like the racial passer, the white characters examined here are "invisibly black," that is, their performance of whiteness is so terribly wrong that they end up playing a role that the southern community would have no problem understanding if they were visibly black. They become artificial Negroes, then, not because they are in blackface but because they are, quite literally, in whiteface: their white faces either render invisible their black psychological interiority or mask their abject class position. For Michaels, "the discourse of race is the discourse of people who can pass but who do not wish to" (235). The fiction I examine opens the unconscious of southern racial discourse by depicting characters who should not have to pass (after all, they are racially white), who nevertheless do pass, but who do not know they do. Unlike the racial passer, then, the artificial Negroes of this study fail to recognize their acts as instantiating a racialized transformation; in fact, the idea of losing their whiteness or of crossing the color line into blackness would be deeply disturbing to them.

One of the ways we might begin to speak of the complexity that emerges when white Southerners begin to reproduce black subjectivity is in relation to the concept of diaspora. African Americans who migrated from the South are doubly diasporic. First, as the descendants of slaves forced to leave their homeland, they constitute an African diaspora. But after generations of living in the American South, those blacks who participated in the Great Migration also experienced a more immediate and personal relation to diaspora. At the beginning of the 1890s, the decade Faulkner was born, 90 percent of African Americans lived in the South; by the 1960s, the decade Faulkner died, only 10 percent of the African American population lived in the South. Forced by the threat of lynching and other violence to leave the only home they knew, these black migrants experienced a southern diasporic identity. The sense of home they carry with them to their new locations creates a second order "historical rift between the locations of residence and the locations of belonging" (Gilroy 124).

It is precisely the southern diaspora constituted by the Great Migration that, in a profoundly ironic way, turns back on the very white racist culture responsible for the intolerable conditions that caused blacks to leave the South. One group to bear the brunt of black migration is the poor white. I am not suggesting that the construct "white trash" emerges at the time of the Great Migration; the poor white as the socially abject was already part of antebellum culture. Rather, the Migration further blurs the boundary between "nigger" and "white trash." Even when remaining on the land as sharecroppers, Faulkner's poor whites become so alienated from home as to be, in a sense, homeless. Perversely, in a kind of mirrored fashion to black displacement, these homeless whites experience identity in diasporic fashion as locationless, hybrid, and uncomfortably mixed. This hybridity is most often represented through racechange, in which their whiteness is simultaneously knowable and unhinged by a figurative relation to blackness.

Doubtless my claim linking diaspora and whiteness will strike many readers as wrongheaded at best and at worst as openly blaspheming the work of postcolonial scholars. The concept of diaspora, quite simply would only seem to be usable in relation to oppressed, displaced peoples. As Paul Gilroy notes, "Slavery, pogroms, indenture, genocide, and other unnameable terrors have all figured in the constitution of diasporas and the reproduction of diaspora consciousness in which identity is focused, less on the equalizing, pre-democratic force of sovereign territory and more on the social dynamics of remembrance and commemoration defined by a strong sense of the dangers involved in forgetting the location of origin and the tearful process of dispersal" (123–24). How could whites, then, possibly participate in such consciousness?

If white identity knows itself in relation to the foil of blackness, what happens when African Americans migrated from the rural South to escape its violent racism? In terms of southern epistemology, there became a need for someone to stand in for the useful category of the vanishing rural Negro. This need is doubled in the realm of economics. If, during the violence of the post-Reconstruction South, rural black workers leave for Harlem, the Midwest, the Southwest, or even the urban South, what do large landowners need? In the absence of black farmworkers emerges the economic need (every bit as much as in epistemology) for artificial Negroes.

The subject position of the sharecropper is perhaps the most obvious one in which black and white bodies inhabit an identical economic subject position. As John Egerton succinctly summarizes it:

> To be a sharecropper or tenant farmer in the South in 1932 was to be caught up in an existence that often was nothing more than peonage or forced labor—just one step removed from slavery. You rented the land from its owner, and made the crop for him with his furnish of seed and fertilizer and mules and tools; he sold you food and other necessities on credit at high interest in his commissary; he kept the books, handled the sales, and divided with you at harvest time. You were lucky if you broke even; some went in the hole, and not one in ten actually came away with a few dollars profit. (20–21)

Faulkner certainly knew about black and white tenant farmers, individuals he had seen since childhood shopping on Saturdays in Oxford, Mississippi. By 1910, approximately two-thirds of all farmers in Lafayette County worked in the tenant system: 80 percent of black farmers and 54 percent of white farmers (Doyle 307). Nevertheless, despite the shared conditions of existence, attempts to unionize tenant farmers met with limited success precisely because of the barrier of race.[7] This same barrier often prevents Faulkner's poor white characters from fully recognizing the ways in which they enact blackness.

In *Absalom, Absalom!* Thomas Sutpen begins his young life as a displaced person, a migrant from his mountain home in (West) Virginia, who comes to see that his being Caucasian is a necessary but insufficient condition to enjoying the status of southern Whiteness. Although sharecropping emerges as a major form of African American farm labor after the Civil War, white tenant farmers did form part of the antebellum South's landscape, and while it is not clear that Sutpen's family worked as tenant farmers on the Pettibone plantation, Faulkner does make clear that his family served as the progenitors of future white sharecroppers. Insulted when a black servant turns him away from the front door of the plantation house, young Sutpen discovers he is raced as much as he is classed; identity ceases to be unmarked. Retreating into a cave, the young Sutpen begins to see how the plantation owner views poor whites such as his family: "as cattle, creatures heavy and without grace, brutely evacuated into a world without hope or purpose for them, who would in turn spawn with brutish and vicious prolixity, populate, double treble and compound, fill space and earth with *a race* whose future would be a succession of cut-down and patched and made-over garments bought on exorbitant credit" (190, emphasis added). When he emerges from this cave, Sutpen is reborn into a strange, newly raced world. Still visibly "white" (after all, his skin color has not changed), he is simultaneously not-white because he no longer enjoys the primary marker of whiteness, which is an experience of the self as unmarked by race. If this is in a sense Sutpen's primal scene, it is also the primal scene of the southern political imaginary: the reification of class as race. The boy now feels himself to be a member of a race apart (one that is subhuman, passing its deserved poverty genetically to its offspring) and, in that regard, difficult to distinguish from the black slave. Both the poor white and the African American are denied humanity by southern Whiteness; indeed, both groups are identified as animals. Beginning as a Caucasian animal, Sutpen seeks nothing less than a species change (from animal to southern white) through his design of land and family.

As a result of this self-consciousness of himself as a member of an oppressed and displaced race, his subsequent southern Whiteness is always performance. As Mr. Compson puts it: "He was like John L. Sullivan having taught himself painfully and tediously to do the schottische, having drilled himself and drilled himself in secret until he now believed it no longer necessary to count the music's beat, say. He may have believed that your grandfather or Judge Benbow might have done it a little more effortlessly than he, but he would not have believed that anyone could have beat him in knowing when to do it and how"(34–35).

While it certainly makes sense to speak of Sutpen's performance of himself as a kind of class passing, class has been reimagined as race, and, as a result, Sutpen has a heightened sense of the danger of racial mixing. This marking of class as race is elsewhere represented by another more literal form of entertainment he provides when he himself owns a plantation, a performance that confuses other white men because they would not do what he does. Sutpen's fighting his slaves becomes a way of denying that he was ever a member of a subhuman race, even as his direct physical contact with blacks (a figurative mixing of the races) points to their metaphorical kinship as the "other" of southern Whiteness.

The complexity of figurative racechange, however, becomes more explicit in "Barn Burning" (1939), where Faulkner imagines another poor white, Abner Snopes, who has a more developed understanding of the interchangeability of "white trash" and "nigger." Once again, class analysis is so coded in relation to figurative blackness that it instantiates a kind of racechanged, minstrel performance of whiteness.

I wish to juxtapose Faulkner's short story with one by another native Mississippian, Richard Wright, because together they underscore the economic slavery experienced by black and white sharecroppers alike. Wright's "The Man Who Was Almost a Man" (1940) also helps us better recognize the performativity of Faulknerian racechange. In Wright's story, Dave Sanders, a seventeen-year-old black male, the son of a sharecropper, suffers at the outset from a sense that, despite performing the labor of man, he is not acknowledged as one in his community. In an effort to gain respect, he buys a gun with which he accidentally shoots the white landowner's mule.[8] When the truth of the accident is revealed to the gathered crowd, Dave receives only ridicule, and the landowner demands fifty dollars for the mule, which Dave will be required to work off at the rate of two dollars a month (or 100 percent of his wages for the next two years). In thinking the gun will grant him respect, Dave fails to realize that manhood is simply not available to the African American male in his southern community. Throughout the story, Dave is addressed by every character as "boy," which points to the fact that any African American male of any age could be hailed by this demeaning designation, since the honorific "mister" was never used to address a black man. At the end of the story, Dave has a dawning, if unarticulated, moment of class consciousness in which he wishes he had another bullet so that he might take a shot at the landowner's big white house before he begins his personal migration to the North. But when the Daves of the South leave home, somebody still has to do the work.

Faulkner's "Barn Burning" might have been titled "The Boy Who Was Almost a White Boy." As both Richard Godden (126) and Matthew Lessig (82) argue, although this story is set in the 1890s, it is in fact informed by Faulkner's understanding of the struggles of sharecroppers in the 1930s. From the outset, the nomadic, sharecropping Snopes family embodies a kind of pastiche of the diaspora consciousness that one associates with the African American experience. The class lesson that Abner Snopes tries to teach his son Sarty in Faulkner's "Barn Burning" is uncannily similar to the one Dave begins to learn. Like Dave, Ab is under a judgment—Dave, if he remains, must pay the landowner for a dead mule; Ab must pay the landowner, Major de Spain, for a rug he has intentionally ruined. Both chose flight, coupled with violence against the landowner. Dave's violence is unrealized for lack of another bullet, but Ab burns barns. If Dave's education begins with his attempt to advance an assertion: "Ahm gettin t be a man like anybody else!" (12), Abner similarly prefaces his lesson to his son: "You're getting to be a man. You got to learn. You got to learn to stick to your own blood or you ain't going to have any blood to stick to you" (8). Based on an essentialist notion of clan-based identity, Ab's bloodpride opposes the pride in lineage of the southern aristocracy, while also marking an absolute line that separates poor whites from black blood. The lessons Abner teaches are uncomfortable both to the boy and to the reader because, though they are correct in terms of class analysis, their articulation is virulently racist. Forced to move to a new tenant home, Ab requires his youngest son to accompany him to the big house, saying: "I reckon I'll have a word with the man that aims to begin to-morrow owning me body and soul for the next eight months" (9). This certainly articulates Ab's understanding that the sharecropper's marginalized existence is a form of economic slavery. After the visit in which Ab stains de Spain's rug with manure, he asks Sarty to turn and look at the plantation owner's house: "'Pretty and white, ain't it?' he said. 'That's sweat. Nigger sweat. Maybe it ain't white enough yet to suit him. Maybe he wants to mix some white sweat with it'" (12). In a fashion that anticipates Ralph Ellison's invisible man and his experience at the

Liberty paint factory, where ten black drops are the special ingredient that makes their white paint so very white, Ab's reading of the white house (in which appropriated African American labor is figuratively what coats de Spain's mansion) correctly sees that his own and other white sharecropper's labor (sweat) is identical to exploited black labor. Clearly, Ab's racism is the only thing that prevents him from fully recognizing that he in fact is an artificial Negro. The sticking point, of course, is the label "nigger." It is the name Abner uses to address the elderly black servant who attempts to block his entrance into the big white house. But the servant has already marked Ab's status in saying "Wipe yo foots, white man, fo you come in here" (11). In the black man's eyes, Ab clearly falls beneath the necessity of addressing him as "sir" or "mister." In other words, Ab may be Caucasian, but falls short of southern Whiteness. Just as the unnamed black servant in *Absalom, Absalom!* initiates young Sutpen's dawning awareness that he is not fully white by turning him away from the planter's front door, it is another unnamed African American in "Barn Burning" who serves as the agent denying Abner his putative racial identity.

As Godden has pointed out, everything about Ab is associated with blackness—his black hat and frockcoat, but most particularly, his relationship with fire. Faulkner's repeated use of the term "niggard" to describe the fire that Ab burns for his family serves as wordplay that points toward, even as its etymological difference deflects attention away from, "nigger" (Godden 127–28).[9] To Godden's analysis, I would add another possibility of Ab's blackness. In the initial courtroom scene in which Harris testifies against Ab, he tells the court that Ab sent a "strange nigger" with a dollar pound fee to collect the Snopes's roaming hog, with a warning that "wood and hay kin burn."[10] But what has become of this African American? This is certainly a question the judge wants to know: "Where is the nigger? Have you got him?" Harris replies, "He was a strange nigger, I tell you. I don't know what became of him"(6).

Too much of what is not stated about this individual who is identified as African American does not quite hold together. Is he a stranger or, as the locution seems to suggest, odd or unusual? The plaintiff, Harris, would likely know by sight most of the black people who lived and worked near him. African American males who were strangers would have been viewed suspiciously by the white community. And what African American would do a favor for Ab? Perhaps a local black man who feared Ab's retaliation, but Ab clearly does not socialize with blacks. How likely would Ab be to trust an African American with a dollar, especially one who might be simply passing through and therefore would not be around to intimidate later?

I wish to suggest that the story's "strange nigger" is actually in the store where the hearing takes place and is the very figure of the man in black, Ab Snopes. Since almost the only person Ab would trust with a dollar is himself (or close kin), it seems plausible that Ab (or perhaps his eldest son) blackened up in order to collect his hog and deliver his warning in person without being recognized. Two objections might be raised to my suggestion of a blackface Ab—one logical and one textual. An immediate objection might be that surely Harris would recognize such a ruse and would be immediately able to distinguish an artificial from an authentic black. But as Eric Lott has pointed out, audiences of minstrel shows in the nineteenth century often were completely fooled by the racial masquerade and assumed that the performers who entertained them were actually black (*Love* 20). A more text-based objection might argue that my assertion is undercut by Sarty's question and comment when he realizes his father intends to burn de Spain's barn: "'Ain't you going to even send a nigger?' he cried. 'At least you sent a nigger before'" (21). However, the detail of the black man carrying a warning is one that Sarty more likely learned about from Harris's testimony, since it is only after the trial that Ab begins to include his youngest son in his plans. Sarty effectively knows no more about the identity of the "strange" black than the reader, and his question in no way proves that he had first-hand knowledge about his father actually sending a racially black messenger to Harris.

If Ab is "black," what finally is Sarty? Following metaphorically the one-drop rule of southern race, Sarty too must be figuratively black. Whether or not one believes that the "strange nigger" is Ab in blackface, in the symbolic logic of the story's second instance of barn burning, Sarty effectively becomes the "strange nigger" who warns de Spain that barns can burn. This strange status is signaled by Sarty's full name, Colonel Sartoris Snopes. Ab might ironically name his son (a gesture that says "the landowner class might appropriate my labor but I can appropriate their names and titles") but that does' not keep Sarty's name from implying a form of miscegenation, inasmuch as the names of many of the African American characters in Faulkner's fiction bear the same names as those that circulate in the aristocratic white families to which they're related. When Sarty escapes to warn de Spain, he does so in attempt to reshape his filiation. He believes he is acting with the discernment of a white man in choosing honor and justice, but just as Dave (who sought a means of claiming manhood through the southern code of gun ownership) remains "boy" throughout Wright's story, Sarty is still only "boy" at the conclusion of Faulkner's story. Sarty's entire exchange with de Spain is rendered as follows:

> "Barn!" he cried. "Barn!"
> "What?" the white man said. "Barn?"
> "Yes!" the boy cried. "Barn!"
> "Catch him!" the white man shouted. (23)

What is striking in this twenty-word passage is the narrator's overt marking of Major de Spain's whiteness, not once, but twice. Sarty and de Spain are racially Caucasian, yet only one of them, the southern aristocrat, is fully white. From his privileged position of whiteness, de Spain fails to acknowledge or even register Sarty's commitment to the aristocracy's sense of itself as the embodiment of honor and noblesse oblige. Sarty is merely something to catch and hold accountable. Eeny, meeny, miny, moe. But they cannot catch this artificial black, and Sarty, much like the earlier "strange nigger," disappears from both his family's and de Spain's spheres of influence; in ways that anticipate O'Connor's poor whites (though without O'Connor's insistence on this racialized moment as an instance of grace), Sarty, utterly adrift at the story's conclusion, is a displaced person who makes clear that whiteness is not a racial essence, but is linked to, and limited by, class. There is an important difference to register between Sarty's and Abner's relation to blackness. By literally blacking up, Ab appropriates blackness as a protective strategy; he is a kind of blackface minstrel. Sarty, however, is not conscious of becoming black. Instead, he is appropriated by blackness. To the extent that he represents the racechanged figure, Sarty becomes something more transgressive because his transformation is invisible both to himself and his culture: he performs cultural blackness in whiteface. In the chapters that follow, my emphasis will be on characters like Sarty who have unwittingly become black, even as they present a white face to the world.

On the one hand, the lives of white sharecroppers suggest a form of economic indenture and nomadic movement that resonate with diaspora; even their offspring who end up in urban areas embody displacement, as Dorothy Allison's fiction suggests. But on the other hand, what one repeatedly sees in southern fiction is that privileged whites—the landowners in Faulkner and O'Connor; the upper-middle class of Barth—also experience home as a dislocation. Complicit with the conditions that cause the black diaspora, these privileged whites find their senses of home disintegrate; if not a literal dispersal and scattering, there is a psychological one. In short, the Great Migration changes things, con-stituting the dislocation of southern culture. When I use the term "white diaspora," then, I am neither referring to a historical phenomenon nor reducing black victimization and white victimizing to an irreducible sameness; rather, I am teasing out a textual strategy employed by white southern authors to image forth the complications of white identity in a way that, like Gilroy's sense of diaspora, "offers a ready alternative to the stern discipline of primordial kinship and rooted belonging" (123).

As Gilroy argues, the concept of diaspora allows for a reconfiguration of identity that challenges the notion of identity as "latent destiny" (104) that results when identity is conceived in terms of one's relation to the land (the South as region) or of one's blood (inescapable biological imperative). Certainly, sectional pride in the post-Reconstruction South is a subject of which southern writers are quite aware, and this forms the basis of one kind of identity, just as a sense of identity based on kinship and clan reverberates throughout southern fiction. From Faulkner's crit-ical discussion of "the old fierce pull of blood" (3) in "Barn Burning" to Enoch Emery's belief that he has "wise blood like his daddy" (79) in O'Connor's *Wise Blood*, an often skeptically treated belief in the notion that "blood tells"—a belief that identity is a hereditary essence—moves through the pages of southern fiction. This is why the concept of diaspora holds out so much promise for the study of white southern literature. Even though there never was literally a white diaspora (beyond the migra-tion of landless white farm labor to urban areas), as a figure, the notion of a white diaspora allows for a different purchase on southern culture by deterritorializing and de-essentializing whiteness, which ultimately grants us a better purchase on the immensely powerful social fiction that is racial identity.

WILLIAM FAULKNER, WHITEFACE, AND BLACK IDENTITY

DESPITE THE ASSERTIONS OF MANY RACIST CHARACTERS IN Yoknapatawpha County, William Faulkner's fiction repeatedly illustrates that race is not a simple matter of essence or biology but is always mediated by performance. Faulkner particularly makes visible an opening between racial and cultural identity through certain reflections on the racist construct "nigger." During his year at Harvard, Quentin Compson comes to realize that "a nigger is not a person so much as a form of behavior" (*Sound* 86). In *Go Down, Moses*, we see a trickster figure, Lucas Beauchamp, who, when the need arises, can manipulate threats from the white world by becoming "not Negro but nigger, not secret so much as impenetrable," who masks his intelligence "in an aura of timeless and stupid impassivity almost like a smell" (58). But if Faulkner opens a space between black performance and racial essence through the depiction of certain African American characters, he is equally aware that not all Caucasians are fully white in a South that wishes to absolutize all racial difference. While Faulkner's fictional world portrays a dizzying variety of masking (whites in blackface, blacks in blackface, whites in whiteface, and blacks in whiteface), what I wish to emphasize here is the performativity of white racial identity in Faulkner, deriving from his figurative use of theatrical minstrelsy; however, it is not primarily American blackface minstrelsy that is Faulkner's frame of reference, but rather an older European whiteface minstrel tradition. My focus on white performances of blackness is intended to articulate the challenge in Faulkner's texts to that piece of southern racial thinking that simply opposed whiteness to "the Negro."

In order to suggest how crucial whiteface minstrelsy was to Faulkner's understanding of his artistic identity as in some sense inescapably black, this chapter is structured in three roughly chronological movements. Beginning with some of the author's earliest writing, in which race, per se, plays little or no part but where the figurative blackness is clearest, I then turn to some of Faulkner's best-known modernist work, which does address race but in which the secret black identity of his white characters has become less immediately visible.

"WHY ARE YOU SO BLACK?" WHITEFACE MINSTRELS, PRIMITIVISM, AND PERVERSION

While Joseph Blotner has laid out connections between the characters in *Mosquitoes* and their probable real-life counterparts (*Faulkner* 514–17), the novel is more than a *roman à clef* of the New Orleans literati. Long derided as one of William Faulkner's weaker efforts, his second novel has undergone a decided resurgence of critical interest since the 1990s, largely thanks to the work of feminist scholars who have shown how significant this novel's engagement with matters of gender and sexuality is to Faulkner's subsequent development as an artist.[1] *Mosquitoes*, we now know, openly portrays sexual multiplicity and dissonances in a fashion that the later Faulkner tends to address more obliquely.

In the novel Mrs. Maurier, an aging New Orleans socialite and self-styled patron of the arts, puts together a yachting party, imagining it will be an occasion for several day trips filled with uplifting conversation about the arts. Her plans go awry, however, when the *Nausikaa* runs aground the first night out. Many of the conversations over the next three days do center on the production of art, but they are far from the respectable and conventional sentiments Mrs. Maurier hopes to have confirmed. In addition to her nephew and niece, Theodore (Josh) and Patricia Robyn, Mrs. Maurier's party consists of a small artistic band—the poets Mark Frost and Eva Wiseman (accompanied by her brother Julius); the painter, Dorothy Jameson; the novelist, Dawson Fairchild; the sculptor, Gordon; and the aesthete, Ernest Talliaferro—as well as a British entrepreneur, Major Ayres, and a working-class couple, the voluptuous Jenny Steinbauer and her bootlegger boyfriend, Pete, whom Patricia meets the morning the trip begins and impulsively invites to come along.

Faulkner's material often has the feel of a Noel Coward farce. Gordon is attracted to Patricia; Patricia is attracted to Gordon's art, but tries to run off to Mandeville with the boat's steward; Ernest ineffectually seeks to seduce Jenny; Dorothy desperately tries to seduce Pete, Mark, and Josh; Pete tries to kiss Patricia; Patricia shares a bunk one evening with a naked Jenny; Eva is interested in Jenny; Major Ayres asks Jenny to run off to Mandeville for a tryst; Josh and Jenny have a petting session; and Ernest accidentally ends up in Mrs. Maurier's bed. None of the shipboard romance is consummated, and the only sex act occurs after the trip when Gordon goes to a whorehouse in New Orleans.

From my brief description of Faulkner's novel, it is easy to see why the recent critical conversation about *Mosquitoes* has focused on matters of gender and sexuality. Race, however, is entirely absent from this sophisticated discussion. And with apparent good reason. Race seems to fall outside of *Mosquitoes*'s field of vision. African American characters in the novel's portrayal of New Orleans and the four-day excursion on Lake Pontchartrain are so minor as to be merely decorative. And yet race, I wish to argue, is actually quite important to the novel through recurring figurations of blackness, figurations that provide one of the earliest indications of the imbricated relation between racial and sexual otherness that would come to characterize Faulkner's major fiction. In Faulkner's second novel, blackness, artistic production, and non-normative sexuality all meet in a strange hall of mirrors in which the novelist appears to be everywhere (and thus finally nowhere) in the text.

Philip Weinstein, writing about Faulkner's depiction of African Americans, quite reasonably claims that, although the author's black characters are crucial for understanding whiteness, they are "largely deprived by the narrative of interior voice, of point of view, of a sense of their own past and future (their memories and desires)"; as a result, Faulkner's "blacks . . . are truncated figures" (*Faulkner's* 44). While not wishing to gainsay the correctness of this assertion about Yoknapatawpha's blacks of African descent, I would nevertheless argue that Weinstein's point becomes less transparent if one acknowledges that not all of Faulkner's black lives are lived by African Americans. These other black figures (Caucasians tropologically linked to blackness), whose inner lives are fully and complexly rendered, and whose identities emerge precisely through a struggle with history, suggest that blackness may be more crucial to an understanding of Faulkner's white southern masculinity than has been previously imagined.[2]

Even before Faulkner turned to fiction, his early work gives strong indications of the black presence shadowing his conception of the white artist. In particular, his use of the Pierrot figure, as Judith Sensibar has pointed out, over and above the contemporary vogue of Pierrot poems, was deeply personal and spoke to a sense of the self as a multiplicity rather than an identity: "Pierrot's paralyzing duality of vision, his doubleness, was something Faulkner recognized. It sprang from a dilemma almost eerily familiar. Pierrot was Faulkner's fictional representation of his fragmented state. In pretending simultaneously to be the wounded war hero, the great airman, the British dandy, the poet-aesthete, and the tramp, Faulkner too was playing forms of Pierrot" (Introduction xvii).

Building on Sensibar's biographical characterization of Faulkner's Pierrot, I would add a consideration of racial masquerade and minstrelsy. John T. Matthews argues that "Faulkner evokes the minstrel tradition to signal his own complex alienation from the South's dominant social and cultural traditions" (80). Matthews, however, is speaking exclusively of the American tradition of blackface minstrelsy. While blackface does resonate with certain instances in Faulkner's work, a different tradition of minstrel masking may more fully express the author's alienation from southern culture by opening a unique epistemology of self and other.

In the pen-and-ink drawings accompanying his hand-produced verse and prose play, *The Marionettes* (1920), Faulkner evokes a long European tradition of Pierrot. First developed in commedia dell'arte toward the end of the seventeenth century, Pierrot, Faulkner's poet figure, was reimagined in the early nineteenth century for French pantomime by Jean-Gaspard Deburau. Deburau established Pierrot as the ineffectual lover, represented on stage as a clown in baggy white clothes and stylized whiteface makeup. Descendants of Pierrot include mimes and whiteface circus clowns. Deburau's is certainly the Pierrot embraced by fin-de-siecle European culture and subsequently modernist art. Pablo Picasso and many other modernist artists represented Pierrot. The poets young Faulkner read and imitated all worked with Pierrot or Pierrot figures, from Mallarmé and Verlaine to T. S. Eliot, Conrad Aiken, and Hart Crane. French pantomime came to England in 1891 and spawned numerous Pierrot troupes that entertained at English seaside towns through the 1920s. These troupes of male and female performers in Pierrot costume presented shows that mixed music, dancing, and comic sketches (Green and Swan 1–24). The Pierrot shows bear an uncanny resemblance to American blackface minstrelsy, but Faulkner chose the European rather than the American minstrel tradition to express his most complicated understanding of an always divided and racially inflected artistic identity.

If blackface minstrelsy raises one set of questions about racial appropriation, whiteface minstrelsy leads us to an odd question about what might be at stake when a Caucasian attempts to "pass" as white. Faulkner's Pierrot appears in whiteface, but his double, Shade of Pierrot, is always in silhouette. Pierrot, to follow Sensibar, is a drunken, impotent dreamer, while Shade of Pierrot is "the Rake . . . a fictionalized ideal, a fantastically successful poet and lover" (Introduction xvii). But Faulkner's fashioning of an idealized sexual and aesthetic self, as I will argue, appropriates blackness in a way that plays on stereotypes of "primitive" sexual license. The first drawing of Pierrot in *The Marionettes* shows him passed out at a table with a bottle and an overturned glass. In Faulkner's next drawing, Pierrot is a tall clown (see Figure 2.1).

From his stylized cupid's bow lips and arched brows to his cap-like hair, Pierrot is not simply white; rather he is in whiteface makeup, which means his identity is masked. Whiteface Pierrot, who is asleep, cannot act, certainly not sexually, and as he stands, his hands crossed in front of his groin suggest a kind of impotence, if not a symbolic castration. It is only the dream figure of the unconscious, the silhouetted black Shade of Pierrot that is capable of sexual performance. In the play's eighth drawing, Shade of Pierrot, standing in the background, plays his lute for Marietta (see Figure 2.2) and so appears perspectivally as a little black man.

What Faulkner suggests through these drawings is that the real artist is not the one who presents a white face to the world but rather resides in the poet's interiority, which turns out to be black. The duality of Pierrot/Shade of Pierrot is crucial to understanding Faulkner's subsequent development of a whiteface minstrelsy that implicitly racializes white male sexuality.[3] The limitation of Faulkner's portrayal of figurative blackness is that it draws on stereotypes of African American sexuality but at the same time significantly unhinges blackness as form of unlicensed sexuality from a biological or essentialist notion of race: in other words, Caucasians, as well as Negroes, can perform blackness.

The most obvious instance in *Mosquitoes* of Faulkner's use of blackness as a way of imagining a kind of male identity comes in an apparently minor metafictional moment, one that ultimately helps to link race and sexual difference precisely by opening a gap between blackness and race. Together in the same bunk, the naked Jenny tells Patricia about being at Mandeville; while her boyfriend and another couple go swimming, Jenny meets someone: "I was waiting for them, and I got to talking to a funny man. A little kind of black man–"; Patricia asks if he was "a nigger?" (144) and Jenny explains, "No. He was a white man, except he was awful sunburned and kind of shabby dressed—no necktie and hat. . . . I think he was crazy. Not dangerous: just crazy" (145). The reason Patricia is confused by Jenny's identification is that "black man" does not really signify in 1920s parlance. As we know from both historical context and Faulkner's other fiction, to have black blood, even only a drop, is to be a Negro, but being

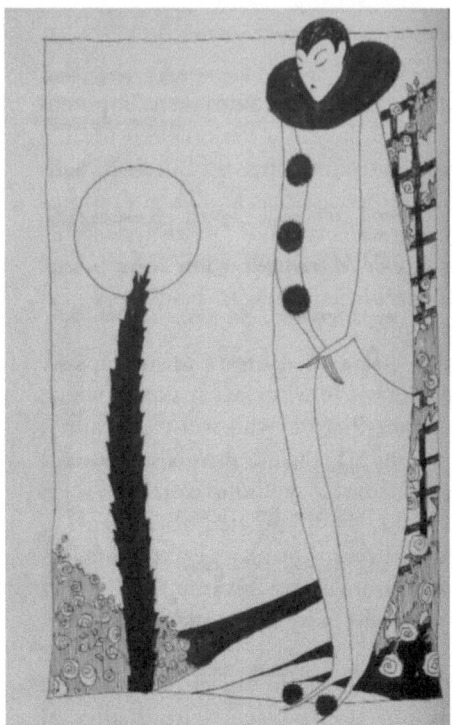

"black" has no immediate unmistakable referent. It is not exactly race but, since naming someone as black raises the question of race, it is not exactly not race either. Jenny finally remembers that this clownish little man, who identifies himself as a "professional liar" and whose racial identity is less immediate to her than the way in which he is in some deep but undefined way "black," is named Faulkner. At one level, the real-life Faulkner pokes fun at his own obscurity through Patricia's response: "Never heard of him." More important to my argument, however, is that the character named Faulkner points to a semantic difference in which an individual can be black without being African American, a situation that ultimately makes whiteness more contingent and less a given. (For the sake of clarity, I will refer to Faulkner the author without quotation marks but to the character as "Faulkner.") This metafictional moment takes a more complicated turn when Jenny tells the rest of her brief story about "Faulkner"; returning to New Orleans from their day trip, she notes: "That crazy man was on the boat coming back. He got to talking to Pete and Roy while me and Thelma was fixing up downstairs, and he danced with Thelma. He wouldn't dance with me because he said he didn't dance very well, and so he had to keep his mind on the music while he danced. He said he could dance with either Roy or Thelma or Pete, but couldn't dance with me. I think he was crazy. Don't you?" (145–46).

This crazy white "black" man who imposes himself on the two couples seems intimidated only by Jenny's voluptuous body, but is ready to dance with (and as?) the other female member of the party. Neither tough-talking Pete nor Roy, presumably, would be interested in coupling with "Faulkner" on the dance floor. But a fictional, trickster "Faulkner" who is willing to "dance" both ways—with male or female partners—hints at the ways blackness becomes a trope for sexual dissonance throughout Faulkner's fiction, even his later fiction that explicitly takes race as its central matter.

This is not to say that Faulkner was not attempting to think about the dynamics of racial difference in his southern community; however, Faulkner's figurations of blackness also frequently carry an extra valence that speaks to the author's struggle to imagine a way to perform an identity as a southern white male. Fictional "Faulkner's" craziness, for Jenny, at least, arises from his refusal to play gender roles straight. Although he appears only in the brief story that Jenny tells, the presence of black "Faulkner" looms over the whole of *Mosquitoes* through his figurative parallels to several other characters.

To the extent that Faulkner does implicitly conflate racial and sexual otherness, he employs blackness to figure certain white characters' (and perhaps his own) fantasized relation to otherness. As an aspiring poet, the young Faulkner could hardly be unaware that his own performance of masculinity differed from the norm of Oxford, Mississippi. His pilgrimage in 1925 to Oscar Wilde's grave, his college drawings in imitation of Aubrey Beardsley (whose illustrations of for Ernest Dowson's *The Pierrot of the Minute: A Dramatic Phantasy in One Act* [1897] may well have inspired Faulkner's illustrations of Pierrot),[4] as well as his friendship with men whom Frederick Karl identifies as homosexual (including Stark Young, Ben Wasson, and Bill Spratling), are just a few indications of Faulkner's awareness of alternative masculinities. Growing up white in the South in the first quarter of the twentieth century, Faulkner found blackness to be an immediately available and flexible trope to serve as a hinge between racial and sexual otherness. Since black women were viewed as promiscuous (thus available to white men) and black men were seen as sexually obsessed with interdicted white women, small wonder that a racially inflected blackness should come to serve Faulkner as a figure for delineating fissures in sexual identities. One result in Faulkner's fiction, then, is that the interdiction of mixed-race sexuality (even as miscegenation between black women and white men was an open secret) could signify taboos in other realms of sexual behavior (homo- and bisexuality, as well as incest) that define culture.

In the South, then, the African American served the role of the primitive other in the terms that Marianna Torgovnick has laid out in *Gone Primitive*. If for the West, "Africa is the quintessential locus of the primitive," in the American South, African Americans could serve a similar role in which "to study the primitive brings us always back to ourselves, which we reveal in the act of defining the Other" (Torgovnick 11). To seek the primitive is, in one sense, to search for what is primal and authentic to our human being prior to the distortions of civilization, since the primitive implies both origin and simplicity (Torgovnick 18). But because the primitive takes us back to a liminal moment, the transition from nature to culture, the primitive also reveals what, in Freudian terms, needs to be repressed in civilized society, most notably, sexual license prior to cultural taboos. Faulkner's fiction often channels a primitivist discourse in which the African American serves as the primitive. Perhaps no better instance of this occurs than in the conversation between Ike McCaslin and McCaslin Edmunds in part 4 of "The Bear," during which Ike's positive assertions about blacks are always countered by McCaslin. Ike claims: "[African Americans] are better than we are. Stronger than we are. Their vices are vices aped from white men or that white men and bondage have taught them: improvidence and intemperance and

evasion—not laziness: evasion: of what white men had set them to";
McCaslin, however, immediately responds, "'All right. Go on:
Promiscuity. Violence. Instability and lack of control. Inability to distin-
guish between thine and mine—'" (281).

For Ike, African Americans are superior because they are pure, and
whatever limitations they exhibit represent the corrupting evils of white
civilization, while for McCaslin, African Americans are subhuman, inca-
pable of ethical reasoning, akin more to mules and dogs than to white
people. Although these perspectives are apparently at odds, both Ike's
positive and McCaslin's negative characterizations of blacks share a central premise that resonates with primitivism. Both men agree that African
Americans are different because they are prior to the effects of white civilization; their disagreement is just a question of how they spin "black"
simplicity and spontaneity. For Ike, blacks retain primitive virtues that
whites have lost, while for McCaslin, their primitive, precultural status
means that it makes no more sense to ascribe virtue to African Americans
than it does to animals. Ike too is implicated in seeing African Americans
as more animal-like, as his word choice to describe blacks' mimicry of
white culture ("aped") reveals.

Torgovnick's linking modernism with primitivist discourse bears a
resemblance to Toni Morrison's thinking about racial figuration and the
Africanist presence in American literature. For Morrison, white writers,
in a fashion akin to blackface minstrel entertainers, have been able to
deploy images of blackness "in order to articulate and imaginatively act
out the forbidden in American culture" (*Playing* 66). While Faulkner certainly uses figurative blackness to map transgressive desire, his working
with a European whiteface minstrel tradition means that he is not using
blackface minstrelsy as a way to assimilate to whiteness, as Irish and
Jewish entertainers did by donning blackface.[5] Rather than as a way to
normalize himself in white southern culture, Faulkner uses his "whiteface"
males to suggest a realm of difference that resists assimilation into the
commonsense divisions that his culture tended to make regarding race.

From the example black "Faulkner" in *Mosquitoes*, I would like to pro-
pose a semiotic square that might be applied to many of Faulkner's texts
(as well as those of the other southern novelists in this study). A semiotic
square can expand a cultural opposition that is used as though it were an
absolute binary (such as on/off or 1/0). The cultural opposition that has
been implicit in my discussion of Faulkner is the one that opposes southern Whiteness to the Negro. However, the mixture of the races in the
South, no matter how much it was denied or legislated against via the
one-drop rule (which states that even a minute amount of African genetic

material makes a person a Negro), reveals that race is a continuum rather than a binary. That is why light-skinned African Americans could pass as white. There exist, then, sharper oppositions to both whiteness and the Negro that function more like true binaries; these can be derived by opposing race to race and color to color. Represented along the diagonal from the original two terms, an additional two terms appear that constitute the square:

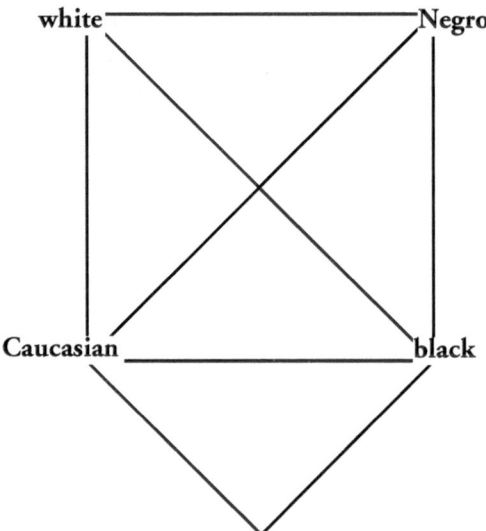

Faulkner's whiteface minstrels:
Pierrot/Shade of Pierrot, *The Marionettes*
"Faulkner" and Gordon, *Mosquitoes*
Popeye and Horace Benbow, *Sanctuary*
Quentin Compson, *The Sound and the Fury*
Ike McCaslin, *Go Down, Moses*

What I hope this square helps to schematize is that southern Whiteness does not simply name a race, but instead covertly speaks a metaphysics of privilege with material consequences. Clearly, whiteness is imperiled by the Negro racial passer, the person who looks white but is "really" Negro, and Faulkner often wrote about the way that characters such as Charles Bon and Joe Christmas (whose doubt about his racial identity alone is sufficient to constitute his position as Negro) can create confusion within the southern community. But whiteness is perhaps more imperiled by that set of Caucasians who fall short of being fully white. All whites must be Caucasian (that is, they must have the geneal-ogy to prove that they are not Negro), but being Caucasian turns out to be an insufficient condition of whiteness. The conjunction where "Caucasian" and "black" meet I take to be the site of Faulkner's whiteface minstrelsy. Faulkner's whiteface minstrels create a kind of obverse reflec-tion of what is at stake with the racial passer. If the racial passer con-sciously denies his or her race in order to participate in the privileges that come with the cultural connotations of whiteness, the whiteface minstrel unconsciously takes on the cultural connotations that are presumed to be the biological essence of the Negro. In a sense, then, the racial passer is less subversive than the whiteface minstrel because the passer does not fundamentally challenge the epistemology of the white-Negro cultural opposition. In other words, the passer accepts the continuum for a binary and so plays a dangerous game, knowing he or she is "really" Negro and may at any moment be exposed as such. But the Caucasian who is not white may well not know that he or she is not accepted as white. As the example of Sarty in "Barn Burning" (which I examined in Chapter 1) makes clear, a poor white may not be white, but does not know it and cer-tainly does not want to be told.

My semiotic square does not begin to address all the connotative cul-tural associations of blackness and whiteness, but if class is one element that can problematize a Caucasian's relation to whiteness, Faulkner's texts suggest that another coordinate of identity—sexuality—can also disqualify a claim to whiteness. Blackness in Faulkner is repeatedly asso-ciated with a kind of undisciplined libidinal energy producing a variety of nonheteronormative possibilities (homosexual, bisexual, incestuous) that defy cultural taboos.[6] Although whites (as we saw in McCaslin Edmonds and Isaac McCaslin's conversation) want to essentialize this form of blackness (a kind of precultural behavior) as a biological essence of the Negro, Faulkner's whiteface minstrel figures unhinge this pre-sumption by revealing Caucasians who are as black as or blacker than any African American. It is precisely this unhinging of blackness from the Negro that creates the possibility of epistemological fissures in the unstable white-Negro opposition.

"Faulkner's" blackness, staged as a kind of playful bisexual orientation, is directly linked to his "crazy" gender performance that embraces either male or female dance partners. If "Faulkner" were the only artist figure linked to blackness in *Mosquitoes*, my discussion might seem overwrought.

But blackness recurs elsewhere in relation to the possibilities of artistic production.

Although neither one of them is among the novel's "blacks," Dawson Fairchild and Julius Wiseman have the most to say about the relation of darkness to artistic and literary production. In another metafictional passage, late on the evening of the fourth day aboard ship, Eva, Julius, and Dawson discuss art and artists. Eva claims that "all artists are insane," to which Fairchild says, "It's a kind of dark thing. It's kind of like someone brings you to a dark door" (248). During their discussion, Fairchild pages through a book of poems Eva has published and claims to have trouble "reconcile[ing] her with this book." Fairchild's problem, Julius claims, arises from innocence regarding recent theories of sexuality, "this park of dark and rootless trees which Dr. Ellis and your Germans have recently thrown open to the public." Fairchild may recognize "emotional bisexuality" in what he reads, but Julius suggests that the relation of poet to poem is something more intimate: "A book is the writer's secret life, the dark twin of a man: you can't reconcile them" (251). This moment, which calls attention to the act of reading Faulkner's book, invites the reader to wonder how *Mosquitoes* might serve as Faulkner's dark twin. As John Irwin points out (167), Eva's poem "Hermaphroditus" is one that Faulkner would publish under his name in his 1933 volume of poetry, *The Green Bough*, evidence Michel later uses as an indication of Faulkner's lesbian identification. But as the poem speaks of the sly smiling figure with "boy's hand" and "woman's breast," desire is always unfulfilled: "canst thou bride/Thyself with thee and thine own kissing slake?" (252). No, says the poem, and the result is "thy twinned heart's grief." While the hermaphrodite clearly suggests androgyny, the completed twinning of this figure is, for Dawson, "a kind of dark perversion" (252), and Havelock Ellis's review of the literature on hermaphrodites shows a considerable degree of confusion between the terms "bisexual" and "hermaphroditism," especially when considered in light of such "sexoesthetic inversion" as transvestitism and cross-dressing (313–15). The implication here is that if art is a perversion, artists themselves are perverts. This implication finds its direct statement in one of the passages that was deleted from the typescript, at the direction of Faulkner's publisher, prior to the novel's publication.[7] In this deleted material, Faulkner inserts a hand-written addition in which Julius tells Fairchild, "Art is against nature: those who choose it are perverts" (ts 43), adding (now back to typeface): "You don't think it is natural for a man to spend his life making little crooked marks on paper, do you?" (ts 43). For a reader trying to decipher Faulkner's cramped and crooked additions on paper, the passage becomes highly self-reflexive.

Turning back to the long conversation on art growing out of Eva's poem, one notes the references to Freud and Havelock Ellis, both of whom frankly discussed homosexuality, although in ways that look less progressive now than they did a hundred years ago. In particular, Ellis's treatment of sexual inversion, while unquestionably arguing for a more enlightened treatment of homosexuals, also clearly participates in the minoritizing taxonomy that Sedgwick has argued ultimately perpetuates homophobia (*Epistemology*, 20–21). Although Faulkner later would claim only a second-hand knowledge of Freud, his characters, as Irwin notes (5), certainly seem familiar with Freud and, one might add, with Ellis as well.[8] Ellis's *Sexual Inversion* is at pains to show the universality of homosexuality—that it occurs in other animal species, throughout human history, and in all cultures. But Ellis singles out certain groups as having particularly high incidences of homosexuality: geniuses ("homosexuality is especially common among men of exceptional intellect" [26]), literary artists, and primitives. As Ellis elaborates on his claim regarding literature as one of the chief avocations of inverts, it is almost impossible not to speculate on how Faulkner might have experienced the following assertion, especially in light of his pose as the failed poet: "[homosexuals] especially cultivate those regions of *belles-lettres* which lie on the borderland between prose and verse. Though they do not usually attain much eminence in poetry, they are often very accomplished verse writers" (294). Ellis's first two categories—geniuses and artists—would seem to overlap, which makes his third category all the more anomalous. If homosexuality in European nations is practiced by a discrete (and discreet) minority, Ellis speaks of the commonness of inversion in a variety of primitive peoples, from American Indians and Tahitians to Africans: "Among the negro population of Zanzibar forms of homosexuality which are believed to be congenital (as well as acquired forms) are said to be fairly common. . . . Among the Bangala of the Upper Congo sodomy between men is very common, especially when they are away from home, in strange towns, or in fishing camps" (19).

"On the whole," Ellis summarizes, "the evidence shows that among lower races homosexual practices are regarded with considerable indifference, and the real invert . . . generally passes unperceived or joins some sacred caste which sanctifies his exclusively homosexual inclinations." Ellis's following paragraph significantly adds class to the mix: "Even in Europe today a considerable lack of repugnance to homosexual practices may be found among the lower classes. In this matter . . . the uncultured man of civilization is linked to the savage" (21). What Ellis misses here is that his extremes meet, for it is not just the uncultured man of civilization who is paired with the primitive (lower races, lower classes) but also the overcultured man (genius, artist) who takes his sexual pleasure in primitive fashion.

In keeping with Ellis's views of homosexuality, Faulkner's self-portraits in *Mosquitoes*, both ironic and idealized, seem to merge both the under- and overcultured. If "Faulkner," the professional liar, seems like the author's wry gesture toward one of his youthful poses as the tramp, the sculptor Gordon represents Faulkner's serious artistic ambition.[9] The tall Gordon, who we are repeatedly told has a hawk's face, is short (five feet five inches) Faulkner's idealized version of himself as a hardworking masculine artist.[10] Gordon (hawk-man/falconer/Faulkner), the dedicated artist as genius, seems opposed to the licensed fool "Faulkner"; however, they share a similar ambiguous relationship to whiteness, since both are merely Caucasians in whiteface. This ambiguity is signaled by the very space in which we meet Gordon. Accessible only by a "darkling corridor" (13) leading to "dark tortuous stairs" (21), Gordon's attic studio/apartment, one learns "had housed slaves long ago" (11).

Early in the novel, Mrs. Maurier, accompanied by her niece Patricia and Mr. Talliaferro, drops by Gordon's studio to try to persuade the sculptor to join her yachting party. Patricia openly admires the statue of the female torso and asks Gordon if he will give or sell it to her. When he refuses, she asks, "Why are you so black?" Since Gordon clearly does not understand her meaning, she tries to elaborate: "Not your hair and beard. I like your red hair and beard. But you. You are black. I mean. . ." (25). Although Patricia is unable to fully identify what constitutes Gordon's blackness, she, like Jenny, identifies the white male artist as black. Like "Faulkner," then, Gordon is not white, which places him in implied relationship to racial otherness. At the same time, as a starving artist, Gordon oddly combines both of Ellis's extremes for inverted tendencies: he is simultaneously overcultured (as artist) and undercultured (as economically lower class). Living in poverty in a space where blacks had lived, Gordon is perceived by Mrs. Maurier in a way that oddly suggests southern attitudes toward race. Because he's an artist, he must be "so spiritual": "He's one of these artists who never have much, lucky people." Mrs. Maurier's attitudes reveal that the dark artist is little different than the happy-go-lucky darkies, who must be equally lucky not to have much, either. When Gordon walks out on her, Mrs. Maurier tries to blame Patricia's behavior, but Patricia points out that, in fact, it is her aunt who has been rude by barging into his studio unannounced. Mrs. Maurier's response is telling: "These people are different," her aunt told her coldly. "You don't understand them. Artists don't require privacy as we do: it means nothing whatever to them" (30). What I hope my discussion to this point has made clear is how easily one might, in the context of the South in the 1920s, substitute "Negroes" for "artists" in the previous sentence. Mrs. Maurier's fascination with artists, her desire to decorate her party with them, reveals that she's slumming for the primitive in much the same way that wealthy New Yorkers went to Harlem's Cotton Club.

And though "black" himself, Gordon sets out to craft whiteness. As initially described, his statue is "passionately eternal—the virginal breastless torso of a girl, headless, armless, legless, in marble temporarily caught and hushed yet passionate still for escape, passionate and simple and eternal in the equivocal derisive darkness of the world." This statue, which "trouble[s] the very fibrous integrity of your being" (11), is explicitly marked as a double for Patricia, who when she first encounters it immediately remarks, "It's like me." Gordon's "growing interest [in] her flat breast and belly, her boy's body which the poise of it and the thinness of her arms belied" nearly reproduces the imagined viewer's response to Gordon's statue: "Sexless, yet somehow vaguely troubling" (24). The statue's marble (linked to the eternal and purity) is knowable primarily by its relation to the world's (and Gordon's) "darkness." Early on the third morning of the yacht party, Patricia goes skinny dipping, and the description of her body makes her the animated version of Gordon's statue: "Her legs and arms were so tan that naked she appeared to wear a bathing suit of a startling white" (164). To the extent that Patricia is delineated in relation to the marble statue, she is raced "white," but this whiteness, as we shall see, is contingent.

As a coded primitive and Africanist presence, Gordon struggles with his desire for Patricia, which, it turns out, is prohibited in more ways than one. Gordon's blackness, in one sense, marks him as artistic primitive, giving him the ability, for example, to see past the layers of civilization to what is elemental and authentic in Mrs. Maurier. Mrs. Maurier may have wished to surround herself with artists, but in bringing Gordon along, she gets much more than she bargained for. Seeing Gordon alone at night on the second day aboard ship, she thinks, "there was that queer, shy, shabby Mr. Gordon, mooning alone, as usual" (151), and then goes over to him to do her duty as hostess. She tries to talk about art but becomes discomfited by his "uncomfortable stare," which produces "a queer cold feeling within her"; his stare makes her think Gordon is "like an animal, a beast of some sort" (153). Although I do not mean to suggest that Mrs. Maurier's use of the word "queer" means that she thinks Gordon is a homosexual (after all, he is not effeminate), by the 1920s, "queer" had become a way to name homosexuals (Chauncey 13–23). If Patricia experiences Gordon's difference as his blackness, Mrs. Maurier experiences it as his "queerness," and she has a direct encounter with blackness/queerness/primitivism when he abruptly lays his sculptor's hands on her face to examine her, a moment she experiences as a kind of sexual violation.

I would like to turn the claim that Julius Wiseman makes about artistic twinning back on Faulkner's representation of Gordon as artist. If a book is the writer's secret life and dark twin, how might that pertain to artists and their work more generally? In sculpting the marble statue of the sexually ambiguous yet still female torso, has Gordon created his own "dark twin"? Gordon suggests as much when Julius and Dawson visit his studio. Dawson admires the statue and begins to idealize it as something to allow one to forget grief. Gordon contradicts Fairchild: "She's not blonde. . . . She's dark, darker than fire. She is more terrible and beautiful than fire" (329). Early in the novel, as he contemplates his desire for Patricia, Gordon seems to merge her back into his work and to see himself in relation both to Jesus and the maternal: "christ by his own hand an autogethsemane carved darkly out of pure space but not rigid no no an unmuscled wallowing fecund and foul the placid tragic body of a woman who conceives without pleasure and bears without pain" (48). One should recall that when Gordon lays his hands on Mrs. Maurier's face, his demand for information about Patricia turns to maternity again: "Why aren't you [Patricia's] mother, so you could tell me how conceiving her must have been, how carrying her in your loins must have been?" (154). Gordon's obsession with Patricia queerly positions his desire as a series of crossings. To the extent that his sacrifice to art (the sublimation of desire) has allowed him to produce a white (yet "really" dark) marble statue that is Patricia's twin, he is simultaneously the young woman's mother (artistic production being analogous to female reproduction), her brother (the statue is his dark twin and she's the statue's double), and even, it seems, her father.

Given all the kissing and fondling in the novel, it is striking that Gordon and Patricia have very little physical contact. Although Gordon desires Patricia, she does not reciprocate his desire. His desire for her, then, is coded metaphorically as father-daughter incest inasmuch as she's only eighteen while he's thirty-six—in other words, old enough to be her father. The prohibited nature of their relationship is made clear by the two main things that pass between them physically: he swings her around and he spanks her when she uses a naughty word. The father-daughter relationship is particularly underscored when, after she has been swimming,

Gordon asks her to give him her hands and begins to swing her around. She admires and touches his muscular forearms and asks him to "do it again." As he obliges her, one sees that in "her taut simple body, almost breastless with the fleeting hips of a boy, was an ecstasy in golden marble, and in her face the passionate ecstasy of a child" (82). After Gordon spanks Patricia, he comforts her by holding her and then places his hands on her face, not as sexual caresses but, as he tells her, to learn her face that he might sculpt it. Gordon apparently sublimates his sexual (and culturally incestuous) desires, but in some sense, the threat of incest is a screen for the more profound prohibition. If he is black and she is white, then he is equally prohibited from acting on his desire by the cultural and legal prohibitions against miscegenation. Here we see how prohibition in one sphere serves to displace another perhaps more disruptive prohibition in the southern imaginary. This is certainly an important facet of Faulkner's major fiction, as in *Absalom, Absalom!* where a story of incest masks a story of miscegenated incest, which, in turn, may mask the imagined threat of homosexual miscegenated incest.

The only other physical contact Gordon has with Patricia is on the final night of the cruise when she accepts his request to dance with her. Remembering that Gordon earlier told her aunt that he could not dance, Patricia tells him he does not look like he can dance. His response, "I can't"(284), reminds us of another dancer with oddly constrained ability, black "Faulkner," who is willing to dance with Pete, Roy, or Thelma, but not full-figured Jenny. If "Faulkner" can't dance with Jenny, Gordon, unlike the other men on the *Nausikaa*, simply won't because he is not attracted to her. What this later scene of dancing confirms in relation to the earlier one is that even male-female pairings on the dance floor may bespeak the range of non-normative desires suggested by Gordon's attraction to Patricia.

It is in the context of my foregoing discussion that I want to examine Gordon's trip through New Orleans' red-light district with Dawson and Julius in section 9 of the Epilogue. Everything about the men's drunken excursion is dark—dark rooms on a dark street in a dark city. It should be noted that the space of purchased sex and that of art are themselves doubles. Just as the part of New Orleans that the prostitutes inhabit is figured through multiple images of darkness, so, too (as I pointed out earlier), is the space leading up to Gordon's studio that had once housed slaves; hence, illicit sex and artistic practice, again, constitute each other as the "dark doors" leading to "dark perversions.

From an external perspective, Gordon's sex with a prostitute could only be described as a conventionally heterosexual (if illegal) act. Gordon's sexual act, however, performs a variety of crossings and certainly hinges on an explicit moment of racechange. Interspersed in the narrative of Julius, Fairchild, and Gordon's drunken ramblings is a different, primitivist narrative that tells of another mythic time and place. Recounting the death of a beggar, the indifference of the priests, and the lamentations of captive women in bondage, the italicized portions of the narrative link up finally to Gordon's claim (made just prior to their trip to the red-light district) that his marble statue is actually black. These italicized passages, however, rather than being simply a freestanding counterpoint to the men's wanderings, suggest Gordon's troubled and alcohol-impaired interiority. The fantasy narrative juxtaposes *"a young naked boy daubed with vermilion"* with *"the headless naked body of a woman carved of ebony, surrounded by women wearing skins of slain beasts and chained one to another, lamenting"* (337). The boy painted with vermillion suggests Gordon's desire for Patricia, the girl with a boy's body, and twin to his statue. This statue, however, has become a racechange totem—instead of marble, the female figure is now carved in ebony. The primitive women, potential sacrifices to the black statue, are doubles for the lower-class prostitutes and their solicitations, offerings of proscribed sexuality. The fantasy scene in which is heard *"the clashing hooves of centaurs"* builds to a crescendo in which *"the headless black woman becomes a carven agony beyond the fading placidity of the ungirdled maiden"* (338). It is at this point that Gordon demands money from Julius and enters a door, lifting a woman, seemingly at random, "smothering her squeal against his tall kiss." But in Gordon's interiority, the physical contact with the actual woman is overwhelmed by *"voices and sounds, shadows and echoes change form swirling, becoming the headless, armless, legless torso of a girl, motionless and virginal and passionately eternal before the shadows and echoes whirl away"* (339). This image, of course, exactly matches the description of Gordon's passionate and eternal statue that one encounters at the beginning of the novel. Black Gordon, it seems, can only steel himself for his encounter with the prostitute if he drinks himself into a near stupor and casts himself as a rapist centaur (man-beast) copulating under the sign of a black totem. Only through this fantasy of violation is Gordon able to consummate his desire for Patricia.

But what, exactly, does this episode say about Gordon's "heterosexuality"? Black Gordon, whose sole sexual performance conflates the body of his epicene marble statue (which simultaneously points to its black racechanged double in ebony and the naked boy marked by red) with that of Patricia, engages in behavior coded in primitivist and Africanist terms. If Patricia stands in a series of metaphorical and metonymical substitutions,

what is she but a figure (both rhetorical and psychosexual) of the reification of desire's multiplicity that goes by the inappropriate name "sexual
identity"? In the dizzying chain of substitutions, where can any form of
sexual identity claim to ground itself or find its original? Looked at from
the psychic interiority of this "black" man, Gordon's "heterosexual" act
simultaneously consummates desire all over the map: miscegenation (he is
"black"), father-daughter incest, brother-sister incest (she is his dark twin's
double), mother-daughter incest (he is her twin's "mother"), even
pedophilia (he is a middle-aged man imaginatively having sex with a sexless
boy-girl). Perhaps all of these possibilities, taken together, answer Patricia's
question, "Why are you so black?" One is black if one's desires transgress culture's sexual taboos, because one is then primitive (prior to the repressions of
civilization) and, implicitly, racially other. Even a heterosexual act, I would
argue, can constitute a decidedly queer moment in Faulkner's text. Recalling
Eva Wiseman's poem, Gordon may be the true hermaphrodite. He has, in
displaced fashion, brided himself through and to his double(s).

There is another way in which "Faulkner" inhabits the novel, even in his
absence. If he shares qualities of artistry and blackness with Gordon,
"Faulkner" is also linked to the aesthete Ernest Talliaferro in a particular
way. If "Faulkner" is the funny little black man, Talliaferro is "that funny
talking little man . . . that dreadful polite one" (141). Little men both,
"Faulkner" and Ernest both represent sides of the youthful William
Faulkner. If "Faulkner" stands in for Faulkner's tramp persona, Talliaferro's
affected English accent and changed spelling of his patronymic both suggest self-parody of Faulkner's pose as the dandy (Arnold 5). Talliaferro
may self-identify as a heterosexual, but everything about his attempted
seductions of women works to ensure that he does not have to actually perform as a heterosexual. For all of his stratagems of seduction aimed toward
Jenny, when she takes him to a secluded space in order to kiss him, Ernest
feels an "unbearable lightness" moving through him, but once it reaches
his feet, he runs away from her (189). His status as heterosexual, then, is
all public performance, literally an act, one undertaken so that he will be
taken as a man by other men. As Gwin points out, Ernest even views his
impending marriage to Mrs. Maurier as a way to avoid having to perform
as a heterosexual ("Did Ernest" 128–29).

Ernest is also oddly related to that professional liar "Faulkner" because
so many of the prefatory sections to the various days of the novel are
voiced through a poetic discourse that is strangely close to Talliaferro's
own overblown rhetoric. The opening of "The Third Day," for example,
exhibits this quite clearly: "the yacht was a thick jewel swaddled in soft
gray wool, while in the wool somewhere dawn was like a suspended

breath. The first morning of Time might well be beyond this mist, and trumpets preliminary to a golden flourish; and held in suspension in it might be heard yet the voices of the Far Gods on the first morning saying, It is well: let there be light" (164).

This purple prose precisely captures Meryl Altman's point: "it is impossible to tell when [Faulkner] is parodying this discourse and when he believes it, or what he does believe, which of the clichéd pontifications about beauty are meant as clichéd pontifications and which are supposed to represent Beauty" (44). But even if the irony spins out of control in *Mosquitoes*, Faulkner's much later and clearly ironic "Afternoon of a Cow" (1943) has another Ernest T. who speaks to what is at stake discursively in his second novel. In this short story set at Faulkner's home, Rowan Oak, Ernest Trueblood reveals that he has "been writing Mr. Faulkner's fiction for years" (424) through a kind of unstable collaboration. The overtly masculine, hard-drinking, taciturn Mr. Faulkner generates the broad outlines and plots, but the effeminate, sensitive Trueblood fleshes them out with the actual words. Strikingly, the story is told through a poetic, euphemistic prose that is unmistakably "Faulknerian," but that rhetoric is here attributed to the fussy and prudish Trueblood. Is Faulkner's story a wry way of acknowledging his own "emotional bisexuality," of allowing, as it were, E. T. to come home?

This figure of the black white man (and by now every time I use these coloring terms they seem to cry out for problematizing quotation marks) recurs throughout Faulkner's subsequent fiction, as the rest of this chapter will try to make clear. But I will make some preliminary observations based on what we have seen. When performing "What Did I Do To Be so Black and Blue?" Louis Armstrong would intone the line "I'm white inside." Faulkner's whiteface minstrels, however, seem to be saying, "I'm black inside." This claim, as I have argued, unhinges black primitivism from the racial category of the Negro by suggesting that Caucasians too could be the primitive other. This use of figurative blackness, I believe, signals the extent to which Faulkner struggled to become an envoy of otherness. But his attempt is always fraught with the ethical problem of how to speak legitimately for (or indeed as) the other. Moreover, Faulkner's racially inflected use of blackness as a way to critically engage southern Whiteness always faces another problem: once white has mixed with black, it ceases to be white. Faulkner's personal relation to whiteness becomes rhetorically imperiled, hybrid, and even miscegenated by his very attempt to imagine nonheteronormative masculine identity. Faulkner's male artists are "black" in some essential way that certain women can immediately recognize. These artists are, then, a kind of photographic negative to blackface minstrelsy: they are "blacks" in whiteface, and therefore experience the world in a way analogous to the racial passer—always in danger of having their whiteness exposed as fraudulent. The point I wish to develop in the rest of this chapter is that if the book is an individual's "dark twin," then rather like black "Faulkner," William Faulkner himself is metaphorically (part) black to the extent that he can repeatedly imagine the queerly proliferating multiplicity of desire.

Before turning to *Sanctuary* in the next section, I would like to address a concern that some readers may have about the gendered nature of my argument. In discussing Faulkner's whiteface minstrelsy, I have largely cast it as a problem of white southern masculine performance. One might reasonably object that feminine examples are as central. Are not Caddy Compson and her daughter, Quentin, examples of women performing black sexuality in whiteface? While they certainly are implicated in black performance, it does not occur in whiteface and fundamentally differs from the way Faulkner's whiteface males experience blackness. If we listen to the male voices that censure female sexuality, we can begin to hear why. Caddy's brother Quentin asks, "*Why wont you bring him to the house, Caddy? Why must you do like nigger women do in the pasture the ditches and dark woods hot hidden furious in the dark woods*" (92). Jason complains about his niece in similar language: "I'm not going to have any member of my family going on *like a nigger* wench" (189, emphasis added).

There is a significant difference between having one's behavior named through a simile (you are acting *like* a "nigger") and being identified as (or sensing that one's identity is) black. In the former, whiteness is not really problematized and in fact is confirmed. There is no social misrecognition: white is white and Negro is Negro. Telling these women that they are behaving "like niggers" merely polices the boundary of their white femininity; it is their behavior (which is correctable), not their being, that is linked to racial otherness. In the latter, however, the recovery of whiteness is quite problematic. Faulkner's whiteface male minstrels have crossed over: they are not *like* blacks—they *are* black. It is precisely this masked black being that creates social misrecognition. Jenny and Patricia may identify "Faulkner" and Gordon as "black," but neither the identifiers nor the identified understand exactly what that means. In the next section, I examine another pair of male characters: Popeye, who is figured as a black man, and Horace Benbow, who initially is linked to racial otherness through simile ("like a nigger," as Caddy and her daughter are described), but who undergoes in *Sanctuary* a process of becoming black.

"A LITTLE BLACK THING LIKE A NIGGER BOY":
SANCTUARY AND THE OBJET PETIT NOIR

In the early Faulkner material I examined in the previous section, race has been absent at the denotative level, though (as I have argued) insistent at the level of connotation. When one turns to the Yoknapatawpha fiction, however, it is difficult to bracket race, the author's most insistent, tragic, and freighted subject. *Sanctuary* thus appears to be an anomaly, a Yoknapatawpha novel largely without race.[11] Doreen Fowler recently has argued that "the bootleggers and prostitutes in *Sanctuary* function as substitutes for a nearly invisible black community" suggesting "the racial segregation that historically characterizes Faulkner's South" (422). Given my previous discussion of *The Marionettes* and *Mosquitoes* as a context for thinking about Faulkner's use figurative blackness, I agree that *Sanctuary* can be read as coded meditation on racial otherness, one that once again cuts close to the bone of authorial identity. But in the logic of whiteface minstrelsy that I have delineated, I would maintain that in *Sanctuary* the social and psychological processes of becoming black map the limits of representational thinking; the racechanges affected by the text blur the boundary between the figural and the real.

At the center of *Sanctuary*'s figurative blackness is the gangster Popeye, who, although Caucasian, activates a southern hysteria over black male criminality and sexuality. For many readers today, Popeye, who rapes the Ole Miss co-ed Temple Drake with a corncob and gets away with it, only to be executed for a crime he does not commit, is the embodiment of blackness. In fact, the last few times I have taught *Sanctuary*, the majority of students, both undergraduate and graduate, has been certain that Popeye is African American. This contemporary misrecognition oddly enacts the stereotypes of the Negro of the 1930s, but a reading that sees Popeye as African American is not simply an error since it leads to the very ambiguity created by the text's deployment of blackness.

There are, in other words, some very good reasons why readers today process Popeye as an African American. Students who have studied other Faulkner novels remember that his fiction often turns on complex issues of miscegenated identity, embodied by racially ambiguous characters. Even for students for whom *Sanctuary* is their first encounter with Faulkner, their skills as close readers lead them to make a racialized sense of repetition. "He smells black" (7), thinks Horace during his encounter with Popeye in chapter 1, a detail that resonates with a clichéd racist sentiment that African Americans smell funny. "Popeye's black presence" (121) looms over the Old Frenchman place; Horace Benbow tells his sister,

Narcissa, and Miss Jenny about "that little black man" (109) with this threatening pistol; and most specifically, Temple Drake twice contemptuously refers to Popeye as "that black man" (42, 49). Oddly, questions of Popeye's size and physical prowess become confused when Horace refers to Popeye as "that gorilla" (128), a term that seems to belie Popeye's diminutive build but that is consistent with the figurative blackness that links the character to racial otherness. "Black" Popeye is a primitive—unevolved and subhuman—an implication that is consistent with white racist attitudes toward African Americans.

Even the way Popeye's skin is described creates ambiguity with its oxymoronic "dark pallor" (5). How can paleness be dark? This ambivalent description of Popeye's skin is no more helpful in fixing racial identity than the description that tells us that his "face had a queer, bloodless color" (4). Like "queer" Gordon from *Mosquitoes*, "queer" Popeye is not necessarily sexually identified by this word, yet the cultural connotation of inversion looms in the designation inasmuch as "queer" was used in the 1930s to name homosexuality. What is queer about Popeye is his combination of violence and nonheteronormative voyeuristic libidinality.

While the mentally challenged Tommy does, at one moment, refer to Popeye as "the skeeriest durn *white* man I ever see" (19), this identification is overwhelmed by the references to Popeye's blackness. It is interesting, however, what Tommy's emphasis of the word "white" implies about the southern racial imaginary, namely, that Popeye's whiteness is anomalous, more like African American masculinity was imagined. On the one hand, Popeye is not manly, since he is scared, it seems, of his own shadow. On the other hand, Popeye inspires fear because he is scary. One never knows when he will draw his gun and kill something or someone. Popeye thus effectively enacts two conflicting stereotypes of the black man: he is seen as an object of derision for his comical cowardice, but he is also known as an unthinking, dangerous brute that white men should fear. This duality means that Popeye, as an artificial Negro, stands apart from white men. Even when identifying Popeye as white, therefore, Tommy names the gangster's difference in a fashion that queers Popeye's white identity.

As we have seen earlier in this chapter, we run into an epistemological problem. Readers today fail to experience Patricia's confusion in *Mosquitoes* when her friend Jenny refers to "Faulkner" as a "little black man," a confusion arising because in the 1920s and 1930s, "black man" was an uncommon locution, one that would not have immediately indicated race. An African American was not "black" but, in polite white society, "Negro," and more commonly "nigger." Moreover, lacking the historical context of southern race relations, readers do not grasp that even in an illegal bootlegging business, an African American male's having a position of authority over whites was simply unthinkable.

Popeye's whiteface blackness does not function in isolation. Just as the relationship between tall Gordon and fictional little "black" "Faulkner" in *Mosquitoes* can trace its genealogy in whiteface minstrelsy to the Pierrot-Shade of Pierrot relationship in *The Marionettes*, the two central male characters in *Sanctuary* have a similarly hinged relationship, one signaled in the opening scene of the novel in which the reflected faces of Horace and Popeye merge in such a way that Horace appears to be wearing Popeye's hat.[12] If the misrecognition of Popeye's racial identity is partially a function of his clothes, this startling visual image of trans-vestment signals the way in which blackness will descend on Horace in the novel. Stated in terms of Pierrot/Shade of Pierrot, Popeye is Horace's black shadow, a visible manifestation of Horace's closeted blackness.[13] Horace and the client he represents, Lee Goodwin, experience cultural and psychological forces that suggest their becoming black, so much so that they, in ways that neither they nor the white community recognize, come to play their roles as if they were African American.

Just as "Faulkner" and Gordon represent aspects of Faulkner's artistic identity and ambition, so too do Popeye and Horace. Diminutive "black" Popeye is a nightmarish version of that funny little black "Faulkner" from *Mosquitoes*.[14] If "Faulkner" represents William Faulkner's tramp persona, Popeye eerily suggests Faulkner's dandyism. One of the first details suggesting Popeye's "blackness" is sartorial: "His suit was black, with a tight, high-waisted coat" (4). Temple's sense of Popeye's blackness surely comes, in part, from the skin-tight black suit he wears. Taunting Popeye after he calls her a whore, Temple asks: "What river did you fall in with that suit on? Do you have to shave it off at night?" (50). This detail also eerily links Popeye with Faulkner. As Joseph Blotner has noted, the young Faulkner's dandyism included having his mother, Maud, alter his new suits to make the legs tighter, so much so that his pants were "close to skintight" (*Faulkner* 180). Beyond the matter of clothing, Faulkner's description of Popeye's face suggests a feared and fantasized authorial self-representation: "His nose was faintly aquiline, and he had no chin at all" (5).[15] While the gangster's physical delineation seems to point toward the author, Faulkner's representation of Popeye, as James Polchin has noted, parallels 1920s popularizations of Freud and Ellis that would position Popeye within the psychopathology of homosexuality (148–51).[16]

Both Popeye and Horace are linked by nonheteronormative performances of masculinity that place them in groups that Havelock Ellis saw as having a disproportionate number of homosexuals. Horace, the Oxford educated lawyer who, even in running away from his loveless marriage, takes a book, represents Ellis's overcultured man, while Popeye, a child of the underclass, suggests the undercultured. As Faulkner's earlier presentation of Horace in *Flags in the Dust* makes clear, Horace is an artist figure. His glass blowing equipment that he brings home with him from World War I allows him to pursue his artistic impulses; working in the garage, he produces after several attempts "one almost perfect vase of clear amber, larger, more richly and chastely serene and which he kept always on his night table and called by his sister's name . . . " (*Flags* 190). Horace's bedside ornament, of course, bespeaks both his incestuous desire for Narcissa and his sublimation of that desire in his art.[17] Despite the displacement, Horace's desire is marked as transgressive and primitive (precultural); if he transgresses in one fashion, he is liable to have other nonnormative desires. In *Sanctuary*, Horace remains the artist figure, and one moment in particular strongly recalls a gesture the sculptor Gordon twice makes in *Mosquitoes*. Speaking to Ruby about his psychological limitations, Horace reaches out and places a hand on her face, "touching the flesh as though he were trying to learn the shape and position of her bones and the texture of her flesh" (17). Art in *Mosquitoes* is a kind of "dark" perversion, yet it is art that allows Gordon, in effect, to pass as a heterosexual even as his interiority produces all manner of transgressive behavior. Horace thinks of his transgression as his incestuous thoughts about his stepdaughter, Little Belle, but as in *Mosquitoes*, the more profound prohibition is against a darkly figured same-sex sexuality.

If Popeye's blackness is queerly positioned between figurativeness (he's really white) and literalness (other characters identify him as black), Horace's relationship to the racial other begins as unambiguously figurative, constructed by simile. Narcissa twice articulates what she finds troubling in Horace's leaving his wife, Belle: "But to walk out just like a nigger," she says, "And to mix yourself up with moonshiners and streetwalkers" (108). A few pages later, she elaborates her dismay: "When you took another man's wife and child away from him, I thought it was dreadful, but I said At least he will not have the face to ever come back here again. And when you just walked out of the house like a nigger and left her I though that was dreadful too, but I would not let myself believe you mean to leave her for good" (117). Narcissa's racialized complaint against her brother, of course, bespeaks her outrage at his compromising her sense of white respectability and gentility, but her simile says much more. What makes Horace "like a nigger" is that he cannot be confined to heteronormative domesticity. Narcissa unreflexively invokes the specter of the presumed unchecked, primitive libidinality of the African American male to name her brother's relation to difference.

Two crucial moments link blackness and nonheteronormativity. The first, strikingly, is generated by a presumptively heterosexual coupling of Temple and Red. Since Red is brought in by Popeye to have sex with Temple while he watches, Red is most often viewed as Popeye's surrogate, a move that tends to read Popeye's desire into a heterosexual paradigm. But Temple says Popeye is "not even a man," certainly not a "real man" (231), and in childhood, his doctor says that the delicate, undersized boy "will never be a man, properly speaking" (308). In the sexological world of the late 1920s, to be less than or other than a man implies inversion, and certainly the slight Popeye, who never develops secondary male sexual characteristics, fits this model. How then does one read Popeye's voyeuristic participation in this sexual threesome? As Temple and Red engage in coitus "nekkid as two snakes," Popeye, fully clothed in his black suit, stands at the foot of the bed "making a kind of whinnying sound" (258). The critical presumption of Popeye's heterosexuality is not supported by his nonsignifying noise. Wherein lies Popeye's identification while he watches—as the penetrator or as the penetrated? His sound does not distinguish. His whinnying expresses, but does not represent, a jouissance that operates beyond the pleasure principle. The second crucial moment in the figurative linking of blackness and nonheteronormativity occurs when Horace visits Temple in Miss Reba's establishment. The story Temple tells of her violation is explicit in its detail but is fantasy, a fabrication that operates with its own symbolic logic that may speak, nevertheless, the truth of her night of terror at the Old Frenchman Place. We know that Popeye was never in the room with Temple long enough for the scenario she describes to have occurred, and moreover, that Popeye rapes her the next morning, not that night. What is of interest, then, is Temple's racially and sexually imagined attempts at avoiding her violation. I am particularly interested in her penultimate and final ruses. On the verge of being raped, she imagines herself as an unattractive middle-aged schoolteacher disciplining "a little black thing like a nigger boy" (219). This reversal of the power relation turns the threatening "black" man into an African American boy who can be controlled.[18]

Temple decides she needs to go one step further and performs a sex-change: "So I was an old man, with a long white beard, and the little black man got littler and littler and I was saying Now. You see now. I'm a man now" (220). By becoming a man, she hopes to unman Popeye and this funny "little black man" is no longer the African American boy but a kind of reverse metonymy, the whole standing (or rather failing to stand) for the part, where the part is the flaccid phallus. And though Temple's words describe Popeye's impotence, the imagined moment of sexuality that ensues is between two men: "Then I thought about being a man, and as soon as I thought it, it happened. It made a kind of plopping sound, like blowing a little rubber tube wrong-side out. It felt cold, like the inside of your mouth when you hold it open" (220). Although she describes the transformation of her vagina into a penis, what "it" in fact represents is the experience of Popeye's penetration of her with the corncob. She may have avoided the literal phallus of the "little black man," but this moment, as will become clear in the trial of Lee Goodwin, constitutes a different kind of black phallus.

Temple's fantasized, sexchanging version of her violation finds its completion in Horace's own sexchange fantasy of violation. When he returns to Jefferson after hearing Temple's story, Horace vomits up a "hot ball" of black coffee that recalls the "hot ball" that Temple had described as part of her anticipation of being raped. In this moment of literal and physical abjection, Horace experiences the psychological abjection of nonnormative desire. As he vomits over the toilet, Horace relives Temple's story about her violation, but as the pronouns shift from male to female, it is not so simple as his incestuous desire for his stepdaughter. As James Polchin has argued, "like Temple Drake's story of her rape in which she creates her physical and mental state as a man, Horace projects himself into a female position in his own recollection of the rape. For Horace, the image evolves as an erotically charged act of anal intercourse" (154). Far from simply an imagined penetration of Little Belle, Horace instead experiences the violation of his own "black tunnel" (223).[19] In this moment, when Horace's desires "go primitive," he ceases to be merely "like a nigger," and is becoming symbolically black.

Given what Temple tells Horace, there is no reason to suppose that he realizes, prior to his own fantasy violation, that Popeye is impotent and committed the rape with a cob. In Horace's imagined reconstruction of the rape, one detail he fixes on ("the shucks set up a terrific uproar beneath her thighs" [223]) suggests that he positions the rape during the night that Temple spent on a mattress filled with corn shucks. Horace is likely unaware of the role of the cob until Goodwin's trial. But if we recall where Temple actually was raped, a strange continuation of the various possibilities of the consumption of corn emerges. Gowan Steven's consumption of corn liquor leads to Temple's night of terror on a mattress filled with shucks. The next morning, she goes to the barn, which is also used as a bathroom, to relieve herself. The rape itself occurs in the corncrib. Considering the rural use of corncobs in toileting, as well as Temple's subsequent excessive bleeding, it becomes unclear which of her orifices Popeye penetrates.

Popeye, the figure of black male criminality (despite quite possibly being a white "invert"), commits the crime that occasions the need for Jefferson's primitive form of justice, a mob vengeance that entails mutilation and lynching. Although on trial for killing Tommy, Lee Goodwin is convicted and punished for raping Temple, who identifies him as Tommy's murderer and her rapist. Rape in the southern imaginary of the 1920s and 1930s is a racialized crime committed almost exclusively by the Negro who lusts after white women. How is it, then, that the victim of the lynching is a white man, Lee Goodwin? The southern practice of castration and lynching of the black sexual offender (whether the offense was real or imaginary) would be inflicted on no white man, and Lee, it turns out, is no white man. But how exactly is Lee stripped of his whiteness during the trial in such a way that he serves as another instance in Faulkner of whiteness becoming black?

Clearly, Lee's relationship to whiteness is already tenuous because of his class position as a poor white. Moreover, as a bootlegger, he operates outside of the law and provides an illicit product that was understood to corrupt social values by lowering inhibitions. One of the reasons for Prohibition was to promote sexual morality. Perhaps most tellingly, in an otherwise segregated South where work itself was often raced (some menial jobs would not be performed by whites), bootlegging was an equal opportunity venture—both poor whites and African Americans produced corn liquor.[20] Nevertheless, Lee's complete racial reassignment requires a prosthetic intervention.

What performs perhaps the oddest moment of racechange in all of Faulkner is the corncob surrogate phallus that Popeye used to rape Temple; it is her "little black thing like a nigger boy" writ large. As such, the cob is not Lacan's "little otherness" (the unconcretizable *object petit a*, that fantasy of desire) but rather what we might call Faulkner's very concrete "little blackness"—the *object petit noir*.[21] When the district attorney, Eustace Graham, introduces the cob into evidence, "it appeared to have been dipped in dark brown paint" (283). The cob, then, overtly marked as the unnatural instrument of violation, is also implicitly raced: in its dark brown coloring, the cob is the disembodied (thus already disciplined and castrated) African American phallus. The effect of the courtroom scene recalls Frantz Fanon's description of the experience of reading a passage from Michel Cournot that carnivalizes the size of the black penis: "one is no longer aware of the Negro but only of a penis; the Negro is eclipsed. He is turned into a penis. He *is* a penis" (Fanon 170). Or perhaps it is Fanon's point with a twist: *Sanctuary*'s surrogate penis *is* Negro. The criminality of the mute, black phallus is reassigned in the courtroom, anticipating the mutilation of Goodwin's lynched body. At the same time, the district attorney's own whiteness and linguistic authority (in Lacanian terms, his phallic authority) derives from his ability to speak the meaning of the black phallus.

As such, the black phallus is the uncannily appropriate object of the white male gaze and white vengeance; it is the object that makes Goodwin's alleged crime "no longer the matter for the hangman [a fit end for a white murderer] but for a bonfire of gasoline [a warning to other would-be black rapists to leave white women alone]" (284). This free-floating surrogate black phallus, while implying the castration of the black man, simultaneously reminds the all-white male jury of the imagined primitive sexual power of the Negro male.

This is why Lee Goodwin can become the object of the white community's peculiar brand of mob justice. In the southern imaginary, the libidinously primitive black phallus, when linked to Goodwin, has the effect of erasing his claim to whiteness, and as he blackens, Temple Drake becomes yet another instance of southern womanhood violated by the Negro. The cob suggests a kind of transubstantiation—the blood of the violated white virgin constituting the surrogate black phallus. Through Temple's testimony that names Lee, rather than Popeye, as the "owner" of the black phallus, we witness the construction of another unrecognized artificial Negro. The crime effectively becomes a black crime and so more readily fits the established southern narrative of white punishment of black primitive libidinality. Symbolically de/re-raced, Lee is thus made available to serve the communal role of the black male in *Sanctuary*'s ritualized lynching.

The blackened cob effectively merges all the text's funny little black-nesses, from Popeye and Horace to Uncle Bud (the African American boy who lives at Miss Reba's whorehouse), and Temple's black fantasy retelling of her rape. During the trial, Goodwin is essentially made to take on the blackness of both Popeye and his double, Horace.

Together, then, these three characters instantiate, once again, Faulkner's whiteface minstrelsy—individuals who beneath the mask of whiteness subliminally function as culturally black. Crime and punishment, taken in this fashion, is about the social construction of whiteness. I have outlined the way Lee stands in for Popeye, but there is also a relation of substitution between Lee and Horace. Sometimes a cigar is just a cigar, but Horace's corncob pipe is hardly just a pipe when read in light of the racial and sexual context of *Sanctuary*'s courtroom and its black cob/penis. The relationship between Lee and Horace is more complex. During the trial, Horace, in a legal sense, "represents" Goodwin. But in the white male community's act of violent retribution that follows, Lee symbolically represents Horace. Effectively switching roles from the courtroom matinee to the open-air evening performance, these two whiteface characters are the odd men out in what Faulkner portrays as the blackface minstrelsy of Jefferson's lynching.

Focalized through Horace's angle of vision, the lynching of Lee Goodwin embodies multiple racialized misrecognitions and appropriations.[22] Approaching the jail, Horace sees a bright fire in the vacant lot next to the jail, which renders the events that he witnesses in "savage silhouette" (295), which turns whiteness black. In lynching Lee, the white men (who appear as though in blackface) literalize Fanon's point that such brutal acts are sexual revenge, revealing the psychopathology of white men and their feelings of "sexual inferiority . . . in relation to the Negro, who is viewed as penis symbol" (159). The lynchers appropriate their stereotype of black sexual primitivism to punish the whitefaced black, Lee. The text reveals that, before dousing him with coal oil and setting him on fire, the blackface lynchers sodomized their victim; one of the men says, when Horace is recognized: "Do to the lawyer what we did to [Goodwin]. What he did to her. Only we never used no cob. We made him wish we had used a cob" (296). Strikingly, the homosexual act is performed in the name of preserving nonmiscegenated heterosexuality and the superiority of the white over the black penis. Here too is Horace's imagined anal rape, fantasized while vomiting, made all too real. For Polchin, Horace's "lack of masculine authority connects his deviancy with that of the rapist" (156). But the sexual deviancy that links Horace and Lee is color-coded: "black" (to the extent that his desire is "inverted," and thus primitive) Horace is metaphorically lynched and sodomized by the mob. The crowd's vengeance may be performed on Goodwin's body, but Horace unconsciously processes the scene as if he were the victim. Horace's brush with the blackface mob completes the transformation of the qualifying simile (Horace is "like a nigger"), turning it into the full-blown identity of metaphor (Horace is another black man who is available for lynching).

The defeated Horace Benbow, who returns to his wife, Belle, in Kinston is a decidedly queer heterosexual white man, his whiteness and heterosexuality called into question by his relationship to that scary little black man named Popeye. Horace's very nearly fulfilled fantasy of anal penetration disciplines him so completely that he returns, in the world's view, to presumptive heteronormative domesticity. Horace, however, is merely passing along the color (and sex) line. Psychologically impotent, Horace again instantiates Faulkner's ineffectual, dreamer Pierrot, while "black" Popeye (even while physically impotent) embodies Shade of Pierrot's transgressive libidinality that once again points to primitivism and racial otherness.

In the final section of this chapter, I continue my thinking about the way blackness queers white male identity in two of Faulkner's most significant meditations on southern masculinity, Quentin Compson and Isaac McCaslin.

WAS IKE BLACK? AVUNCULAR
RACECHANGE IN *GO DOWN, MOSES*

> If he was not to recant the convictions so dear to him, then Egypt had no more to give him; he had lost his native country. In his hour of need he found an unusual solution.
>
> Sigmund Freud, *Moses and Monotheism*

The beginning of *Go Down, Moses* immediately identifies the centrality of one supposedly racially unambiguous character to our understanding of the various stories that follow: "Isaac McCaslin, 'Uncle Ike', past seventy and nearer eighty than he ever corroborated any more, a widower now and uncle to half a county and father to no one" (3). This opening, part of the material Faulkner added to turn his several previously published short stories into a more unified narrative, points directly to a doubling—Isaac McCaslin and Uncle Ike—two signifiers to name one body: the first, his birth name; the second, what he is known by in his old age. But this sentence fragment also introduces matters of gender and sexuality. As "father to no one," Isaac has no heir, a fact that raises a question about his sexual performance, which in turn opens the issue of his enactment of white southern masculinity. Yet, as "uncle to half a county," we are aware, initially, that others of his clan must be fertile and, retrospectively, that this description is less hyperbolic when we acknowledge his African American, as well as his white, kin.

Ike's failure to enact the scripts of white southern masculine identity, I wish to argue, leads to his symbolic racial reassignment, one that is misunderstood in the text both by the white southern community and by Ike McCaslin himself (as well as by readers who have learned the significance of the "one-drop" rule to matters of racial identity in the South). Elsewhere, I have argued that heterosexuality alone, in Faulkner's fiction, is not sufficient to ensure a correct performance of southern masculinity

("Faulkner's Crying" 60). What I similarly would argue here is that the absence of African genetic heritage may be a necessary, but finally insufficient, ground for constituting whiteness in Faulkner's South. So, despite the title of this section, which nods toward Shelley Fisher Fishkin, my discussion does not uncover some heretofore unnoticed evidence of Ike's biology or literary genealogy.[23] To remove the suspense, then, I am not claiming that Ike truly is an African American or that Faulkner based his portrayal of Ike on some particular African American, yet, I believe the answer to my title's question may still be "yes" if we consider Uncle Ike's final position in the southern imaginary. By the end of *Go Down, Moses*, Ike has become a "funny uncle" indeed, one his white community consciously misrecognizes, yet unconsciously recognizes, as a "black" white man.[24]

The ways in which Faulkner's earlier writing explicitly deploys blackness as a form of authorial self-fashioning creates a context for understanding what may be at stake in Ike's racechange. With characters such as Popeye and *Mosquitoes*'s "Faulkner," as I argued previously, their sexual performance causes other whites to associate them with blackness, which reflexively means that, for Faulkner's white characters, an association with blackness queers their white identity.

Quentin Compson continues Faulkner's minstrel exploration of identity, though in a more oblique fashion. As a 1933 draft of an introduction to a never-published special edition of *The Sound and the Fury* attests, Faulkner was aware of the extent to which he placed bits of himself into both his white and black characters: "I was Quentin and Jason and Benjy and Dilsey and T. P." (Cohen and Fowler 278), an awareness that may have led to his disavowal of this introduction in 1946, and his refusal to allow its publication in a subsequent edition of *The Sound and the Fury*. The first character mentioned in this list, Quentin, is undoubtedly first for a reason—a sensitive young man who agonizes over his failures to enact "appropriate" (heterosexual) masculine behavior—repeats elements of the more autobiographical fragment "Elmer" that Faulkner had previously abandoned. If Elmer was an artist, Quentin is the artist manqué, who on the final day of his life leaves the city for the country. There he meets three boys who are fishing, one of whom asks if Quentin is Canadian, which produces this exchange:

> "He dont talk like them," the second said. "I've heard them talk. He
>   [Quentin] talks like they do in minstrel shows."
> "Say," the third said. "Aint you afraid he'll hit you?"
> "Hit me?"
> "You said he talks like a colored man." (120)

Quentin's southern accent queerly positions him as a whiteface minstrel, and as a young man at odds with his cultural heritage, like so many of Faulkner's male protagonists, he becomes another white colored man. Quentin's "blackness," then, is subliminal, a function of his voice and his shadow that follows him throughout his final day. Within the larger symbolic logic of *The Sound and the Fury*, what may shadow Quentin and his failure to find an artistic voice is another of Faulkner's funny little black men, one who this time is actually an African American. Reverend Shegog begins his Easter sermon in what may be linguistic whiteface, but suddenly modulates to an African American dialect. Because he a visiting speaker from St. Louis, however, it is unclear which of his two voices are authentic, and so what part of his sermon is in fact the most performative. Nevertheless, because he constructs his rhetorical authority by modulating race in different voices, Shegog figures the possibility of an artistic identity that is black.

The relationship between Quentin Compson and Ike McCaslin is generative, since, as Faulkner initially conceived of his hunting stories "Lion" (written in 1935) and "The Old People" (drafted in 1939), it is Quentin who learns the ways of the wilderness from Sam Fathers (Blotner, "Notes" 690–91). Ike quite literally, then, is born out of Quentin, and the two characters serve a similar function by allowing Faulkner to think southern masculinity. And if Faulkner, in some respects, *is* Quentin, and Ike had originally been Quentin, the metonymic chain of displaced author figures continues. Like Quentin, Ike shares the problem of trying to negotiate an adult identity, of seeking how to be a southern white man, when that subject position embodies barbarisms to which these young men cannot reconcile themselves. As is well known, Quentin's problems are largely psychosexual: aware that it is he, and not his sister, Caddy, who should be sexually active, he fears this inversion of the gender order, a situation only underscored by the other students at Harvard who identify Quentin's roommate, Shreve, as his husband. But related to his sense of sexual otherness, part of what unfits Quentin to return home and embrace his destiny as a white male Southerner is his experience of race in Massachusetts. Meeting African Americans outside the South, as I noted at the outset of this chapter, makes Quentin realize the constructedness of his community's enactment of race. If in his sojourn north Quentin comes to realize that African Americans are people too, Ike makes an even more startling discovery for a white Southerner—African Americans are, in fact, kin. Quentin's "solution" to his problematic relation to white southern masculine identity is suicide, which serves as a total renunciation of identity itself. Ike's attempted resolution is a renunciation of his patrimony, a refusal to accept property that in a more coded way turns out to kill his white identity as effectively as Quentin's flatirons.

Ike's communally misrecognized blackness comes into sharper focus if one draws on Weinstein's meditation on a "poetics of identity" that emerges through the honorific "mister" as it functions in a southern context from the end of slavery through the Civil Rights movement. Only white men could be addressed as "mister." For an African American male, this minimal designation of respect was simply unavailable, as Richard Wright's story "The Man Who Was Almost a Man" illustrates. Therefore, as Weinstein cogently notes,

> "*mister* both betokens male adulthood as achieved insertion within the symbolic order—one can only be a *mister* within a larger community of misters—and simultaneously declares a certain measure of autonomy. . . . *Mister* further implies . . . a completed negotiation of the Oedipal crisis itself. All misters are deemed to have passed through the crucible of potentially crippling infantile confusions and to be credentialed as successfully individuated human beings within the social order." (*What Else* 88–89)

Weinstein specifically applies his insight to two African American characters (Lucas Beauchamp in *Go Down, Moses* and Paul D in Toni Morrison's *Beloved*), but I believe this poetics of identity might extend to Uncle Ike as well. Further teasing out the role of southern honorifics, one begins to grasp how Uncle Ike's name is his destiny. In this system, if an African American was always required to address a white man as "mister," naming the African American adult male was a problem.

But the system of naming was more complicated than what is revealed by "mister." For example, a white man named John Smith might be addressed formally by another white adult as "Mr. Smith," but by custom, polite children and adult African Americans would address this white man as "Mr. John." Mr. Smith's wife Jane, similarly, would be Mrs. Smith in formal address by another adult, but "Miss Jane" if addressed by children or African American adults. (This formula still exists in the South to the extent that children in pre- and early elementary school are expected to use the Mr./Miss-plus-first-name formation, although, now, white children might address African American adults in this manner, too.)

The importance of southern honorifics should not be underestimated when reading Faulkner's fiction. It is, for example, why in *Absalom, Absalom!* Quentin is so annoyed with Shreve for repeatedly misidentifying Rosa Coldfield, calling her "Aunt Rosa" when custom demands that she, as a southern lady, be addressed as "Miss Rosa." This act of misnaming is particularly fraught with racial meaning because, typically, the only elderly female, other than a blood relative, that a mannered white Southerner would hail as "aunt" would be black; hence, "Miss Rosa" is unambiguously white, but "Aunt Rosa," quite likely, would be black. Something similar occurs in the naming of the African American male. Since a black man could not be a mister (and, hence, a man), one understands both why the designation "boy" was used by whites, and why this name is so offensive to African American men. But even white Southerners felt the contradiction of calling a black man over sixty "boy," which is why, at a certain age, the pliant African American male graduated from "boy" to "uncle." Growing up, Faulkner had such an "uncle," the family's African American male servant, known as Uncle Ned Barnett. This southern system of naming that distinguishes white folks from blacks has an odd afterlife in contemporary consumer culture in the form of Aunt Jemima pancake mix and Uncle Ben's instant rice—Miss Jemima and Mr. Ben just do not signify in southern culture.

On his trip home for Christmas, the Quentin Compson of *The Sound and the Fury* encounters an instantiation of the black uncle. When the train stops in Virginia, Quentin sees an old African American on a mule and experiences the moment as though it were a sign reading "You are home again"; this leads him to initiate the following exchange:

> "Hey, Uncle," I said. "Is this the way?"
> "Suh?" He looked at me, then he loosened the blanket and lifted it away from his ear.
> "Christmas gift!" I said.
> "Sho comin, boss. You done caught me, aint you."
> "I'll let you off this time." [. . .] "But look out next time. I'll be coming back through her tow days after New Year, and look out then." I threw the quarter out the window. "Buy yourself some Santy Claus." (87)

By enacting this southern custom—a game played between blacks and whites in which whoever says "Christmas gift" first wins—Quentin attempts to stabilize his whiteness, which, as noted earlier, becomes more contingent as he experiences different racial codes in the North; for a brief moment, in this ritualized instance of *noblesse oblige*, Quentin can be what his cultural and family traditions tell him he should be—the "young marster."[25]

Not all unrelated "uncles" are black, of course, as evidenced in *Go Down, Moses* by Uncle Buck and Uncle Buddy (whose given names are

Theophilus and Amodeus). Initially, then, we might suppose that Ike's honorific "uncle" functions in the same good-old-boy fashion as it does for Buck and Buddy. The difference is that in the appropriate social setting, Buck becomes Mr. Theophilus, just as Uncle Buddy can be Mr. Amodeus. (Certainly no African American would risk addressing these white men as "uncle.") From the time of his majority at age twenty-one, however, Ike can never be Mr. Isaac. This, I believe, creates a fundamental misrecognition that operates in *Go Down, Moses*, one that renders Ike a "boy" until he becomes an "uncle," and thus positions Uncle Ike in the symbolic logic of *Go Down, Moses* as black, more akin, finally, to Uncle Luke (Lucas) and Aunt Molly Beauchamp than to Uncle Buck and Uncle Buddy. Unlike the character "Faulkner" in *Mosquitoes* or Popeye in *Sanctuary*, Ike becomes a sort of invisible man because no one, certainly not Ike himself, can see or name his blackness.

Ike's racechange comes about in part from his claim to be the spiritual son of Sam Fathers. From Sam's marking Ike's face with the blood of the first deer he kills, to Ike's help in providing Sam with appropriate Native American funeral rites, Ike's metaphorical refiliation is signaled, but in a misleading way. Quite simply, Ike thinks he is choosing "Indianness," but misses that he also is linking himself to blackness. Although Sam is a curiously hybrid figure, the son of a Chickasaw chief and his female quadroon slave (which makes Sam one-half Indian, three-eighths white, and one-eighth black), to the larger southern community that rigorously wished to absolutize racial divisions, Sam's small percentage of African heritage means that he can only be seen as "Negro." To the nine-year-old Ike, though, there is a difference. He recognizes that the white hunters acknowledge Sam's difference and treat him with greater respect than other blacks precisely because of his special knowledge of the woods and hunting. Moreover, Ike sees that Sam only does "white man's work," and that, "although Sam lived among the negroes, in a cabin among the other cabins in the quarters, and consorted with negroes . . . and dressed like them and talked like them and even went with them to the negro church now and then, he was still the son of a Chickasaw chief and the negroes knew it" (163).

For Ike, then, becoming the son of Sam Fathers means embodying a Native American ethos toward the land. What Ike misrecognizes is Sam's status as a black man in the white community. And in the South, if the father you claim (no matter how figuratively) is black, then you yourself can only be black too; it may simply be that the indirectness of Ike's claim to be Sam's son prevents both the community and Ike from articulating how he has positioned himself.

This positioning is indicated by Ike's final return to Major de Spain's old hunting camp a year and a half after Sam Father's death. Ike, now eighteen, waits with the old African American cook, Ash, for the arrival of Boon Hogganbeck. The alcoholic Boon, himself part Indian (though still "white" in the southern context because he has no African heritage), is a character that typically does not have the respect of other white men, and yet, when speaking about Boon to Ash, Ike refers to him as "Mr. Boon" (307). What is noteworthy here is that Ike addresses Boon as a black male would be required to. Although one could attribute Ike's addressing Boon as "Mr. Boon" to the youth's respect for an elder, no other white character ever grants Boon the honorific. An index of Boon's marginal performance of whiteness is that even Ash does not employ "mister" when referring to Boon.[26]

Over and above the matter of honorifics, a different, yet no less significant indication of Ike's blackness resides in the book's title, *Go Down, Moses*, which appropriates the name of the African American spiritual based on the story in Exodus of Moses and the freeing of the Hebrews. In order to liberate Pharaoh's slaves, Moses, who was born of poor Hebrew parents, but raised by Pharaoh's daughter in wealth and privilege, must identify with the suffering of the enslaved. Moses's killing of the Egyptian who beats a Hebrew results in his loss of privilege and patrimony. Moreover, Moses's act leads to his transformation from Egyptian back into Hebrew. The biblical account of Moses and the African American appropriation of this narrative, however, are not the only ones on which Faulkner could have drawn to construct mythological resonances in his 1942 text. Published in 1939, Sigmund Freud's *Moses and Monotheism* posits a different Jewish lawgiver, one who more closely resembles the racechange experienced by Isaac McCaslin; since Freud's Moses is not originally a member of the enslaved race, he cannot experience a return to a true Hebrew identity. In his opening chapter, Freud, having analyzed the etymology of Moses's name and reviewed the biblical story from the perspective of Otto Rank's monomyth, concludes that "Moses is an Egyptian—probably of noble origin—whom the myth undertakes to transform into a Jew" (15). Freud's analysis of Moses resonates with my sense of Faulkner's Isaac: Isaac is a southern white (from a family with some aristocratic pretension) whom the narrative undertakes to transform into a black. Like Moses's renunciation of class privilege that Freud imagines, the renunciation of property and status by Faulkner's Moses figure is willed and deliberate, not accidental as it is in the biblical story. The deliberateness of Freud's Moses, however, goes much further than Ike's; Moses's "unusual solution" (39), which I quote at greater length in the epigraph to this section, is his dream of empire not with God's Chosen People, but with the people he has chosen. He willingly undergoes a racechange to become the Jewish leader. Faulkner's Ike is less self-aware than Freud's Moses. Ike, in addition to having no alternative patriarchal scheme, neither recognizes how his renunciation of class position chooses his new people for him nor that he has, indeed, stumbled onto a most "unusual solution" to the problem of white identity, namely, covert black identity.

But whether we follow the biblical or the Freudian account, it is primarily Moses's loss of his status as an aristocratic Egyptian that prepares Moses for his prophetic role. Long before his encounter with the ledgers of his family's plantation, in which he believes he finds proof of Lucius Quintus Carothers McCaslin's incestuous miscegenation, Ike unconsciously attempts to play the role of Moses in relation to his hunting mentor, Sam Fathers.

In "The Old People," when Ike's older cousin and father figure, McCaslin (Cass) Edmonds, tries to tell Ike about what haunts and imprisons Sam Fathers, Ike pleads "Then let him go! [. . .] Let him go!" (161), words that echo Moses's words in Exodus (9:1) and the spiritual that gives Faulkner's novel its title. At this juncture, McCaslin can laugh at Ike's presumption and dismiss the plea by saying that Sam's "cage aint McCaslins" but, rather, the mixture of his "wild" Indian and African blood that overwhelmed his white blood. McCaslin confidently assumes, at this point, that young Ike will grow up to see race from the essentialized perspective of the white southern male.

The dense and difficult part 4 of "The Bear" records Ike's long conversation with McCaslin in which the young man explains his decision for repudiating his patrimony, a section that reveals that Ike's relation to Moses is overlaid with Christological meanings. The section also provides various contexts for understanding Ike's repudiation, particularly his reading the ledgers of the plantation that cryptically record his grandfather's incestuous miscegenation. Having read the ledgers, but before his majority, Ike tries to enact the role of the adult southern male to the extent that he executes the conditions of his grandfather's will in seeking out the unacknowledged black McCaslin heirs. This becomes particularly pointed in the case of Fonsiba, who marries a northern black man and moves to his Arkansas farm. When Ike finally finds them and sees the poverty of the young couple, he asks her if she is all right, to which she replies only, "I'm free" (268). In a paternalism worthy of the southern white male, Ike decides not to give Fonsiba her one thousand dollar legacy outright but goes to town and arranges with a bank president, "a translated Mississippian who had once been one of Forrest's men" (268), to dole out the money, three dollars per month, for the next twenty-eight years.

During his debate with McCaslin, Ike makes several claims about his freedom that echo Fonsiba's. Early in their discussion, Ike positions himself as a kind of Moses, claiming that God chose his grandfather to redeem the land, not for what L. Q. C. McCaslin would do, but rather that "maybe He had foreseen already the descendants Grandfather would have, maybe He saw already in Grandfather the seed progenitive of the three generations He saw it would take to set at least some of His lowly people free" (248). In short, God foresaw in old McCaslin the grandson, Isaac, who would play the role of freeing His people. But as the impassioned argument of these two men plays out, it becomes clear that Ike, who takes up carpentry in imitation of both Sam Fathers and Jesus, enacts a version of Moses that suggests why the Jewish lawgiver serves in biblical typology as an Old Testament figuration of Christ.

Later in their debate, McCaslin returns to Ike's sense of God's providence in order to drive home the point that Ike must accept his inheritance. Ike may focus on the inheritance claims of his grandfather's unacknowledged African American heirs, but McCaslin insists that Ike is the exclusive legitimate heir. Here Ike interrupts to proclaim "I am free" (285). Undaunted, McCaslin attempts a different argument, one that would unite Ike's white claim to the land as the McCaslin heir with the older Native American title claim: "You said how on that instant when Ikkemotubbe realised that he could sell the land to Grandfather, it ceased forever to have been his. All right; go on: Then it belonged to Sam Fathers, old Ikkemotubbe's son. And who inherited from Sam Fathers, if not you?" Again, Ike interrupts, claiming "Sam Fathers set me free" (286).

Ike's relation to freedom, though, is fundamentally different than Fonsiba's. Born two years after the end of the Civil War, Ike cannot in any literal sense do what Moses did for the Hebrews because African Americans already have been granted their freedom by the U.S. government. The literal slavery that African Americans experienced becomes, in part, a metaphor for Ike's personal sense of bondage to the crimes against humanity perpetrated by his grandfather. Therefore, although Ike postures as Moses, the one who frees the slaves, his real purpose in the Christ-like sacrificing of his patrimony and identity is to redeem the land and white southern masculinity itself. Ike's aspiration is fully ironized, however: the freedom he ostensibly gains from repudiating his patrimony may allow him to construct what he believes is an alternative enactment of southern manhood, but in fact this "freedom" only turns him into "black" Uncle Ike, a not-man who can say nothing that will influence the behavior or thinking of a "real" white man.

Stated differently, what Ike fails to realize is that, from the moment he denies his patrimony and argues for the superiority of African Americans, he has chosen a different people and thus becomes a *faux* Moses inasmuch as he does not want to lead blacks and he has disqualified himself from leading whites. He may wander in the wilderness for more than forty years, but there is no Promised Land for him even to glimpse because he makes his journey alone. In this sense, he is less the patriarch Moses than his biblical namesake, Isaac, a sacrificial figure, even if God spares his life. Oddly, like the sacrificial role that the biblical Isaac was made to play, Ike's self-sacrifice, far from disrupting patriarchy, ultimately serves to ensure its endurance.

Giving up their argument in disgust, McCaslin tosses an envelope with thirty dollars onto the bed, which Ike claims he will take only as a loan. But Cass says, "You cant. I have no money to lend you. And you will have to go to the bank and get it next month because I wont bring it to you" (294). Even though Ike insists on paying this money back, in a southern context, from his majority through his reincarnation as Uncle Ike, he cannot be "white" because he is cast by a white man as the object of *noblesse oblige*. What Ike does for Fonsiba, McCaslin attempts to do for Ike, namely, arrange with a banker to provide a monthly income to ensure the well-being of an individual who is deemed incompetent to handle her or his own money.

Although Ike's repudiation of his inheritance overtly focuses on the land, it also effectively serves as a disavowal of his heterosexuality. Having repudiated the McCaslin plantation once, he does so again in the marriage bed when faced with his wife's sexual blackmail. What is striking, though, is that the second repudiation, which causes his wife to terminate their sexual relations, seems to be of little moment to Ike; his passion is always for the big woods and not any woman. In retreating from heterosexuality, Ike repairs into the extreme homosociality of the hunters' world. "Delta Autumn," which briefly telescopes the missing years of Ike's life between his youth and old age, sings no song of sexual suffering, but rather of having no male heir: "that same wrong and shame from whose regret and grief he would at least save and free his son and, saving and freeing his son, lost him" (335). Although he continues to live with his wife until her death, and afterward with her "widowed niece and children," Ike's real sense of family is wholly masculine. He sees his true home as the brief period spent in a tent each fall with men "some of whom he only saw during these two November weeks and not one of whom even bore any name he used to know" because they "were more his kin than any" (335). By vacating his role as husband (thus denying the possibility of fatherhood) and being passionate only about hunting, Ike retreats from sexual adulthood and returns himself to the state of boyhood until he is granted the honorific "uncle," which, once again, in the racially fraught world of *Go Down, Moses*, can scarcely be without meaning.

While the marriage bed is a site of shame, recrimination, and betrayal, the bed (oddly enough), when shared by two males, becomes a site of ideal communion. At the end of "The Old People," ten-year-old Ike is in bed with McCaslin. After their bodies stop shaking from the cold, they slip into conversation. Ike tells his cousin about seeing the spirit of the big buck with Sam Fathers. When Ike becomes agitated, thinking that McCaslin does not believe him, the older cousin calms the boy by putting his hand on his "flank beneath the covers" (180). Old General Compson also instinctively knows where special intimacy arises, where one man can fully reveal himself to another. After Ike has repudiated his family's farm, Compson wants to know why and offers to share his bed with the young man on the grounds that "You sleep with me and before the winter is out, I'll know the reason. You'll tell me" (295). Ike's most intimate intercourse is always verbal rather than sexual and is always between men.[27]

Ike may cast himself as the latter-day Sam Fathers, seeking to lead a new generation of southern men to a higher plane of ethical intercourse, but among the hunters of November 1941, Uncle Ike gets no respect. These middle-age men patronize Ike and speak in thinly coded language about Roth Edmonds's affair, language that the "innocent" Ike does not understand. No one is more brutal to Ike than Roth, the current owner of the old McCaslin plantation and grandson of McCaslin Edmonds. In *Go Down, Moses*, we see Roth harassed by two uncles, one white and one black—Isaac and Lucas: the latter by his illegal or shady business deals; the former by his moralizing. Roth, however, cannot put Lucas in his place by calling him "Uncle Lucas," because to do so would be to articulate the southern community's unspeakable (the very thing that McCaslin Edmonds will not allow to be spoken when the northern African American comes to him to ask for Fonsiba's hand), namely, that whites and African Americans are related. Significantly, Roth speaks to Uncle Ike, his supposedly acknowledged kinsman, using the same degree of contempt with which he addresses Lucas and does not defer in the least to the ideas of either old man.

And to this new generation of hunters, Uncle Ike has some mighty queer notions about heterosexuality. Around the campfire, Ike speaks of the instantiation of God as follows: "I think that every man and woman, at the instant when it dont matter whether they marry or not, I think that whether they marry then or afterward or dont never, at that instant the two of them together were God" (332). Ike's theological valuation of the sex act, based on his memory of the one time he saw his wife naked, seems strange to the other men who know of Roth's affair with a light-skinned African American woman. A contradiction in Ike's conception of God is that it necessarily embraces L. Q. C. McCaslin's forced sexual congress with his slave Eunice and their daughter, Tomasina, the very sins of the father that Ike has sought to counterbalance.

Ike's conception of the God of heterosexuality, then, serves a useful context for considering the scene in which he is confronted by Roth's African American mistress and her child, a scene that condenses the multiple *méconnaissances* surrounding Ike's identity. Ike initially assumes the woman is white and wonders why Roth abandoned her in a language that recalls the way he delineates God: "Not marriage. He didn't promise you that. Dont lie to me. He didn't have to" (341). But Ike misses the clues in her language that might have prepared him for the revelation of her identity as his black kin. She calls him Uncle Isaac, not Uncle Ike, and she knows a great deal about the genealogy of the McCaslin family and about the descendants of the McCaslin slaves. It is only when she mentions that her aunt took in washing—something that only an African American woman would do—that the scales fall from Ike's eyes, but his response seems overdone (especially for someone who had argued at length with McCaslin that African Americans are better than whites): "*Maybe in a thousand or two thousand years in America*, he thought. *But not now! Not now!* He cried, not loud, in a voice of amazement, pity, and outrage: 'You're a nigger!'" (344).

The full effect of Ike's identifying moment can be unpacked more completely if we read it as an instance of racial panic, where racial panic works in ways that are parallel to the psychological structure of homosexual panic that Eve Sedgwick has described.[28] In this flash of recognition and identification, Ike's confidence in the supposed stability of black-white racial difference temporarily evaporates. Earlier in their conversation, this young woman had asserted that Ike was responsible for Roth's failure: "You spoiled him. You, and Uncle Lucas and Aunt Mollie" (343). Speaking as she does, her white identity had seemed secure to Ike, her utterance only indicating that she knew how to politely name an elderly black man and woman such as the Beauchamp couple. But when Lucas and Molly are literalized as biological uncle and aunt, something happens: Ike stands in relationship to these African Americans as just another of this young woman's relatives (her Uncle Isaac). Looking into the mirroring face of his kinswomen, Ike is not simply identifying her in his exclamation "You're a nigger!";[29] rather, his amazed and outraged outburst suggests that the claim is self-reflexive, one in which Uncle Isaac recognizes that Uncle Ike is, socially speaking, a "nigger," too. Openly acknowledged as kin to blacks, without land, money, or possessions, Ike is not a self-possessed "mister." At the same time, this young woman's unashamed declaration of her interracial heterosexual desire exposes the impossibly idealized conception of heterosexuality that Ike has articulated, an idealization that had protected him from actually having to himself perform as a heterosexual. In this doubled sense of racial and sexual identity, Ike *is* black.

This racial (self-)identification is a shock to Ike, and the moment of recognition seems also to entail a nearly simultaneous repression of his new knowledge. He initially wants to be rid of this young woman but then attempts to do what no other McCaslin or Edmonds ever does, namely, acknowledge an African American woman's kinship by presenting her infant son with General Compson's silver hunting horn. The only legacy Ike has he passes to a black heir. The advice he gives this woman, however, is but a milder version of his panicked response when he leans her identity: "Marry: a man of your own race. That's the only salvation for you—for a while yet, maybe a long time yet. We will have to wait. Marry a black man" (346). To the extent that he vaguely recognizes his blackness ("*We* will have to wait"), Uncle Ike is now an Uncle Tom, speaking for the "go slow now" school of racial progress.

Not surprisingly, there is no more room for Uncle Ike than for Uncle Luke to maneuver in the concluding narrative, "Go Down, Moses." In her grief over her grandson's death, Molly may cry out that "Roth Edmonds sold my Benjamin. . . . Sold him to Pharaoh" (362), but Ike cannot intervene, cannot be Moses coming down to free his people. In renouncing his white patrimony, in becoming symbolically black, Ike is disbarred from speaking in the white contexts of the law and *noblesse oblige*. Ike's fall into silence typifies the conundrum of Faulkner's "black" white characters—ranging from that funny little black man named "Faulkner" in *Mosquitoes* to the minstrel Quentin Compson of *The Sound and the Fury*. Such characters consistently avow a liminal space of difference that the author's southern community can never acknowledge in its urge to make absolute all racial and sexual difference. In this regard, these characters serve as yet another way to expose the historical contradictions of a culture that believes in racial purity but in which the races in fact have already been mixed. But there is a price to be paid for attempting to construct an alternative white masculine identity; even the most minimal figurative relation to blackness queers these characters' attempts to enact an alternative to white southern masculinity.

From his early writing onward, Faulkner had been playing in the dark, using figurations of blackness to think about and question white masculine identity. In some sense, Uncle Ike culminates the author's use of racechange as a strategy to reimagine whiteness. By 1942, Faulkner may have acquired the trappings of the southern patriarch, such as an antebellum home and a farm, but his increasing family responsibilities made his attempt to enact the role of the southern patriarch a kind of unintentional pastiche. Most of his novels were out of print, and he simply could not make enough money fast enough from his short stories to support the fiction that he was adequately fulfilling his proper masculine role.[30] One wonders, then, to what extent Ike's panicked response to Roth's mistress may not, in some sense, be Faulkner's own expression of anxiety about his subject position and the very contingency of his own identity as a "mister." If Ike's blackness maps the limits of Faulkner's own black brinksmanship, perhaps we can better understand why the author pulled back from the precipice, as it were, and increasingly turned in his later fiction to the more restrained southern liberalism of Gavin Stevens in order to have an unambiguously white position from which to extemporize about race.[31]

In the world of Yoknapatawpha, African Americans are not the only ones who lead "black" lives, and a whole range of issues surrounding whiteness and sexual identity comes into sharper focus if one is willing to make visible Ike's blackness. Whatever one finally thinks about Faulkner's appropriation of blackness in Go Down, Moses, his text remains a site of proliferating misrecognitions, and we can perhaps locate the "true" Faulkner everywhere and nowhere: from his well-intentioned but racist dedication to "Mammy" Caroline Barr to the racial panic of Uncle Ike, Faulkner risks the grotesque and self-exposure. But it is precisely his foolhardiness that means that Faulkner's fictions are never merely personal but always open out to larger social and historical issues of the inevitably raced and gendered body.

Faulkner's minstrelsy complicates southern racial thinking by illustrating that whiteness is not so much a race but actually a metaphysics of class privilege. The differences between Negro and Caucasian are unknowable because they are always overwhelmed by a constellation of cultural values placed on blackness and whiteness. Faulkner's whiteface minstrelsy uncouples blackness and the Negro, meaning that cultural blackness may reattach itself to racial whiteness. To make this claim is neither to cast William Faulkner as a forerunner of critical whiteness studies nor to see him as a traitor to whiteness. Faulkner the man was clearly of two minds, as his February 15, 1931 racist letter on lynching, sent to the editor of the Memphis *Commercial-Appeal*, so shockingly shows.[32] But if his fiction is populated by white characters that are not exactly white, then it is a testament to an artistic imagination that recognized the contingency of racial identity. We can never know precisely how the man born (and who signed his lynching letter) Falkner experienced race, but the artist William, whose first fiction was merely one letter long, created the self-progenitive nom de plume Faulkner, a signifying difference that proleptically resonates with African American Lucas Beauchamp's recasting of his white name Lucius. As his early fictional portrait of "Faulkner" as a funny little black man suggests, racial identity was never precisely a given for the Nobel Laureate from Oxford and that "Faulkner," whether the artist or the character, always served as a mask enabling a performance of blackness through a minstrelsy of whiteness.

CHAPTER 3

FLANNERY O'CONNOR, (G)RACE, AND COLORED IDENTITY

IN THE PREVIOUS CHAPTER, WE SAW HOW WILLIAM FAULKNER'S FICTION takes the otherness of African Americans' presumed relation to primitivism and maps that primitivism onto nonheteronormative white masculinity. Stated more simply, Faulkner finds in blackness a central trope for his largely failed search for a usable southern white male identity. His white characters' "blackness" almost always signals sexual dissonance. In Flannery O'Connor's fiction, the tropologicial function of blackness shifts from the sexual to the theological. Living in a culture in which whites were supposed to exclusively possess mind and intellect, while African Americans represented the body and emotions, O'Connor found in blackness a trope for reconciling a different binary—body and spirit.

For a long time, readers of O'Connor have noted her relation to blackness. In 1962, John Hawkes saw similarities between O'Connor and Nathanael West on the grounds that both "reflect the verbal mannerism and explosively reductive attitudes of [diabolical] figures in their own 'black' authorial stances" (400). Hawkes here equates "blackness" with an immoral impulse in O'Connor's authority, and while O'Connor vigorously denied being of the devil's party, the issue of color, of course, resonates with the theological context that she insisted was the only appropriate frame for reading her fiction.[1] Following one of the deeply engrained binaries of Western metaphysics, Christianity aligns whiteness with purity, while blackness figures humanity's fallen nature, an opposition that cannot help but have social implications in the context of O'Connor's South.

But what happens when blackness appears to offer a path to salvation? For Claire Kahane, this is what is most troubling about O'Connor's fiction. Kahane sees O'Connor's African American characters as racist stereotypes, "while the metaphor of 'the Negro' in her fiction typically signifies divine humility"; by appropriating blackness, O'Connor is guilty of "transforming the particular brutalizing experience of black men in America into a symbol of the condition of Everyman . . . [and] universalizing their victimhood" (184). While acknowledging that O'Connor is aware of the way African Americans use the blackface mask as a protective device, Kahane nevertheless finds O'Connor's characters "one-dimensional" because of the author's inability to imagine the interiority of African Americans (Kahane 187). Kahane certainly marks an important limitation to O'Connor's ability to depict African American life, but there are ways that O'Connor's figurative blackness does more than simply assert: "We are all niggers" (Kahane 184).[2]

Hawkes suggests a different aspect to O'Connor's relation to blackness. In his opening sentence of his 1962 essay, Hawkes identifies her writing as "black humor" (395). As William Solomon has pointed out, black humor was a term coined by André Breton in the late 1930s to designate surrealism's take on humor. This obsolete term, superceded by "postmodernism," came to be used in relation to a number of writers in the 1950s and 1960s, including Hawkes, Thomas Pynchon, John Barth, Joseph Heller, Valdimir Nabokov, and Ken Kesey. The reason for recovering the concept of "black humor," Solomon argues, is that the humor in these authors' texts has a "comic thrust [that] often strikes at the vicissitudes of whiteness, lucidly analyzing the extent to which this social construct takes shape, by and large, in relation to hallucinatory impressions of blackness. The texts in question may well have contributed to our present understanding of the structure and effects of racialized fantasies, helping clarify the function of embodied images of the Other in the acts that enable persons to feel like individuals" (471). Like the novelists Solomon names, O'Connor creates a humor in her figurative blackness that also strikes at the vicissitudes of whiteness.

The figurative blurring of racial binaries in O'Connor's fiction is often closely related to the possibility of salvation, but it is a salvation predicated on whites' traumatic awakening to a shocking discovery that they are colored, even if that epiphany encompasses an almost simultaneous repression. Whatever theological symbolism color may have in O'Connor's fiction, color cannot be completely uncoupled from the matter of racial identity. O'Connor's characters frequently believe in (or even assert) their whiteness, and this awareness corresponds to their sense of social privilege. Almost invariably, these Caucasian characters are unconcerned about a spiritual searching, either because they are certain that they are already saved or because they thoroughly disbelieve.

Such smugly complacent characters, O'Connor readers know, are heading for a fall. Robert Brinkmeyer, Jr., is surely correct when he observes that "any number of O'Connor stories conclude with bodily injury that signal the penetration of the divine" (83) and that such violence returns characters "to their bodies" (84). As O'Connor has said herself, "I have found that violence is strangely capable of returning my characters to reality and preparing them to accept their moments of grace" (*Mystery* 112). But the fall is not just theological, but social as well. For a person whose identity hinges on a belief in his or her whiteness, to experience a moment revealing that whiteness is a socially conferred distinction that can be withdrawn is to be surprised by race as much as it is to be surprised by sin. In such instances, these returns to the body are moments of *race* as much as they are moments of *grace*. So, even if O'Connor's fiction does risk universalizing black suffering, there is an equally strong countercurrent in her appropriation of blackness that repeatedly underscores the contingency of whiteness.[3]

The world O'Connor writes about has a rigid social hierarchy based on race, class, and gender, but the racechanging moments I explore in this chapter repeatedly suggest how precarious this hierarchy is, threatened as it is by more fluid, transgressive possibilities and becomings. One character who self-consciously maps the social terrain is Mrs. Turpin in "Revelation." Apparently confident in her whiteness, we see her in the doctor's waiting room dividing the other patients into various social categories based on their clothing, particularly their shoes. She pointedly thinks about the choice she would make if Jesus were to tell her that she could "either be a nigger or white-trash," ultimately deciding she would have Jesus make her "a neat clean respectable Negro woman, herself but black" (491). While Mrs. Turpin places poor whites beneath the better sort of colored people, those who most fully embody the position of the poor white (for example, the woman in the doctor's office with the snuff-stained lips) most rigorously maintain their superiority over blacks. Mrs. Turpin's apparent confidence in her social place actually marks an anxiety, namely, that without the proper ongoing performance of whiteness, one risks losing this status. So, every day and in every way (right down to her shoes), Mrs. Turpin performs her whiteness, until a not-so-veiled authorial figure, college student Mary Grace, attacks her and calls her a warthog from hell, a moment that ultimately reduces Mrs. Turpin to a bestial level below that of the poor white or African American.

What "Revelation" underscores is a radical contingency: if whiteness is a performance, rather than a racial essence, one can wake up one day and cease being white. Much of what follows is based on a logic of "it takes one to know one"; that is to say, in O'Connor's fiction, those whites who identify African Americans as "niggers," in fact, speak reflexively, simultaneously identifying something in themselves that problematizes their privileged status as white and reconstitutes them as "artificial niggers." By referring to the title of one of O'Connor's best-known stories (and the story she thought was one of her best), I do not mean primarily those whites who consciously "blacken up," but rather those who at some deeper level fail to recognize that they, in some socioeconomic or psychological way, are positioned as "black" within southern culture and, thus, are always obliviously passing. As we saw in the previous chapter on Faulkner, not all black lives are led by African Americans, and the fact of being racially Caucasian does not ensure southern Whiteness.

Like so many of Faulkner's "black" white characters, such as Quentin Compson and Ike McCaslin, O'Connor's characters often have a problematic relationship to home. Having left home for various reasons, wherever they go, they end up oddly displaced from that home. O'Connor's fiction, I believe, uncannily positions its "colored" whites as diasporic figures. They carry a sense of home with them but cannot go home again precisely because of the distances—whether literal or psychological—that they travel from the rural South. These "black" white characters' relationship to home oddly mirrors the diaspora of African Americans who fled the rural South to escape racist violence. The Great Migration of southern blacks to Harlem, the Midwest, and the Southwest, however, has an important impact on those who remain behind.

I invoke Freud's notion of the uncanny because it resonates with a sense of an estrangement from home. The combination of the familiar with the unfamiliar, the homey with the unhomey, is precisely the experience of disrupted personal identity that so many of O'Connor's characters experience. Heavily invested in a sense of their whiteness in distinction to the Negro, these characters figuratively become racial hybrids in a variety of racechanging moments. The result of these uncanny moments for so many of O'Connor's characters is that, in ways just beyond their ability to name or grasp, they experience a sense of difference from the white self they thought they possessed, which leaves them with a fundamentally changed sense of home.

This chapter, then, will take up a number of O'Connor's narratives in which the very white characters who perpetuate racism find themselves becoming colored. That is, the stable ground that they assumed ensured their whiteness (and thus their ability to name social otherness) crumbles away, leaving them in a strange, newly raced world. Two characters who perpetuate racism and have a problematic relationship to home are Mr. Head in "The Artificial Nigger" and Hazel Motes from *Wise Blood*. Both serve as complementary examples of "displaced persons": Haze literally has no home to which he can return, while Mr. Head's home, while still physically there, has figuratively vanished in his sojourn to the city. But before turning to the problems of these two poor white racists, I wish to consider the more literal representation of diaspora that appears in "The Displaced Person" because it vividly illustrates how an apparently minor change can refigure the epistemological landscape of racial and class hierarchy and helps us better understand the problem of home and homelessness in O'Connor's fiction.

HISTORICAL AND PSYCHOLOGICAL DISPLACEMENTS OF THE PERSONAL

All you colored people better look out.
Flannery O'Connor, "The Displaced Person"

In "The Displaced Person," originally published in 1954, the landowner, Mrs. McIntyre, decides to take on the literally displaced Guizac family from Poland. Looking particularly at O'Connor's expressions regarding the Holocaust, Rachael Carroll argues that O'Connor's portrayal of the South and its relation to the Holocaust operates "by denials and displacements" (98) so that the victims of the Holocaust (the Guizacs) become the perpetrators of displacement. After the liberation of Europe by the Allies, one immediate problem was what to do with all the people who had been taken from their homes and placed in Nazi concentration camps. They could not be immediately repatriated since there often was no home for them to return to. As a result, these people were housed in displaced persons (DPs) camps, which in many instances were former concentration camps. As Carroll notes, the United States was ambivalent about allowing DPs to immigrate to America, and the Displaced Person's Act of 1948 discriminated against Catholics and Jews (107). As political refugees, the Guizacs remind us that the Holocaust was not simply about the extermination of Jews, but also of Slavic peoples. As Mrs. Shortley so dismissively and grotesquely puts it, the Guizacs are "from Poland where all them bodies were stacked up" (206–7). In immigrating to the rural South, the Guizacs upset the sense of social difference predicated on the white/Negro binary.

If Mrs. McIntyre hopes to shore up her sense of noblesse oblige (already signified by her sticking by her black help, Astor and Sulk) by giving these refugees a new home, something profoundly unsettling happens to her own sense of home in the wake of her interaction with this Polish family. Her noblesse oblige toward blacks and foreigners makes Mrs. McIntyre's relationship to the putatively white hired workers, the Shortleys, both more and less complicated. Although these employees are Caucasian and she appreciates Mrs. Shortley's company in the kitchen, Mrs. McIntyre comes to see the Shortleys as white trash who have less of a claim on her charity than her black workers. Such a distinction allows her to see her relationship with the Shortleys as primarily economic. Astor and Sulk are expected, as Negroes, to be unreliable workers, and they are quite willing to "blacken up" to play the role expected of them precisely so that they can benefit from Mrs. McIntyre's paternalism. Mrs. Turpin, as I discussed earlier, might explain the social hierarchy of the South, but Mr. Guizac turns out to be so different as to be nearly impossible to categorize; he becomes a liminal figure who obliviously crosses and recrosses the customs and culture of the color line. And because he can figuratively cross the color line, it turns out to be less absolute than southern culture imagined.

We can see the social system's urge to mark absolute difference in miniature when Mrs. McIntyre wishes to introduce the Guizacs to Mr. Shortley. Mrs. Shortley says, "He don't have time to rest himself in the bushes like them niggers over there" (197). Referring to Astor and Sulk, Mrs. Shortley can assert her husband's whiteness by what he is not—a "nigger." But Mrs. Shortley's belief in this binary is already implicated in a minstrel theatricality made legible in her exchange with old Astor, who is perfectly willing to play along. When Astor asks about the Guizacs ("Who they now?"), the story briefly becomes a pastiche of minstrelsy, with Mrs. Shortley serving as an unrefined Mr. Interlocutor to Astor and Sulk's Tambo and Bones:

"They come from over the water," Mrs. Shortley said with a wave of her arm. "They're what is call Displaced Persons."
"Displaced Persons," he said. "Well now. I declare. What do that mean?"
"It means they ain't where they were born at and there's nowhere for them to go—like if you was run out of here and wouldn't nobody have you."
"It seem like they here, though," the old man said in a reflective voice. "If they here, they somewhere."
"Sho is," the other [Sulk] agreed. "They here." (199)

Irritated by "the illogic of Negro-thinking," Mrs. Shortley responds with a comment that underscores her own faulty logic and her limitation as Mr. Interlocutor: "'They ain't where they belong to be at,' she said. 'They belong to be back over yonder where everything is still like they been used to'" (199). Mrs. Shortely's misunderstanding, though comically worded, is appalling in its ignorance. As displaced persons, the Guizacs are the remainder (and reminder) of the Nazi occupation of Poland, a place where things most definitely are not "still like they been used to." Her failure to comprehend is linked to the contingency of her claim to whiteness and, in fact, suggests that her class position is only minimally different than that of the Negro. Ultimately, in her minstrel performance, Mrs. Shortley is nothing more than a black in whiteface.

Her statement about the homelessness and "being run out" is oddly prophetic, and speaks more broadly than Mrs. Shortley can know, not only to the whole of this story but also to O'Connor's fiction in general. We see in this story how one actual diasporic presence, the displaced Guizacs, creates a kind of chain reaction that dislocates both the notion and the actuality of home, not just for the Shortleys but eventually for Mrs. McIntyre as well. Claims of whiteness, as a result, become unstable, and everyone's identity becomes figuratively miscegenated. This hybridizing occurs through an unhinging of the racial and class assumptions of southern culture.

Mrs. Shortley, as noted previously, initially stands confident in her whiteness, certain that she is not "trash," since she can talk with Mrs. McIntyre about her previous white trash tenants. But after the Shortleys' depart (once they know that they are about to be fired), Mrs. McIntyre sees the Shortleys as indistinguishable from all the other white help she has employed previously: "The people she hired always left her—because they were that kind of people," and that kind is white trash (214). But if Mrs. McIntyre demotes the Shortleys from white to white trash, the story itself has always, as I hope to show, marked Mrs. Shortley as colored. Her colored status is signaled at the outset by her relation to the peacock that follows her in the opening two paragraphs, because in the symbolic logic of "The Displaced Person," African Americans and peacocks are figuratively linked in a way that speaks to historical displacements. In order to show how O'Connor's story colorizes Mrs. Shortley, I will elaborate on the narrative's almost psychoanalytic use of displacement, one that attempts to shift the accent away from (even as it points toward) race.

Mrs. McIntyre's entire sense of home—the house and fifty acres left to her by her first husband, the Judge—depends on her maintaining this space as a kind of memorial to her late husband. The Judge particularly wanted to keep two things on the farm—peacocks and "niggers." Having peacocks "walking around the place made him feel rich" (218), but in this regard, these good-for-nothing birds are closely aligned with his impression of African Americans, who are in his imagination simultaneously lazy and shiftless, yet valuable because "they don't have sense enough to know when to stop working" (219). Both peacocks and African Americans, then, are crucial to the Judge's fashioning his proper white identity as a southern gentleman, an identity itself dependent on diasporic displacements: if Astor and Sulk represent the African diaspora, the non-native peacocks also signal literal displacement as they were taken from their Asian homeland to serve a decorative function in the New World.

Astor and Sulk are the last blacks left on the Judge's property, something again signaled by the reduction of the Judge's once large flock of peafowl to one cock and two hens. The text mangles diasporic identity through Chancey Shortley, who comes to see Guizac, rather than Mrs. McIntyre, as responsible for Mrs. Shortley's death. Despite his grotesque representation of slavery and the Holocaust, Chancey's portrayals of these events to Sulk do serve to link the concepts:

> "Whyn't you go back to Africa?" he asked Sulk one morning. . . . "That's your country, ain't it?"
> "I ain't goin there," the boy said. "They might eat me up."
> "Well, if you behave yourself it isn't any reason you can't stay here," Mr. Shortely said kindly. "Because you didn't run away from nowhere. Your granddaddy was bought. He didn't have a thing to do with coming. It's the people that run away from where they come from that I ain't got any use for." (232)

Although Chancey clearly refers to Guizac in his complaint about people who run away, the reason that Mrs. McIntyre hires such people as the Guizacs is that there has been an exodus of African Americans away from the rural South. Just as the Guizacs have fled the oppressiveness of the displaced person camps, blacks also have moved away from the racism of the agrarian South. The Great Migration effectively reduced the pool of African Americans to exploit for farm labor. If there are not African Americans left to serve as underpaid labor, clearly, landowners need to find artificial Negroes to fill the void.

To the extent, then, that the peacock suggests both diaspora and the subject position of the African American, one can better appreciate the way racechange is signaled by the opening image of Mrs. Shortley, an image that makes her seem almost genetically engineered. When the peacock stops "just behind her" and opens its multicolored tail (194), to the viewer positioned in front of Mrs. Shortley, the plumage appears as though it belongs to the woman. Colored by the peacock's plumage, Mrs. Shortley stands revealed as the text's secret colored woman, a situation confirmed by her involuntary physical response to learning that her husband will be fired.

Overhearing Mrs. McIntyre tell the priest that she intends to fire Chancey, Mrs. Shortley literally stops being white and starts becoming colored: "Her face was an almost volcanic red" (212). The transformation brought about by this loss of caste is emphasized in her efforts to get her family quickly packed up and out of their rented house: "All the time she had been working, her face was changing rapidly from red to white and back again" (212). At the literal level, of course, these changes of color simply signal her body's warning of the impending stroke that kills her. But figuratively, Mrs. Shortley's becoming colored points us toward the "artificial Negro" paradigm that I have argued grows out of Faulkner's practice of whiteface minstrelsy. For Mrs. Shortley, so certain that she could define her whiteness against the otherness of "niggers" and "displaced persons," to suddenly become displaced herself (and thus to suffer the fate she assumed would be Sulk and Astor's) forces her to a degree of recognition that she and her family are substitutes for the blacks. This realization (or perhaps more accurately, her struggle not to articulate what she intuitively knows) effectively kills her white identity so that her sudden death is merely a coup de grace.[4]

White identity is even more problematic in the Polish refugees. Guizac clearly does not know how to act white according to the codes of the South. As Mrs. Shortley tells her husband, "I'd rather have niggers than them Poles. . . . [Y]ou recollect how he shook their hands, like he didn't know the difference, like he might have been as black as them [Astor and Sulk], but when it come to finding out Sulk was taking turkeys, he gone on and told her" (207). Lacking southern prejudices, Guizac is willing to socialize with African Americans but expects that they will honor their employer's property. Mrs. McIntyre tries to explain to Guizac that "all Negroes would steal" (202), a "fact" that is not problematic for her (after all, just as it does for Mrs. Shortley, it confirms her whiteness) and is certainly not grounds for firing Sulk. (What Mrs. Shortley does not realize is that Mrs. McIntyre also "knows" that all white trash also steals, which blurs the line between "trash" and "nigger.") With his new knowledge that stealing does not injure an African American's merit, Guizac concocts a plan to have his cousin escape the displaced persons camps in

Poland by marrying Sulk. Guizac's willingness to mix the races strips Mrs. McIntyre's racism of its civilized pretense: "You would bring this poor innocent child over here and try to marry her to a half-witted thieving black stinking nigger! What kind of monster are you! [sic]" (222). In the light of Guizac's intention to violate this primal southern taboo by facilitating the mixing of white women and black men, the Pole's attitudes toward African Americans suddenly ceases to be an amusing cultural confusion (how droll—he expected blacks to be honest) and becomes a serious problem. Mrs. McIntyre envisions two interchangeable monsters—Sulk and Guizac. Sulk ("the half-witted thieving black stinking nigger") and the now oddly colored Guizac: "Monster! she thought to herself and looked at him as if she were seeing him for the first time. His forehead and skull were white where they had been protected by his cap but the rest of his face was red" (222). Like Mrs. Shortley before her red-faced death, Guizac becomes colored. With this colorization comes a social demotion—Mrs. McIntyre's perception of him shifts from white to white trash, signaled by her placing him in a series of all her other poor white tenants: "They're all the same . . . whether they come from Poland or Tennessee. I've handled Herrins and Ringfields and Shortleys and I can handle a Guizac" (224).

But she cannot finally handle Guizac, and if "The Displaced Person" initially shows Mrs. Shortley's and Guizac's fall from whiteness, the story finally reveals that even the one who has erstwhile been the arbiter of whiteness, Mrs. McIntyre, becomes tinged with the very redness that marks a subliminal racechange in Mrs. Shortley and Guizac. Once colored in this fashion, she too becomes displaced hybrid, who, at the end of her life, performs a kind of whiteface version of the southern African American diaspora. We see the coloring of Mrs. McIntyre's whiteness when she speaks with the priest about getting rid of Guizac. The priest wants to turn the conversation to the peacock that has spread its colorful tail, which he takes a metaphor for Christ's coming. When she hears the priest speak of Christ, "she reddened. Christ in a conversation embarrassed her the way sex had her mother" (226). The two continue to speak at cross-purposes, which leads to a strange conflation of Guizac and Chirst. Mrs. McIntyre complains that "He [Guizac] didn't have to come in the first place," to which the priest responds, "He [Christ] came to redeem us" (226).

This moment of red-faced embarrassment recalls an earlier scene in which Mrs. McIntyre had already made an unintentional link between Guizac and Christ when she tells Mrs. Shortley, because the Pole is such a good worker, "at last I'm saved," by which she means saved economically from the thieving lazy ways of blacks and poor whites. But Mrs. Shortley warns that it is "salvation got from the devil" (203). The color red, traditionally associated with the devil, adds weight to Astor's repeating one of the Judge's favorite lines to Mrs. McIntyre when the two talk following the Shortleys' departure: "Judge say the devil he know is better than the devil he don't" (217). In this context, Mrs. Shortley is the devil Mrs. McIntyre knew, while Guizac is devil she does not know.

On the day of his murder, Guizac combines both roles (devil/temper, Christ/savior) as Mrs. McIntyre's racechange is completed. She wears "a heavy black coat and a red head-kerchief with her black hat pulled down" (234). Falling prey to temptation, her desire to be rid of Guizac, she fails to save him from the "accident" that Chancey has staged: "She had felt her eyes and Mr. Shortely's eyes and the Negro's eyes come together in one look that froze them in collusion forever" as the tractor runs over Guizac (234). Her complicitous gaze creates a hybrid identity that empties whiteness of any privilege; quite literally, there is an "identity" in the gaze which renders her indistinguishable from the poor white and the Negro. All three had seen their self-interest in Guizac's death, but that death turns them all into displaced persons. As Laurel Nesbitt notes, "far from returning everyone to their initial places, Mr. Guizac's death brings about a more thorough displacement for them all" (160). Shortley and Sulk literally leave the farm, and Astor, who does not want to work alone, quits.

But for Mrs. McIntyre, although she remains in her house at the story's end, her uncanny experience in the aftermath of Guizac's death makes her the final, and perhaps fullest, embodiment of displacement. She sees the "bent bodies" of his family over Guizac's corpse, as well as "a black one." This black bent body, however, is no African American, but one of O'Connor's near-ubiquitous "men in black," here, the Catholic priest who had helped the Guizacs find a place with Mrs. McIntyre. Dressed in black, the priest stands to reveal "bloody pants legs" (235), which makes his outfit a strange double of Mrs. McIntyre's black and red clothing. As she looks into the priest's face, there is a second shared gaze from which he does not avert his face; in the space between the shared gazes of racial and priestly blackness, Mrs. McIntyre "felt she was in some foreign country where the people bent over the body were natives, and she watched like a stranger while the dead man was carried away in the ambulance" (235). This moment, which encapsulates both her loss of home and her moment of diaspora consciousness, precipitates her physical decline. At the end, she is an invalid and a displaced person.

What Guizac (as both artificial Negro and Christ figure) redeems Mrs. McIntyre from is not so much her fallen human nature, but rather from her whiteness, an "innocent" belief in her moral and intellectual superiority over the otherness of white trash, Negroes, and foreigners. As the cases of Mrs. Shortley and Mrs. McIntyre make clear, only by becoming colored can white characters experience the often devastating effects of the unification of body and spirit, a unification that hinges grace and race.

To the extent that becoming colored serves as a loss of white identity in "The Displaced Person," one can register the effects of colorization in stories that mimetically have much less to do with racial otherness. The intellectual and self-named Hulga in "Good Country People," for example, predicates her identity on her ability to see through social delusions, particularly religion. She decides to seduce the bible salesman, Manley Pointer, but in the barn loft where they go for their tryst, she discovers that she does believe in something, namely, that Manley is an authentic example of the concept of "good country people," the very group against which she defines herself. Having removed her artificial leg at his request, doubt about him creeps in and she demands he return her leg. When he refuses, her face turns "almost purple" as she berates him for being a hypocrite, a "perfect Christian" (290) who says one thing but does another. But her criticism completely misses the mark since his professions of faith, he reveals, were a con. Hulga's disbelief, then, turns out to be grounded on her belief that a set of people—good country people—do believe. Taking her artificial leg merely is an emblem of the way Manley has already shattered her intellectual pretense; he takes not her virginity, as the reader might suppose he will, but her whiteness (wherein whiteness is the unexamined presumption of class superiority). This racial transformation is confirmed by Hulga's mother, who sees Manley exit the woods and decides he "must have been selling [bibles] to the Negroes back in there" (291). While not displaying his wares to African Americans, he was in fact showing Hulga his hollowed out bible with the whisky flask, the pornographic cards, and the condoms. Obviously, O'Connor's racialized thinking is in play if she imagines that the precondition for receiving God's grace is to become raced, to occupy, at least figuratively, the social abjection of the African American. In "Good Country People" we see again what is the most problematic and the most potentially disruptive about O'Connor's appropriation of blackness: it risks always sliding into racist stereotype, and yet, the appropriation repeatedly works to de-essentialize whiteness.

THE ARTIFICIAL NEGRO AS THE NEW JESUS:
MR. HEAD AND HAZEL MOTES

In the previous section, I referred to Mrs. Shortley as an instantiation of the artificial Negro paradigm, which in O'Connor's ficiton means those Caucasian characters who experience a disturbing revelatory moment in which their whiteness vanishes. This paradigm, not surprisingly, is strikingly evident in one of her best-known stories, "The Artificial Nigger," which ostensibly takes as its matter Mr. Head's desire to teach his ten-year-old grandson, Nelson, about the evils of the city and to instill in the youth the value of being good country people.[5] I agree with Jeanne Perreault, however, who argues that "Mr. Head must take Nelson to the city to teach him to be white" (391). If whiteness knows itself in relation to blackness, there is simply no way for Nelson to assume the mantel of white southern masculinity in his rural community, since Mr. Head notes with pride that they ran all the blacks out of his remote community twelve years ago.[6] While Nelson argues that this will be his second time in the city (since he was born there), his grandfather maintains that the boy exists in a state of innocence about the city, an innocence most profoundly identified as never having seen a "nigger."

The story, focalized as it is through Mr. Head or Nelson, never grants us an angle of vision that is not that of a poor white. But given the poverty they live in, it is apparent that everyone they meet on the train and in the city, white or black, is financially better off than they are. Here, of course, is where the hierarchy of class confronts the hierarchy of race. Mr. Head, who is proud of his wit and wisdom, is oblivious not only to the annoying entrance he and his grandson make on the train as they wake their fellow passengers but also to how little these whites want to interact with him. The old man immediately begins a one-sided conversation with the man seated across from him, for Mr. Head assumes his whiteness is entrée into the social world of the Jim Crow train. He tells his fellow passenger that this is Nelson's first train ride and that the boy is "ignorant as the day he was born, but I mean for him to get his fill [of the city] once and for all" (254); however, Mr. Head is oblivious to the reflexivity of his remark, which applies equally to him. From the outset, these characters are marked as doubles who "looked enough alike to be brothers and brothers not too far apart in age, for Mr. Head had a youthful expression by daylight, while the boy's look was ancient" (251). While Nelson looks to his grandfather ("who would be his only support in the strange place they were approaching" [257]) for guidance in the city, Mr. Head, himself grossly inexperienced with all things urban, previously had gotten lost in a large city store "and had found his way out only after many people had insulted him" (258). Mr. Head proves to be an equally unreliable guide to whiteness because he erroneously believes that difference is legible at the body's surface.

Before they leave home, Nelson asserts, "I reckon I'll know a nigger if I see one" (252). On the train, however, he fails to make good on this assertion. When Mr. Head points out three "coffee-colored," well-dressed individuals—a large man and two younger women—Nelson cannot identify their difference. This is where Mr. Head's pedagogy of poor white racism, in which racial identity always trumps class identity, is implicit. If the Negro is always inferior, Mr. Head's ability to recognize the black who is not actually black is an important ability for Nelson to learn. Yet, Nelson's assertion about a knowledge of blackness predicated on seeing comes into play, I believe, at a key moment in the narrative.

Before embarking on their journey through the city, Mr. Head warns his grandson of the physical dangers of the city and its "lower parts," the sewers, an underworld everywhere underneath them. Making the boy squat down to look at a sewer entrance, the grandfather explains "how a man could slide into it and be sucked along down endless pitchblack tunnels" (259), which in its figurative use of blackness creates a weird symbolic logic. If whiteness privileges mind (as the very name "Head" impiles), then blackness is the body (inasmuch as the sewer suggests not just the city's bowels, but the human lower parts more generally). The ideological message the grandfather teaches resonates literally and figuratively by merging the social and the bodily abject—to be black is to be shit.[7]

Nelson's experience with the maternal black body, however, seems to contradict his grandfather's dire warning. During their day in the city, Mr. Head and Nelson become lost and find themselves in the African American part of town. Since his grandfather is unwilling to show weakness by asking for directions, Nelson approaches not black men (whom he fears) or black children (who he believes will laugh at him), but a large black woman.[8] Nelson realizes her responses to his questions are mildly teasing but is overcome with a powerful urge: "He suddenly wanted her to reach down and pick him up and draw him against her and then he wanted to feel her breath on his face. He wanted to look down and down into her eyes while she held him tighter and tighter. He had never had such a feeling before. He felt as if he were reeling down through a pitch-black tunnel" (262).

Far from the terrifying experience his grandfather had described, the dark tunnel now seems an inviting place. While not a sexual awakening (the black woman's body is maternal rather than erotic), Nelson's sense of this woman's pitch black tunnel reminds the reader that the body's lower parts encompass the reproductive as well as the excremental, the vagina as well as the anus. This motherless child, on the verge of becoming figuratively the black woman's son, rather than the white man's grandson, must be violently pulled away from this woman by Mr. Head, who upbraids the boy for his response to her, which had only been an inarticulate stare.

Mr. Head's decision to trick Nelson in order to prove to the boy that he needs his grandfather's direction backfires spectacularly. When Nelson wakes from his nap and cannot see his grandfather, he panics and runs away, knocking over a white woman who calls for the police. In his terror of the police, Mr. Head denies his kinship to his grandson, a moment he soon realizes has disgraced him in the boy's eyes. But since this story allegorizes the psychological as much as the theological, the doubling of grandfather and grandson is crucial. To the extent that Mr. Head and Nelson are twins, Mr. Head's denial of his grandson is simultaneously a denial of himself and what he holds dearest—his socially constructed sense of what it means to be white. And without his whiteness, he is truly lost: "He knew now that he was wondering into a black strange place where nothing was like it had ever been before" (267). As Mr. Head, who is abjectly ashamed, contemplates throwing himself into a sewer opening to be swept away down that black hole, "a fat man approach[es] with two bulldogs."

I believe that this "fat man," who will direct the pair back to the train, doubles and substitutes for Nelson's "fat man" whom he saw on the train that morning. In the morning the boy existed prior to a knowledge of racial difference, so that when his grandfather asks Nelson what kind of man he sees, he replies "a fat man" (255). Just as the coffee-colored fat man on the train leads his two female companions, the afternoon's fat man (who is clearly white since his race is not marked) has two bulldogs on leads. Both men's dress signals their superior class status, if in different ways—the African American with his ruby tie pin and black walking stick and the suburban white man in his golf knickers. Mr. Head desperately calls out to the fat white man, an appeal that ends "Oh Gawd I'm lost! Oh hep me Gawd I'm lost!" (267). With his trembling hands and the thickening of his country dialect (no different, really, than many renderings in southern fiction of black dialect), Mr. Head has positioned himself as the clown-like figure in need of white charity. The point is that, prior to identifying the "artificial nigger," Mr. Head has already performed the role of artificial Negro in a kind of unconscious minstrelsy. In a white suburb, Mr. Head comes to play precisely the role he will ascribe to the racist statuary—the embodiment of stereotyped blackness where there are no African Americans.[9]

The sole witness to this scene is Nelson, whose "eyes were triumphantly cold" (268). Nelson's triumphant gaze, I would argue, results from his now having made good on his initial assertion that he would recognize a "nigger" if he saw one. At the same moment that Mr. Head is enthralled in anxiety about blackness, just prior to his appeal to the fat man for directions, Nelson "felt, from some remote place inside himself, a black mysterious form reach up as if it would melt his frozen vision in one hot grasp" (267). Nelson's internalized feeling of blackness is less threatening than his grandfather's and recalls his urge to be hugged by the fat black woman ("one hot grasp"); it also anticipates the "vision" of the black statuary, with its one chipped, all-white eye, which is forever frozen. In witnessing his grandfather's breakdown in asking the white man for directions, Nelson's vision becomes temporarily unfrozen, and the boy subliminally grasps that Mr. Head has become what his socioeconomic position might have told him he already was—a Negro in whiteface.

Mr. Head, then, even though he knows how to catch the train home, is also on the verge of a conscious recognition of his loss of whiteness; however, at this moment he spies a piece of grotesquely stereotyped statuary depicting a watermelon-eating African American, a moment that he experiences ultimately as an instance of grace: "An artificial nigger!" (268), the purpose of which he can then "explain" to Nelson: "They ain't got enough real ones here. They got to have an artificial one" (269). What the reader recognizes (even as the characters cannot) is that the racist statue is another double for Mr. Head and Nelson (who have already been marked as doubles). If "Mr. Head looked like an ancient child and Nelson like a miniature old man," the statue, which is "about Nelson's size" mirrors them since "it was not possible to tell if the artificial Negro were meant to be young or old" (268).[10] The statue's look of "wild misery" captures exactly Mr. Head's "black" despair over being lost. In identifying the statue as "artificial nigger," Mr. Head names himself and his grandson but remains unaware that he has done so.

For Mr. Head, identifying the racist statue as an "artificial nigger" allows him a way of scapegoating his shame onto this inanimate object. It is, therefore, Mr. Head's way of repressing the painful (though not yet fully conscious) knowledge that, both in denying Nelson and in his pathetic appeal to the fat white man, he has blackened up. Mr. Head's repression comes in the form of denial that might be articulated as follows: "My uncomfortable sense of blackness, whatever that may mean, does not make me black because, look, over there is the real artificial Negro."

Mr. Head and Nelson return home physically but, in a figurative sense, that home is no longer there. Leaving their cabin in darkness that morning, where everything was bathed in white moonlight, they step off the train that night to notice that "the clinkers under their feet gave off a fresh black light" (269). Although the grandfather comes to understand the journey to the city as proof of his salvation, Nelson's final words underscore the kind of diaspora consciousness that now goes hand in glove with whatever compromised sense of white identity that the day has given him. Before acceding to his grandfather's denial of blackness that resides in the identifying moment of naming the artificial Negro, Nelson finds the fat man's directions to the suburban train stop pointless: "Home was nothing to him" (268). A stranger in a strangely raced land, he is estranged from home. But where is home for Nelson? At the outset, despite his grandfather's dismissal of the notion, he claimed to be from the city since he was born there. For Nelson, home is literally neither here nor there, as he resides in diaspora consciousness between the place he was born (the racialized city) and the place he now lives (the black-free country). Though the "artificial nigger" statue allows the boy to return to his grandfather's rural home, one may need to read Nelson's final words with a full sense of his encounter with his other black homeland: "I'm glad I've went once but I'll never go back again!" (270). Nelson can never return to the city because to do so would be to risk losing the now fragile sense of whiteness that the "artificial nigger" has granted him. To go back, his (as well as the text's) unconscious knows, is to go black.

I have waited until now to examine O'Connor's first novel, *Wise Blood*, because I believe that my discussion of two interrelated figures—the artificial Negro and the displaced person—helps us better approach Hazel ("Haze") Motes, a character in which these figures are latent. Intimately tied to these two figures is a third, the new Jesus, which serves as the foundation of Haze's theology. Taken together, these three figures help us to better understand the imbricated nature of grace and race in O'Connor's fiction.

The first words in the novel spoken to Hazel, who is in a train heading toward the city, are "I guess you're going home." When Haze does not respond, his fellow passenger, Mrs. Wally Bee Hitchcock, taking his silence for consent, opines, "there's no place like home" (10). But the twenty-two-year-old Haze, during his journey to and through the unreal city of Taulkinham, can never click his heels three times to return to his childhood home because *Wise Blood* makes literal the notion that you can't go home again. As a displaced person riding a train, Hazel might recall Faulkner's Quentin Compson, who becomes a displaced Southerner at Harvard. On Quentin's train ride back to Mississippi at the end of fall semester, he needs the old African American on the mule to play the game of "Christmas gift" to temporarily reaffirm his white identity. For the quarter that Quentin throws him, the old black man is willing to wear the mask of "Uncle," and thus become the object of Quentin's noblesse oblige.

Hazel, however, has no aristocratic past and no home left. Returning from military service in World War II, he finds that his small, rural hometown of Eastrod has been abandoned by its final few residents. Yet, like Quentin, Hazel tries to stabilize his white identity in relation to blackness through the figure of the high yellow porter. As his defunct Tennessee hamlet, "fill[s] his head," Haze is certain that the porter is "a Parrum nigger from Eastrod" (12). But what Haze "knows" is in fact what he desperately needs the porter to be—the social construct "nigger" who is ready to service white desire; only the porter can confirm for Haze both his whiteness and his home. But while Quentin's "Uncle" is willing to play along, the porter whom Haze encounters refuses to provide any salvation for whiteness.

Haze's certainty about the porter's identity, even in the face of this African American's repeated assertions that Haze is mistaken, speaks directly to the young man's inherent faith. He may deny Jesus, but he firmly believes in the stereotype of the Negro. What he does not realize is that, in light of actual African Americans abandoning the rural South (and with it the role of the "nigger"), someone still has to fill that role in order to maintain the fiction of southern Whiteness. And that someone is him. If African Americans are no longer available to play Jesus and save whiteness, the artificial Negro must leap into the breach and become the new Jesus (a surrogate of a surrogate), one who offers a different, more terrifying brand of salvation. Haze's role is one that will be played subsequently by such trickster figures as Mr. Shiftlet, Manley Pointer, and the Misfit. But just as these whites fail to understand the ways in which they are becoming black, they do not comprehend or intend the role they play in the salvation of others.

By insisting on the porter's black identity, Haze, in effect, accuses the porter of passing, not in the racial sense, but by denying his rural origins. If, however, Haze accuses the porter of masking his identity, just about everyone Haze meets accuses him of trying to closet his truest identity. His encounter with the steward in the dining car underscores the way in which Haze functions as a rather unsuccessful passer. Having accompanied Mrs.

Hitchcock to the dining car, Haze is rebuffed by the steward, who only has seats for Mrs. Hitchcock and another woman, and pushes Haze back through the doorway. As we have seen in O'Connor's depiction of "colored" whiteness, this gesture of exclusion causes Haze's face to turn "an ugly red" (15). His embarrassment is the most obvious source of his blush, but in turning him into the object of the white gaze, Haze is transformed into the Other, and seems to function in the scene as a surrogate colored person.[11] Once finally seated, Haze is treated in a way that signals a kind of second-class status of the not entirely white. The steward does not call him boy, but by addressing Haze as "sonny," there is an analogous condescension. Seated with three unpleasant young women, Haze is subjected to a variety of small slights. One of the women repeatedly blows cigarette smoke in his face, and the steward, exchanging a conspiratorial wink with the three women, refuses several times to take Haze's money. While not racially black, Haze, as the poor rural white, nevertheless serves the object of ridicule in a way that implies something akin to racial otherness.

In *Wise Blood* the color line is troped as a kind of theological line because Haze's spiritual life is intimately tied to blackness. Like Faulkner's essentially "black" whites, O'Connor's Haze has a relation to figurative blackness so strong that, spiritually at least, it becomes his truest identity. At age twelve, Haze is aware of "a deep black wordless conviction in him that the way to avoid Jesus was to avoid sin," a belief that is linked in the boy's mind to his knowledge that "he was going to be a preacher"; young Haze pictures Jesus as a "wild ragged figure motioning him to turn around and come off into the dark" (22). Jesus is a threatening figure in the boy's imagination, almost a pedophile trying to lure boys into the woods.

Haze may wear a glaring new blue suit, but his black hat is the telltale sign that gives him away to white people. Haze is trying to pass as not-preacher, but he fools no one. From Mrs. Hitchcock and the women in the dining car to the taxi driver and the prostitute, Leora Watts, everyone can see Haze's black hat and know, however much he might protest to the contrary, that he is a preacher. His claim to the women in the dining car that he "wouldn't believe even if He existed. Even if He was on this train" (16) points to what gives him away. Not a doubting Thomas, but a denying one, Haze would still hold it as an absolute article of faith that one should not believe in Jesus even if there were undeniable evidence that Jesus existed. His eventual assumption of the role of preacher whose message denies Christ is but to affirm the irony of his anti-faith, which is so strong as to be indistinguishable from faith. Jesus may not be on the train, but the African American porter is.

After dinner, Haze asks the porter for help getting into his berth, and the porter, as part of his job, complies. Once in his berth, however, Haze experiences this confined space as a nightmare of blackness in which he recalls his spiritual journey toward what he takes to be his faithlessness. In the army, Haze "had all the time he could want to study his soul in and assure himself that it was not there" (24). His fetishizing denial of his soul, like his denial of Christ, is based on a certainty of the existence of that which is denied. Haze's contradictory and paradoxical relationship to the theological should warn the reader about the accuracy of his self-knowledge that follows his reflection on his soul: "The misery he had was a longing for home; it had nothing to do with Jesus" (24). As another of Haze's denials of Jesus, we may need to turn this around. His sense of homelessness has everything to do with Jesus and, hence, blackness.

As the opening chapter ends, Haze seeks to be released from his night-mare that turns his berth into his coffin. Thrusting his head out of the berth (birth/death), he sees the porter as "a white shape in the darkness" and appeals to the porter to get him down. In doing so Haze calls out "Jesus . . . Jesus" (27), which can be taken as an exclamation of his fear, but also has the uncanny effect of seeming like a direct address to the porter. William Faulkner, of course, had played on the Jesus-as-Negro figuration in naming the sinister lurking character that Nancy knows is coming to kill her in "That Evening Sun." Faulkner's Jesus interestingly conflates two white southern conceptions of the African American into one disturbing figure—the black as a simple, devout Christian and the black as violent murderer. In *Wise Blood*, the porter, whom Haze has unin-tentionally figured as Jesus, replies, "Jesus been a long time gone" (27).

The porter's response helps to illustrate the way in which Jesus and blackness are implicitly linked. In crying out to his African American Jesus, Haze (in a kind of dreamwork logic) is in fact crying out to a par-ticular white conception of the serviceable African American, the black man who will be his salvation by stabilizing whiteness—the nigger Jesus. Neither the Uncle Tom whom Quentin Compson encounters nor the razor-carrying Jesus whom Nancy fears, O'Connor's porter continues the dream logic in his response to Haze. In short, the porter's claim that Jesus has been a long time gone tells the uncomprehending Haze that, in the postwar world, the old southern conception of the happy-to-be-of-service Negro is indeed a white fantasy, one in which the porter refuses to par-ticipate. This porter renders the services for which he has been paid but is unavailable and unwilling to grant Haze his white identity by becoming a "Parrum nigger."

The porter's assertion about the absent Negro/Jesus speaks to Haze's subsequent articulations regarding Jesus, giving them a racialized valance. When Haze tells Asa Hawks, the "blind" street preacher, at their first meeting that "Nothing matters but that Jesus don't exist" (54), or when Haze later preaches to a crowd that: "Nothing matters but that Jesus was a liar" (105), one hears professions of faith. In both instances, his absolutizing pronouncement (nothing matters) is meaningful only in its exceptional relation to Jesus—either the one who does not exist or the one who is a liar. Recalling the porter's claim about Jesus's disappearance, one might hear Haze's dark Jesus anxiety. In his first assertion, Haze confirms the porter's message that African Americans no longer play the "Negro Jesus" role, while, in the second, the porter/Jesus is a liar.

If Haze's black hat is the dark mark that gives away his attempt to pass as not a preacher, then he has a chance to refine his performance when the prostitute, Mrs. Watts, ruins his old hat. He buys a white panama that the salesman says are just the thing for a trip to Florida, but Haze responds, "This hat is just the opposite of the one I used to have is all." The salesman quickly says that Haze can "use it anywhere" because "its new" (111). In fact, it is the hat of the new jesus. If his old black hat was what gave him away as a preacher, his attempt to pass is again frustrated because after Haze adjusts the white hat to his liking, "it looked just as fierce as the other one had" (111). Even whitening up, it seems, fails to hide Haze's more deep-seated blackness.

Each of Hazel's three main doubles plays on the dark Jesus motif in *Wise Blood*. Asa Hawks wants Haze as a disciple; Enoch Emory wants to be Haze's disciple; and Solace Layfield is hired to be Haze. Each of Haze's doubles are blackface minstrels, in the same sense that Faulkner's Ab Snopes is also. (See my discussion of '"Barn Burning" in Chapter 1). That is, like Ab, they appropriate blackness for personal gain as scam or scheme. Haze, however, is more like Sarty Snopes, because he is appropriated by blackness. In other words, Haze is unaware that he is becoming culturally black.

The reader first meets Asa Hawks when he breaks up a street vendor's presentation by begging for money. Wearing a black suit and a black hat (which, of course, recalls Haze's black hat that repeatedly marks him as a preacher), he is accompanied by his daughter, Sabbath Lily, who wears a black dress. With his white cane and black glasses, the apparently blind Asa instantiates one kind of artificial Negro, in the sense that he is willing to become the object of white charity, offering other Caucasians an easy way to confirm their sense of whiteness. In the absence of African Americans, Asa serves in their stead.

Although professing distain for Hawks, Haze is clearly infatuated with the older preacher, and takes a room in the same boarding house as the blind man who has called on Haze to repent. Haze becomes nearly obsessed with Hawks after the older man shows Haze a newspaper clipping from ten years earlier that tells how Asa would blind himself the following night at a revival to "justify his belief that Christ Jesus had redeemed him" (112). What Asa does not show Haze is the subsequent clipping that tells how his nerve failed him. Asa's false blindness enacts a minstrel show. It is a kind of "blackface" because the lime-streaks around his eyes, along with Asa's dark glasses, present a front of authenticity that says "I live in a world of blackness." This unspoken claim leads back both to Haze's childhood belief in a dark Jesus and to Haze's encounter with the porter, who proclaims that dark Jesus has left the building. Hence, Haze's obsession with Asa develops from his sense that the older street preacher's "faith" represents a serious challenge to his own anti-faith, which is as absolute in relation to Jesus as any fundamentalist's. This is why Haze plots to seduce Sabbath: he believes if he "ruins" the preachers' daughter, the old man will lose his faith. Since Haze believes that the old man's blindness/blackness is real, he also erroneously believes that Asa truly wants to save him, just as he had hoped the porter would. Asa does hawk salvation but for cash flow, not conviction. In this sense, then, Haze enters a struggle with Asa over who will convert whom.

The conflict between these doubles is symbolized in one particular scene in which animals become their totemic substitutes. When Haze's car breaks down in the country, he finds a store with a gas pump and a mechanic. At the store, there is a bit of free entertainment in a cage marked with a sign proclaiming "TWO DEADLY ENEMIES": "There was a black bear about four feet long and very thin, resting on the floor of the cage; his back was spotted with bird lime that had been shot down on him by a small chicken hawk that was sitting on a perch in the upper part of the same apartment. Most of the hawk's tail was gone: the bear only had one eye" (125).

As if entering a dream, Haze witnesses a symbolic performance of his struggle with the older preacher. By its very name, the chicken hawk is linked to Hawks, while the one-eyed, thin black bear represents the gaunt Haze. The bear's partial blindness points both toward Haze's failure to recognize Asa's false blindness, as well as to Haze's eventual blinding of himself as a way to prove the superiority of his conviction that there is no salvation over Asa's apparent conviction in salvation. More interesting, though, is the bear's blackness, which serves as another indication of Haze's racechanged identity. If Haze is in the dark about Asa's ruse, he is equally blind to the ways in which he is coming to fill the role of black-ness in the southern city that the porter refuses to play. Culturally black in ways that he cannot see, Haze is like the bear whose blackness is being hidden by the white bird droppings. In short, Haze's status as a "white-face" black is encoded in the bird-lime covered black bear.

If Asa doubles Haze in their inverted relationship to blackness, Enoch doubles Haze through their relationship to primitivism, as well as to blackness. Like Haze, the eighteen-year-old Enoch is also displaced from his rural Tennessee home. Though claiming a degree of sophistication for having arrived in Taulkinham two months earlier than Haze, Enoch is as alienated in white urban space as Haze. Enoch, like Haze, seeks someone to confirm his identity. But while Haze attempts to use the African American porter to confirm his whiteness, Enoch tries to use Haze's sameness to stabilize his rural identity. Just as Haze insists on the train that he knows the porter to be from his hometown, Enoch maintains that Haze is familiar and that they have met before.

Even before Haze begins preaching, Enoch is literally a follower of the newcomer, shadowing Hazel down the street and ignoring Haze's annoy-ance, one that grows into active dislike. Haze eventually bloodies Enoch by throwing a rock at him. Despite this ill treatment, Enoch feels drawn to Haze in the same way that Haze is drawn to Asa, sensing that Haze might possess some greater truth. The greater truth Enoch seizes on is Haze's teachings about "the new jesus," in which Jesus is stripped of the divine. When Haze preaches the new jesus on the street, Enoch happens by and hears Haze's words: "What you need is something to take the place of Jesus, something that would speak plain. The Church Without Christ don't have a Jesus but it needs one! It needs a new jesus! It needs one that's all man, without blood to waste, and it needs one that don't look like any other man so you'll look at him. . . . Give me this new jesus, somebody, so we'll all be saved by the sight of him!" (140–41). Haze means his message metaphorically. The notion of redemption through the death of the new jesus is meaningless because his new jesus's blood has no supernatural power. For Haze, who had been left hanging in his berth by the porter, people need to be saved from the notion of salvation.

In his fundamentalist literal mindedness, Enoch feels he is the some-one who can deliver the new bloodless jesus. To Enoch, Haze's descrip-tion can only be that of the mummified man that he has already shown to Haze at the museum. The three-foot-long naked, dried, yellow figure cer-tainly does not have any blood to waste, and undoubtedly looks different than everyone else. Although Enoch eventually identifies the new jesus as a "shriveled-up part-nigger dwarf" (176), there is nothing to suggest that the mummified man was African. Enochs' characterization of the mummy as "part-nigger" derives from its color. As Susan Edmunds points out, the yellow mummy recalls the yellow skin of the African American porter, and, as such, are figures of the threat of miscegenation (575).[12] To the extent that the yellowish mummy (new jesus) is a repetition with a difference of the yellow porter (the hoped for old black Jesus), then Haze, whose face is reflected in the glass case housing the mummy, has a metaphorical kinship to both these figures.

In order to steal the mummy from the museum, Enoch resorts to a disguise, much as Asa does, that instantiates a blackface minstrel performance: "He had darkened his face and hands with brown shoe polish so that if he were seen in the act, he would be taken for a colored person" (174). Prior to stealing the new jesus, Enoch had prepared the washstand cabinet in his room, painting its interior with gilt. Though he did not know why he prepared the cabinet at the time, "he had dreamed of unlocking the cabinet and getting in it and then proceeding to certain rites and mysteries that he had a very vague idea about" (132). This cabinet, which was designed to house a slop jar, becomes the site where the bodily abject meets the socially abject—blackness and shit are again equated, much as Mr. Head does. Having stolen the mummy, Enoch installs his new jesus in the cabinet and waits for its magic to transform his life. Enoch's ritual with the cabinet takes us back to Haze's two coffin experiences. The first is his berth on the train, where he expects deliverance from the porter, but the second is his childhood experience of an adult carnival attraction. Left outside by his father, Haze imagines the forbidden entertainment first as something to do with a privy (suggesting the slop jar cabinet), then as something being done to an African American (the installation of the new Negro jesus in the cabinet). When the barker finally lets Haze in, he discovers the white male audience viewing a naked white woman in a coffin. The object of the male gaze, this woman recalls Haze's experience of watching his dead mother have the coffin lid shut on her. Haze, in his nightmare experience in the train berth, becomes his mother at the moment of the coffin's closing, which suggests a subliminal awareness of his own precarious white masculinity. Rather than being the male subject performing the gaze, Haze, like the carnival woman and his mother, becomes the object of the gaze.[13]

Enoch enacts, then, "strange rites" when he installs the new jesus in the slop jar cabinet, and after nothing happens, crawls into this enclosed space. He experiences not renewal, but a sneeze. Enoch's experience in a coffin-like space serves as a farcical repetition of Haze's train berth/coffin terror. Disgusted that he had believed in Haze's new jesus, Enoch decides to give the mummy to Haze in case the authorities are looking for it. In delivering the new jesus to Haze, Enoch acts unintentionally as a midwife in a strange family romance that makes Haze the father of the new jesus. When Enoch arrives, Haze is asleep, so he gives the mummy to Sabbath, who begins treating it as though it were her child, identifying herself as its momma and Haze as its daddy. What her designation metaphorically suggests is that, as the father of a "nigger dwarf," Haze either has engaged in miscegenation or that he himself is black too. Haze responds with violence to Sabbath's playful characterization, destroying the mummy. By destroying this new jesus/artificial Negro, Haze attempts to deny a part of himself, a kind of objective correlative that identifies his own condition as the novel's secret black man.

The way that Enoch blackens up in minstrel fashion, as opposed to Haze's more profound whiteface blackness, is underscored in their relation to primitivism. Prior to their first sexual encounter, Sabbath identifies Haze as "king of the beasts" (170). But if Haze is called to sexual performance in this fashion, Enoch attempts to literalize the primitive and become "Gonga, Giant Jungle Monarch" (193). On his way to Haze's, after his initial disappoint in the cabinet with the new jesus, Enoch sees a poster announcing a chance to meet the movie gorilla Gonga, which temporarily restores his faith in the new jesus: "To his mind, an opportunity to insult a successful ape came from the hand of Providence. He suddenly regained all his reverence for the new jesus. He saw that he was going to be rewarded after all and have the supreme moment he expected" (178). Previously, when he and Haze had walked through the zoo, they encountered "black shapes" (93) behind bars. Enoch points out an ape in order to insult it: "If I had an ass like that . . . I'd sit on it. I wouldn't be exposing it to all these people come to his park" (94). In the city of Taulkinham, curiously devoid of African Americans, the closest thing to the African primitive is the African primate.[14] To the extent that Enoch seeks confirmation of his whiteness through blackness, his pejorative comment about the caged ape's body helps explain why the "opportunity to insult a successful ape" in person is so appealing. But the plan backfires. Like early audiences of minstrel performances who thought they were witnessing real African Americans, Enoch is convinced that the gorilla is real. So when his turn comes and Gonga extends his warm, soft hand to Enoch, the young man is flooded with a sense of communion. Here is the "black" who offers salvation to the rural youth, alienated in an urban setting. Rather than insulting the artificial ape, Enoch begins to spill out his life story; Gonga, however, cuts him short. Rather than the promise of salvation that seems to be offered by the opportunity to authentically commune with the primitive other, the man in the ape suit tells Enoch to "go to hell" (182). In the sense that a hoped for redemption via an encounter with blackness is frustrated, Enoch's negative experience with Gonga obliquely recalls Haze's failure to elicit the porter's sympathy.

Enoch, however, gets his revenge, but only by taking his own earlier blackface masking one step farther. Chancing on a notice in the paper regarding Gonga's final public appearance that evening, Enoch goes to the theater, murders the man who wore the gorilla costume, and steals the suit. Enoch's initial naivety about the artificial gorilla is replaced by another. He believes that all he has to do to become Gonga, the movie star, is to don the gorilla suit and act as he has seen "Gonga" act in film and at public appearances. It never occurs to him that this is just one of many gorilla suits. His attempt to become the successful ape and to begin basking in his newfound celebrity fails spectacularly when he sees a young couple and approaches them from behind. He only succeeds in scaring them. As ludicrous as Enoch's attempt to become Gonga are, his instincts are based on historical precedent. Like the Irish and Jewish entertainers who earned whiteness by donning blackface, Enoch seeks to attain full whiteness by blackening up. That Enoch, like Haze, falls short of full southern Whiteness is signaled by Enoch's trip to the movie theater (the space of Gonga's fame). He is confronted with a literal sign of racial differentiation that lists "the price of a ticket for adults was forty-five cents, balcony, thirty-five" (138). Having only forty-three cents, Enoch grudgingly goes through the foyer "then up a darker tunnel and then up a higher, still darker tunnel. . . . He didn't like any picture shows but colored musical ones" (138). In the Jim Crow South, movie theaters restricted African Americans to the balconies. Enoch, an economic artificial Negro, sits not in the section reserved for whites (or "adults" as the text labels it), and is therefore constituted as a "boy" with its racial connotation. The narrator's claim that Enoch only liked "colored musical" shows, of course, literally refers to the rise of the use of color in Hollywood films, but in this racialized context it cannot fail to point toward an older entertainment, the blackface minstrel show.

If Asa Hawks and Enoch Emery instantiate versions of blackface minstrelsy, Solace Layfield, another poor rural white, stands as the postmodern double to Haze's status as artifical Negro/new jesus. Asa, Enoch, and Haze each have some chance to begin to recognize their subject position in the New South, but Solace, as simulacrum, becomes so embedded in the system of commodified religion that there is no critical purchase for him to ever recognize what he is, namely, the *artificial* artificial Negro.

Solace is employed by another religious con-man (with whom Haze refuses to work) to imitate Haze's style and message about the "new jesus." Wearing the same style glare-blue suit and kind of hat that, willy-nilly, marks Haze as a preacher, Solace publicly professes that he does not believe in Jesus, which Haze interprets as a mockery of his true faith in no Jesus. Solace becomes a figure for the cultural logic of postmodernism to the extent that he participates in turning religion into pure commodity. He does so because it delivers the goods, three dollars a day and use of a car, which he earns for his weird minstrelsy in which he stands in for that whiteface "black," Hazel Motes.

The murder of Solace, then, reveals Haze as the first instance of O'Connor's many new "black" Jesuses, such as the Misfit, who populate her later fiction. Running over the false prophet, Haze provides the bodily shock that lifts Solace out of his complacency within the economy and returns him to ultimate questions. Listening to Solace's dying confessions, Haze enacts an anti-priestly role; as the dying man spills out his failings, Haze repeatedly tells him to shut up. Solace's final moments are reduced to a plea:

"Jesus . . . " the man said.
"Shut up like I told you to now," Haze said.
"Jesus hep me," the man whispered.
Haze gave him a sharp slap on the back and he was quiet. (205)

Just as Haze had called out to Jesus in the form of the African American porter, Solace calls out to Jesus in a way that conflates Haze with Jesus. In other words, as artificial Negro, Haze provides Layfield with a harsh solace, a path to salvation that Haze himself had hoped to find from the porter. Unlike the porter, whom Haze assumed to be ready to serve whites in their moment of need, Haze (the surrogate black) is the agent who, strangely enough, leads Solace to realize that Jesus is his only hope, thus providing the dying man the harsh solace that effectively makes his salvation possible.

In the conclusion of chapter 13, which inverts yet mirrors the scene between Haze and Solace, a policeman with a "red pleasant face" (208) in a black patrol car pulls Haze over and punishes him for not having a license by pushing Haze's old Essex over an embankment. This act completes Haze's displacement, for the car had been his truest replacement for the rural home he had lost. When Haze collapses on the edge of the embankment, the policeman—in a gesture paralleling Haze's leaning down to hear Solace's last words—bends down to the inconsolable Haze to ask if he needs a ride anywhere. The policeman's act has the potential to redeem Haze from his abject status, but Haze persists in his faith in no Jesus and chooses instead to finalize his the role as the novel's central artificial Negro: he returns to his boarding house and blinds himself, literally immersing himself in a world of blackness.

As the novel draws to a close, Haze's blindness, explicitly marked as a form of blackness, is just one way that we see the logic by which Haze is now the new jesus. His expression of faith (albeit faith in no Jesus) in blinding himself clearly has an impact on his landlady, Mrs. Flood. Initially, she resents the prospect of having to look after a disabled man and equates his pension with foreign aid, equating "blind fools" with "foreign niggers and a-rabs" (214). Her equation points us back to the initial description of Enoch's new jesus, since the mummy, also figured as a "foreign nigger," had been reduced to his small stature by "A-rabs" (98). With "eyes drawn almost shut," the mummy's "vision" anticipates Haze's blindness. Mrs. Flood's resentment, however, gives way to fascination as she tries to imagine how Haze experiences the world:

> She thought of her own head as a switchbox where she controlled from; but with him, she could only imagine the outside in, the whole black world in his head and his head bigger than the world, his head big enough to include the sky and planets and whatever was or had been or would be. . . . She imagined it was like you were walking in a tunnel and all you could see was a pin point of light. . . . She saw it as some kind of a star, like a star on Christmas cards. She saw him going backwards to Bethlehem and she had to laugh. (218–19)

While Mrs. Flood, in her unreflexive whiteness, sees her own mental activity as rational and controlled, she casts Haze's mind as the repository of remote black primitive spirituality—all encompassing but irrational. The tunnel Mrs. Flood imagines walking through to enter Haze's "black world" recalls the black tunnel Enoch must ascend in order to reach the theater balcony reserved for African Americans. Her thoughts, moreover, link Haze's "black world" to Bethlehem, which almost constructs Haze as a version of W. B. Yeats's rough beast, slouching to Bethlehem in "The Second Coming." And though Mrs. Flood laughs, her fascination turns to obsession. When she asks Haze to marry her, he leaves and she reports him to the police for not paying his rent.

After he dies in the police car that returns him to Mrs. Flood's, Haze's apotheosis as the artificial Negro/new jesus becomes complete. Unaware that he is dead, Mrs. Flood hails Haze as the police carry his corpse into her boardinghouse: "I see you've come home!" (231). Mrs. Flood's final address to Haze, now the supremely displaced person, about the home he can have with her completes the novel's meditation on a white diaspora initiated by Mrs. Hitchcock, whose line—"I guess you're going home" (10)—serves as the first words in the novel spoken to Haze. Embraced by Mrs. Flood much as Sabbath had embraced the "part nigger" new jesus, Haze is nothing so much as mummy-like, his hand she holds to her heart "resistless and dry. The outline of a skull was plain under his skin" (231). Closing her eyes, Mrs. Flood experiences the dead Haze "moving farther and farther away into darkness" (232).

By the end of the novel, the dead Hazel Motes is the (artifical) Negro (new) jesus, and he anticipates all of the O'Connor's "men in black," the poor white outcasts, misfits and one-armed men who are the agents of the rough work of salvation. These whitefaced minstrels, who substitute for the vanishing rural African American, do not reproduce the stereotype of the serviceable black, the protective mask worn by African Americans for self-preservation. Instead, these "artificial Negroes" go about their work oblivious both to their figurative racial transformation and to their theological mission. Like Haze, they do not doubt their whiteness and profess not to believe. Even as other Caucasians wish to confirm their whiteness in southern culture against these surrogate blacks, O'Connor's white "black" men produce, in the smugly white, the bodily shock that the author believes produces moments of grace, but which are also invariably moments of race.

If O'Connor discovers in the racial other a striking trope for encoding her theological concerns, John Barth, the subject of the next chapter, is able to turn blackness to use in his explorations of secular, existential identity. What is a constant, however, in the very different worlds of these writers, is a masked identity that cannot help but point toward minstrelsy. If Faulkner and O'Connor conceive of a minstrel mask that is white, Barth directly explores blackface minstrelsy in *The Floating Opera*. Nevertheless, Barth's narrator, Todd Andrews, still performs in whiteface since he appropriates the black cultural role of trickster, even if he remains oblivious to the fact that the Mr. Interlocutor he fools the most is himself.

CHAPTER 4

JOHN BARTH, BLACKFACE, AND INVISIBLE IDENTITY

ALTHOUGH FLANNERY O'CONNOR'S POSTWAR REPRESENTATION OF whiteface minstrelsy shifts Faulkner's concern with masculine identity to the matter of salvation, at least Faulkner and O'Connor seem to write from a relatively shared sense of place. As writers from the Deep South, Mississippi and Georgia, Faulkner and O'Connor are at the core of what most readers think of as Southern Literature. John Barth's Tidewater Maryland might seem to stretch the limits of what one might wish to identify as a coherent set of texts addressing similar regional concerns. As Judith Fetterley and Marjorie Pryse have argued, "conventional under-standings of region (the South, Midwest, Northeast, and West)" tend to flatten out differences within those broad designations; regions, they believe, are best though of as "local and specific" (11). From Fetterley and Pryse's perspective, Faulkner's region is north Mississippi and Barth's is Tidewater Maryland, neither of which "can be consolidated into any monolithic 'South'" (12). While I agree that any construction of the South that vacates the specificity of place is problematic, I think there are two good reasons—one literary, the other sociological—for including Barth in this study.

The first reason has everything to do with Barth's literary apprentice-ship, in which William Faulkner played an important role, even if it was one that Barth discovered he had to move past. During his undergradu-ate career at Johns Hopkins University, Barth recalls that his "very first fiction-writing coach [was] a Marine-combat-veteran teaching assistant from the Deep South at work on the university's first-ever doctoral dis-sertation on the sage of Oxford, Mississippi" ("My Faulkner" 193–94). As a result, Faulkner's voice in his major novels of race (such as *The*

Sound and the Fury, Light in August, and *Absalom, Absalom!*) became for
Barth a "mesmerizing" influence:

> It was Faulkner at his most involuted and incantatory who most enchanted
> me, and while I had and have never though of myself as a capital-S
> Southerner (nor a Northerner either, having grown up virtually astride
> Mason's and Dixon's Line), I felt a strong affinity between Faulkner's
> Mississippi and the Chesapeake marsh country that I was born and raised
> in. My apprentice fiction grew increasingly Faulknerish, and when I stayed
> on at Johns Hopkins as a graduate student, my M.A. thesis and maiden
> attempt at a novel was a heavily Faulknerian marsh opera about sinisterly
> inbred Chesapeake crabbers and muskrat trappers. . . . [B]ut the finished
> opus didn't fly—for one thing, because Faulkner intimately *knew* his
> Snopeses and Compsons and Sartorises, as I did not know my made-up
> denizens of the Maryland marsh. A copy of the manuscript made the
> rounds of Manhattan in vain until my agent gave up on it; I later destroyed
> it as an embarrassment. ("My Faulkner" 194)

As Barth casts it, Faulkner was an influence he had to overcome in
order to become a published author.[1] One of the things that I wish to
suggest in this chapter is that Faulkner's figuration of racial masquerade
serves as a modernist residue in Barth's postmodern metafiction.

The second and more significant reason for placing Barth in a study of
southern fiction is that there are certain structures of feeling regarding
race and racial difference that derive from Maryland's history and that
come into particular focus in Barth's nihilistic Maryland trilogy, which
consists of his first three novels—*The Floating Opera, The End of the
Road,* and *The Sot-Weed Factor.* What I am referring to is a historical
sense of race that wishes to make absolute the difference between white
and black. Maryland, of course, was a border state that remained part of
the Union during the Civil War. However, it remained a slave-holding
state even during the war, and there were a number of regiments that
fought for the Confederacy as Marylanders. This history of slavery, as
well as its dehumanizing effects on African Americans, remains part of
Barth's legacy as a white writer attempting to negotiate matters of masculine identity. To the extent that one emphasizes racial ideology, Fetterley
and Pryse's emphasis on the specificity of place works for, rather than
against, seeing Barth as a *southern* novelist, one who can be grouped with
the other white southern writers in this study.

An example of what I mean by Barth's racialized sensibility occurs in
Lost in the Funhouse, a book that can be read as a collection of stories or
(like Faulkner's *Go Down, Moses*) as an experiment in novelistic form.

Taken as a novel, Barth's book looks more like a Künstlerroman. In the title story, "Lost in the Funhouse," the artistic adolescent Ambrose takes a trip to Ocean City with his family. While metafictionally playful about the possibilities and limits of storytelling, the narrative at the same time realistically tells of young Ambrose's sexual rivalry with his older brother, Peter, for the affections of a girl, Magda, who has been invited along on this excursion.

During the car ride, Ambrose recalls a sexual initiation that occurred three years earlier when he was ten and Magda was eleven. They had "played Niggers and Master in the backyard; when it was Ambrose's turn to be Master and theirs to be Niggers Peter had to go serve his evening papers; Ambrose was terrified to punish Magda alone, but she led him to the whitewashed Torture Chamber between the woodshed and the privy in the Slaves Quarters; there she knelt sweating among bamboo rakes and dusty Mason jars, pleadingly embraced his knees, and while bees droned in the lattice as if on an ordinary summer afternoon, purchased clemency at a surprising price set by herself" (77–78).[2]

It is "the surprising price" that Barth's narrator encodes in Ambrose's minutely detailed memory as a sexual experience: "He even recalled how, standing beside himself in the reeking heat, he'd stared the while at an empty cigar box . . . beneath the words *El Producto*, a laureld, loose-toga'd lady regarding the sea form a marble bench; beside her, forgotten or not yet turned to, was a five-fingered lyre. Her chin reposed on the back of her right hand; her left depended negligently from the bench-arm. The lower half of the scene and lady was peeled away; the words EXAMINED BY _____ were inked there into the wood" (78). Sometimes, Freud assures us, a cigar is just a cigar, but Barth's figurative language reveals that Ambrose has had his not-yet-fully-formed "cigar" handled and examined by Magda.

Although he could not successfully write an ersatz Faulknerian style, Barth could, as the above scene from *Lost in the Funhouse* shows, take up Faulknerian themes. One such theme is the inevitable fall from childhood innocence into the knowledge of racial and sexual difference that one sees so clearly in the opening section of *The Sound and the Fury*. Another Faulknerian theme that strongly resonates in Barth is the formation and contingency of white masculinity. Ambrose's experience with Magda, who plays a faux black girl in a whitewashed shed, may be read intertextually with the moment in *Light in August* when an adolescent Joe Christmas enters a shed for a sexual encounter with an African American girl. For Faulkner's character, the experience activates his unconscious memories of his primal-scene humiliation in the dietician's closet, a moment in which forms of otherness—racial and sexual—become blurred. The inarticulate Christmas can only react with violence toward the black girl, unable as he is to process the traumatic psychic energy that his encounter with her unleashes. A similar blurring of racial and sexual boundaries happens to Ambrose, though Ambrose is more Quentin Compson than Joe Christmas; that is, like the overly sensitive artist figure Quentin, Ambrose intellectualizes the moment. He has an almost out-of-body experience: "But though he had breathed heavily, groaned as if ecstatic, what he'd really felt throughout was an odd sense of detachment, as though someone else were Master. Strive as he might to be transported, he heard his mind take notes upon the scene: *This is what they call* passion. *I am experiencing it*" (84).

While Magda unselfconsciously plays the role of black female, Ambrose cannot identify with his role as white master. At the core of Ambrose's emerging sexual "identity" is a multiplicity that is imbricated with (because unknowable from) race. Ambrose thinks his problem is with mastery, but his problem actually is how to enact whiteness. Stated within the dynamics of the childhood game they play (a game that parodies southern racial politics), if he is not a master, he is slave, and, if he is a slave, he is black. Because this initiation into sexuality occasions a disease with white mastery, sexuality itself comes to be racially suspect.

To the extent that Ambrose may be read as a portrait of the artist as a young man, he provides an important context for understanding the complex racial figuration of Barth's early male characters: Todd Andrews, who is obsessed with masking and mastery; Jacob Horner, who experiences a pathological difficulty in acting; and Henry Burlingame, who constantly enacts various roles. Each of these characters instantiate versions of what I have been calling whiteface minstrelsy. However, unlike Faulkner's tragic heroes, who never find a viable way to embody southern white masculinity, Barth's comically disturbed and decentered characters chart a way toward an acceptance of a contingent (yet still socially privileged) whiteness.

"TURN[ING] BLACK FACES WHITE AGAIN": TODD ANDREWS AS MISCEGENATED MINSTREL

Near the end of her chapter on the racial ventriloquism (or "black talk") that white modernist writers used as a form of linguistic experimentation, Susan Gubar turns to a more contemporary text, *The Floating Opera*, in order to argue that "admissions of white guilt about linguistic racechange often present white black talk . . . as an indefensible but enthralling trope of condescension" (166). In the (anti)climax of Barth's first novel, the narrator, Todd Andrews, tells the reader about how he nearly blew up himself and 699 of his fellow citizens of Cambridge, Maryland, during a minstrel performance on a showboat known as the Floating Opera. For Gubar, Todd's decision not to commit suicide results from "the nihilistic hilarity, the threadbare facticity and absurdity of the [white] actor's impersonations" of blackness, which "provide an ironic but sustaining image of the games people play not only in art but in life" (167). Gubar finds this curious since Todd immediately sees through the "pathetic attraction" of blackface minstrelsy. The discrepancy that Gubar notes between Todd's ability to read the ideology of minstrelsy and the novel's puzzling use of this same minstrelsy owes something to the genesis of the novel. In the foreword to the Anchor edition of *The Floating Opera* and *The End of the Road*, Barth explains that in his research he ran across photos of Captain James Adams's Original Floating Theater and, because of the allegorical implications of the name, "made notes toward a fiction in the form of . . . well, a philosophical blackface minstrel show." Barth continues: "I had picked up from the postwar Zeitgeist some sense of the French existentialist writers and had absorbed from my own experience a few routine disenchantments. I imagined myself something of a nihilist, not the grim-faced kind. I would write some sort of nihilist minstrel show" (vi). And while Barth modified his original design for the novel during its composition, he retained the minstrel show as part of the narrative's climax.

In Faulkner's *The Sound and the Fury*, Quentin Compson, on the day he commits suicide, is accused of speaking like the white actors do in a minstrel show.[3] Barth's novel tells the story of what was to have been the final day in the life of Todd Andrews; however, since Todd is telling his story years after his failed suicide attempt, Barth travesties Faulknerian tragedy, in part by raising the stakes of what it means to speak in the fashion of minstrel performers. Despite his turn to black humor, Barth, like Faulkner, uses figurative blackness to explore various queer possibilities regarding white southern identity.

Minstrel masking is doubled by the two authorizing characters in Barth's novel. Todd Andrews most centrally presents himself as the author of *The Floating Opera*, but Capt. Adam, the owner/impresario/cast member of the Floating Opera, also serves as an author/ity figure. In the minstrel show that comprises much of chapter 27 ("The Floating Opera"), Capt. Adam initiates the performance with the traditional cry of "Gentle-men-n-n-n . . . BE . . . SEATED!" (238). In doing so, he ceases, in a sense, to be Capt. Adam. As Todd notes: "In his new role as Mr. Interlocutor, Capt. Adam was transformed into an entirely different person—grammatical, florid, effusive—so that one doubted the authenticity of his original character" (238). As well one should, because as Adam himself makes clear when Todd first meets him, he is not the uneducated old salt that he pretends to be; rather, he has always been a showman: "I never set foot on a boat in my life till I built the *Op'ry*. Not even a row-skiff; now, then. I run a two-car ten-cent vaudeville show all over the country, sir, from 1895 till 1905, and did so good I had to quit, 'cause ever'body I hired cut out to start a ten-cent show hisself" (200). In his ability to exchange one linguistic mask for another, Adam is a figure for Todd, who has come to see his life as a series of masks. Adam, then, underscores the relation between performativity and passing. His minstrel show, in which whites pretend to blacks, parodies the politics of racial passing, wherein light-skinned African Americans pretend to be white for their social and economic advantage. Moreover, Adam passes in the world for a sea captain, but his passing seems to conceal no true identity, since his other performance as the educated white straight man, Mr. Interlocutor, is but a stage role too.

Barth's representation of the minstrel show is historically accurate, particularly in the interactions between the white Mr. Interlocutor and those blackface racial stereotypes, Tambo and Bones. In their jokes, the "black" characters consistently upstage the supposedly more linguistically sophisticated Mr. Interlocutor. Indeed, Todd understands the full range of minstrelsy's confirmation of white identity, not only as it figures racial difference, but gender and class difference as well; the objects of the minstrels' jokes and humor define otherness:

> Negroes were shiftless and ignorant, foreigners suspect; the WPA was a refuge for loafers; mothers-in-law were shrewish; women poor drivers; drunkenness was an amusing but unquestioned vice; churchgoing a soporific but unquestioned virtue. Tambo and Bones deserved their poverty, but their rascality won our hearts, and we nodded to one another as their native wit led the overeducated interlocutor into one trap after another. Tambo and Bones vindicated our ordinariness; made us secure in the face of mere book learning; their every triumph over Mr. Interlocutor was a pat on our backs. Indeed, a double pat: for were not Tambo and Bones but irresponsible Negroes? (239)

But while reading minstrelsy's not-so-subtle subtext, Todd (as well as Barth) finds himself repeatedly implicated in the very black masquerade he critiques. But this implication goes beyond participation in racialized discourse: in Todd's case his implication simultaneously problematizes his whiteness.

As with so many of the other texts this study has examined, *The Floating Opera* opens curious epistemologies of self and other. Like Bakhtin's notion of carnival, minstrelsy can be read as a licensed inversion of hierarchical relations, turning them upside down, since the "blacks" Tambo and Bones repeatedly get the better of Mr. Interlocutor. But it is a very circumscribed challenge, since minstrelsy is all masks and perform-ance—masked whiteness ultimately confirming whiteness. As ostensible author of *The Floating Opera*, Todd, it turns out, is running a minstrel show every bit as much as Capt. Adam is on his Floating Opera. But Todd's minstrel show is more subversive (even if it too is finally con-tained); rather than focusing exclusively on the white appropriation of blackness, it underscores the performativity (and ultimately the impossi-bility) of whiteness. Todd himself becomes unstably positioned between the roles of Mr. Interlocutor and Tambo and Bones.

It is in Todd's attempts to be Mr. Interlocutor that Barth's fiction is most problematic to contemporary readers. One expects a heavy dialect from the blackface performers in their grotesque appropriation of black language, as when Tambo explains to Mr. Interlocutor why he will not buy his son an encyclopedia: "*Ah say to dat boy, ah say, 'Cyclopedia nuffin'! Y'all gwine walk like de other chillun!*" (239). But even though Barth understands the limitations of minstrelsy, he seems to reproduce its stereotyping of African American linguistic performance outside his por-trayal of the minstrel show. African Americans are not prominently fea-tured in the novel, but when they are, they are depicted in ways that are hard to distinguish from blackface minstrels. The interchange between Todd and Eustacia Callader, a longtime servant to the Mack family whom Todd is trying to enlist to provide information that will help his client, Harrison Mack, Jr., is a case in point. Included in the estate of Harrison Mack, Senior, are a number of jars of his excrement, and though Mrs. Mack appears to have the upper hand in her legal battle with Harrison Junior, she may not dispose of any of the "assets" while the case is still under review:

> "Where does Lizzie keep the old man's fertilizer," I asked. "Is it still in the
>   wine cellar?"
> "De ferilize'?" 'Stacia chortled. "What fertilize'?" She laughed so hard that
>   I knew she didn't understand.
> "The crap, 'Stacia," I demanded. "How does Lizzie feel about all those bot-
>   tles of crap?"
> "Oh, *dat's* what you mean de fertilize'!" (105)

Despite the similarity between the minstrel and non-minstrel appropriations of black language, there are crucial differences. Like the joke in
the minstrel show, the confusion turns on the meaning of a word. Yet,
here the tables are somewhat turned. Rather than being the object of
laughter (as Tambo is), Eustacia is the agent of laughter, clearly seeing
this white man (Todd) and other white men (such as Harrison Mack,
Senior) as crazy. Unlike Tambo, who failed to understand the denotative
meaning of "encyclopedia," Eustacia cannot follow Todd's contextless
figure ("fertilizer") and forces him to speak more plainly ("bottles of
crap"). Within the philosophical minstrel show that Barth writes, Todd's
attempt to assume the linguistically superior (and white) role of Mr.
Interlocutor is constrained by black risibility. His mastery of the situation
is limited and depends on another black linguistic performance, the letter
written by Eustacia, that provides him the evidence that will win his case.[4]

The novel's other instance of black laughter also comes from a black
woman. Early in his sexual relation with Jane, Todd feels the need to
reign in the Macks' sense of proprietorship toward him. He does so by
playing a race card. When Harrison drops by Todd's office one day,
Todd uses Dorothy Miner, "a plump Negro girl of eighteen," whose
divorce suit he is handling, to shock his friend. He tells Harrison that
because Dorothy is poor that he "takes it out in trade," at which she
"clapped her hand over her mouth to hold down laughter." Harrison is
incredulous and upset, but Todd insists:

> "No indeed," I grinned. "I'm getting to be real good at this business. Isn't
> that so, Dorothy?"
> "Whatever you say, Mister Andrews," Dorothy giggled; it was a tremen-
> dously funny joke. (40)

This of course is a freighted moment. By exposing Harrison's racial
prejudice, Todd must draw on a stereotype of black promiscuity in order
for his performance to elicit the desired effect from Harrison. Todd,
therefore, is guilty of perpetuating this racialized stereotype, which
Harrison readily believes. To the extent that Todd uses Dorothy, a reader
might dismiss the moment as Barth's degradation of African Americans.
At the same time, though, Todd empowers Dorothy in a very particular
way. Unlike the "black" laughter in the context of the minstrel show,
where the blackface performer's ability to show up white Mr. Interlocutor
is already contained by the fact that the black is in fact another white
man, Dorothy's laughter at the expense of the white man is not contained
by a theatrical stage. Dorothy's laughter is directed not only at Harrison,

who is not in on the joke and leaves the office humiliated and embarrassed, but also at the joke's author, Todd. His interactions with these
two African American women illustrate the unstable makeup of Todd's
identity, at once Mr. Interlocutor and the trickster figure. Eustacia might
laugh at Mr. Interlocutor Todd and Dorothy at trickster Tambo Todd,
but both women find him crazy.

Todd is the man who would be Mr. Interlocutor but who willy-nilly
finds himself playing his part as though he were black, enacting the very
black laughter that he experiences with Eustacia and Dorothy. That is
because in the symbolic logic of the novel, Todd is more black than
white; indeed, he comes to be another instantiation of the black in whiteface. But rather than being a tragic figure (as Faulkner's whiteface blacks
so often are), Todd, in his comic guise as trickster, manages to fool not
only the novel's white men, but also himself at the very moments when
his urge toward whiteness emerges. In the novel's ironic treatment of
Sartrean existentialism, one can trace a curious link to Ralph Ellison's
Invisible Man, one that suggests an intertextual commentary that points
toward the racialized nature of Barth's treatment of whiteness.[5]

For Jean-Paul Sartre, existentialism meant, first and foremost, the pri-
ority of existence over essence. Since no god authored human essence,
human beings are radically free—free, particularly, to choose how to act.
But with this freedom comes profound responsibility: "Man is responsible for what he is. Thus, existentialism's first move is to make every man
aware of what he is and to make the full responsibility of his existence rest
on him. And when we say that a man is responsible for himself, we do not
only mean that he is responsible for his own individuality, but that he is
responsible for all men" (*Existentialism* 19).

Sartre's is a philosophy both of radical self-making and of radical
implication. We construct ourselves by our choices. Our choices, however, are never individual but involve all humanity because what we
choose as the good, we assume to be the good for everyone. Our responsibility, then, is very large indeed. If one chooses, for example, whether
from patriotism or indifference, not to oppose the U.S. war on Iraq, then
one is, from the Sartrean perspective, personally responsible for the civil-
ian casualties caused by operations carried out by U.S. forces. Our being
emerges only through the decisions we make, and these choices make our
natures. Condemned by a freedom to choose so absolute that one can
never free oneself from that freedom, human beings, for Sartre, live in a
world in which there are no accidents. As he claims in *Being and
Nothingness*, "what happens to me happens through me, and I can neither

affect myself with it nor revolt against it nor resign myself to it. Moreover everything which happens to me is *mine*" (554).

What invites us to read *The Floating Opera* against *Invisible Man* (1952) is their similar engagement of the Sartrean notion of responsibility. Toward the end of the Prologue in *Invisible Man*, Ralph Ellison, an avid reader of Sartre, clearly and critically engages the existential notion of responsibility.[6] Having described how he attacked a white man who insulted him, as well as his underground life stealing electricity from Monopolated Light & Power, the narrator says:

> I can hear you say, "What a horrible, irresponsible bastard!" And you're right. I leap to agree with you. I am one of the most irresponsible beings that ever lived. Irresponsibility is part of my invisibility; any way you face it, it is a denial. But to whom can I be responsible, and why should I be, when you refuse to see me? . . . Responsibility rests upon recognition, and recognition is a form of agreement. Take the man whom I almost killed: Who was responsible for that near murder—I? I don't think so, and I refuse it. I won't buy it. You can't give it to me. *He* bumped *me, he* insulted *me*. (14)

What Ellison points out is a logical limitation to the notion of Sartrean responsibility. If everything that happens to us belongs to us, then are racial others "responsible" for the racism directed at them? Ellison, while usefully raising the issue, returns us to the notion of Sartrean responsibility by the end of the passage:

> And if he had yelled for a policeman, wouldn't *I* have been taken for the offending one? Yes, yes, yes! Let me agree with you, I was the irresponsible one; for I should have used the knife to protect the higher interests of society. Some day that kind of foolishness will cause us tragic trouble. All dreamers and sleepwalkers must pay the price, and even the invisible man is responsible for the fate of all. But I shirked that responsibility; I became too snarled in the incompatible notions that buzzed within my brain. (14)

Interestingly, in the name, ultimately, of Sartrean responsibility and existential ethics, the invisible man decides that killing the white man was the truly authentic choice he should have made. Couched in the terms of the enlarged sense of responsibility so dear to Sartre, Ellison constructs an existentialist argument for the ethics of racial violence, thus ironically underscoring his earlier point about reciprocal recognition being a necessary precondition for responsibility.

Turning back to Barth, we should recall that, in critiquing the stereo-typing of minstrelsy, Todd speaks of his culture's universal acceptance of the notion of African American irresponsibility. With this in mind, Todd's characterization of himself as a figure of the law (since both he and the law are "uncommitted") seems to engage both Sartre and Ellison:

> if you have followed this chapter so far, you might sensibly ask, "Doesn't your attitude—which is, after all, irresponsible—allow for the defeat, even the punishment of the innocent, and at times the victory of the guilty? And does this not concern you?" It does indeed allow for the persecution of innocence—though perhaps not so frequently as you might imagine. And this persecution *concerns* me, in the sense that it holds my attention, but not especially in the sense that it bothers me. . . . Irresponsibility, yes: I affirm, I insist upon my basic and ultimate irresponsibility. Yes indeed. (85)

In *Invisible Man*, the ultimate figure of irresponsibility is the shape-shift-ing Rinehart, for whom the invisible man is mistaken in chapter 23. Through Rinehart, the invisible man sees one possible response to the alienating condition of the invisibility that results when others see him not as a person but a stereotype. But what Ellison's protagonist backs away from in horror, Todd embraces: Rine the pimp, Rine the numbers runner, Rine the preacher becomes in *The Floating Opera*, Todd the rake, Todd the saint, and Todd the cynic. Both Rinehart and Todd acknowl-edge that when it comes to existential authenticity and subjectivity, there is (as Gertrude Stein might say) no there there, since anything that aspires to identity is always a performance. While I do not want to be guilty of the faulty logic of the undistributed middle (all Negroes are irresponsible; Todd is irresponsible; therefore, Todd is a Negro), the fact that Todd embraces a characteristic that his culture generally associates with black-ness creates an implication that other elements of Barth's novel work to reinforce.

Most particularly, the circumstances surrounding the suicide of Thomas Andrews, Todd's father, indicate the subliminal way in which racial impersonation leads to ambiguity about racial identity. Todd, who, on the day that he plans as his last, comes to see his life as nothing but a series of masks, fails to register that his theatrical trope for identity derives from the condition of his father's dead body. In chapter 7, "A note, a warning," Todd, in the middle of telling how he learned the habit of doing manual labor in good clothes from his father, springs his father's suicide on the reader: "When one day in 1930 I came home from the office and found Dad in the cellar, one end of his belt spiked to the floor joist and the other fastened around his neck, there was not a smudge on dirt anywhere on him, though the cellar was quite dusty. His clothes were perfectly creased and freed of wrinkles, and *although his face was black and his eyes were popped*, his hair was neatly and correctly combed" (71, emphasis added).

Todd fails to explicitly recognize, even as his description makes clear, that in death his father is the very image of the minstrel—with a blackened face and exaggerated eyes (the minstrel's, of course, appear to bulge because of an unblackened ring of white). But Thomas Andrews is more than simply an artificial Negro in blackface; the manner of his death cannot help suggesting the primal scene of white southern vigilantism—the hanged black body. The trauma of his father's death marks Todd in a fundamental way, which he reveals through a series of questions: "Does one's father hang himself for a simple, stupid lack of money? And is one expected to set up again the chair one's father has kicked over in his strangling? Can one actually, with a kitchen knife, saw through the belt? Carry one's father up to the bed whereon one was conceived, and laying him on it, dig one's fingers into the black and ruptured flesh to release the dead neck from its collar?" (183).

Strikingly, Todd, beginning with the second question, describes the sequence of actions he in fact performed after discovering his father's body.[7] The answer, then, to each of these rhetorical questions is "yes"; however, Todd refuses to accept "yes" as the answer to the first question he poses. Indeed, he resolutely rejects the notion that his father has killed himself as a result of his stock market losses, despite the fact than it is a cartoon cliché of the 1929 market crash to see formerly wealthy speculators leap to their deaths rather than face a life of poverty. While this pop culture image of mass suicide is a grotesque exaggeration, a number of people did kill themselves in the aftermath of the market crash because they could not face a life of poverty and reduced social status.

A prominent lawyer, Thomas Andrews speculated with money borrowed from friends and his mortgaged properties and lost nearly everything. Why, then, is Todd unable to understand his father's death in the most logical and straightforward fashion? Why must Todd turn this suicide into a problem that becomes an obsession in a significant portion of his *Inquiry*? A clue to answering this question, I believe, is found after Todd cuts down his father's body. Todd carries the body "to the bed whereon [he] was conceived." Handling his father's "black flesh" at this particular site, Todd experiences the moment as a kind of primal scene, but one more involved with a disruption of racial rather than sexual identity. Clearly, to someone in 1930s Maryland, to have a black father is to

be black oneself. If we follow the one-drop rule of southern culture ana-
logically, what does it mean to discover one's father in blackface? In the
symbolic logic of *The Floating Opera*, Todd is a natural-born minstrel.
But things are more complicated still because Thomas Andrews's black
face is more than just a blackface mask, as Todd's subsequent meditations
on his father's suicide suggest.

The fact of his father's suicide erupts at several moments throughout
The Floating Opera. One of the most telling instances comes in relation to
the despair his friend Harrison Mack experiences after learning from
Todd's analysis that the Court of Appeals will surely confirm the judge's
ruling that gives the three-million-dollar estate to Harrison's mother.
Disgusted with his friend's despair over losing the money, Todd
responds: "What'll you do—hang yourself in the cellar? There's a twen-
typenny nail right there, in a joist—you'll find it. It's already been broken
in. And I know an undertaker who can *turn black faces white again*" (99,
emphasis added). If it requires an undertaker to turn Thomas Andrew's
black face white, then in death he is more than a minstrel representation
of blackness; he apparently has *become* black, so that becoming white
again is now the true crossing of the color line. At the same time, Todd's
piqued response may be read as an admission of what he denies regarding
the reason for his father's suicide. By suggesting to Harrison the same act
(suicide) at the exact site of his father's death, Todd reveals that he unconsciously believes that his father's suicide resulted from something similar
to Harrison's emotional response—despair over lost financial and social
position.

Much of Todd's *Inquiry*, then, can be read as a kind of denial, but one
less focused on the reason for his father's suicide (which Todd already, if
unconsciously, knows) than on the racechange implied by that suicide. In
other words, Todd says he does not know why his father killed himself,
but, in fact, what he does not want to acknowledge is that by killing himself, his father made him the son of a black man. And to be the son of a
black man is to be a black man oneself.

The racialized trauma of his father's death resonates in curious ways
with Todd's earlier traumatic experience that "happened in the dark"
(62) during the trench warfare of World War I. Completely stupefied
with fear, Todd finds himself lost and alone in a shell hole, only to be
suddenly joined by a German soldier, which causes Todd to soil himself.
To make the German understand that he means him no harm, Todd
places his bayonet on the man's neck until he too experiences the same
animal terror Todd had felt moments before. The result? "Never in my
life have I enjoyed such intense intimacy, such clear communication with

a fellow human being, male or female, as I enjoyed with that German sergeant. . . . If any American, even my father, had jumped into the shell hole at that moment, I'd have killed him unhesitatingly before he could kill my friend. . . . For the space of some hours we had been one man, had understood each other beyond friendship, beyond love, as a wise man understands himself" (66). This perfect communication, however, does not last; when morning comes, doubt returns. Todd tries to slip out of the hole, but when the German soldier awakens, Todd panics and lunges at the German with his bayoneted rifle; after a brief moment the blade slides through the German's neck. This moment of perfect communication, then is consummated by an act of penetration, but Todd, who always attempts to control his readers responses, has already warned us: "If the notion of homosexuality enters your head, you're normal, I think. If you judge either the German sergeant or myself to have been homosexual, you're stupid" (65). Yet, before killing the German, Todd wonders if the other might not think he was a "homosexual crank" (67).

By invoking the notion of trauma, I in no way am suggesting that Barth was trying to represent a historically accurate picture of the "shell shocked" war veteran. Todd is neither a poster child for what now goes by the name of post-traumatic stress disorder, nor would his war experience, which occasions no obvious symptoms, qualify as an instance of traumatic neurosis. Todd is far too conscious of the event, which he says "cured" him of daydreaming, expectations of others, prejudice, and overvaluing the opinion of others: "To be sure, I don't call that one incident, traumatic as it proved to be, the single cause of all these alterations in me; in fact, I don't see where some of them follow at all. But when I think of the alterations, I immediately thing of the incident" (68). Todd suffers no nightmares that return him to the scene of his war horror or survival. Nevertheless, Todd's war experience and his father's suicide are uncanny repetitions. In both cases, against his expectations, he survives. (Given what he knows about his heart condition, Todd fully expects to die before his father.) To the extent that Todd is a figure for trauma, it is that he embodies the incomprehensibility of his own survival (Caruth 64), obsessively chronicled in his *Inquiry* that leads to his rationale for suicide and mass murder. Todd's text itself, one might say, is the site of trauma's unknowing.

Both his perfect communication with the German soldier and Todd's imperfect communication with his father end in the other's death. But while Todd takes no responsibility for the German's death (for which he is clearly responsible), he takes full responsibility for his father's death (which he could not reasonably have foreseen) in the form of his *Inquiry*.

Read against his subsequent trauma of finding his dead father, Todd's conscious and curious insistence regarding his war story (I am not sexually deviant) lines up in interesting ways with the repressed knowledge of his father's suicide (I am not white). The presumed primitive and transgressive libidinality of blacks—part and parcel of Todd's Maryland world picture—in fact can be seen in his subsequent sexual performance.

Though he never broaches the topic of race in all his years of his investigation into and obsessive writing about his father's suicide, Todd is caught in the dynamics of southern racial politics. More than a loss of class position, Todd suffers his father's suicide as a fundamental trauma to his sense of white identity. What Todd cannot articulate, yet what effectively drives him, is his unconscious knowledge that, at least figuratively, he is not white. Todd becomes, from this moment onward, quite literally of two minds. Consciously, he never questions his whiteness and privileged position in the social hierarchy as a successful attorney, a Mr. Interlocutor of the bar. Yet, his unconscious is obsessively caught in the dynamic that he describes to Harrison; it constantly strives (and fails) to turn his black face white again. As a result, Todd becomes minstrelsy's obverse reflection—a black in whiteface, passing for white even as he plays the role of a sexually ambiguous black trickster. Hence, Todd's philosophical minstrel show in *The Floating Opera* is a far more subversive challenge to whiteness than the minstrel show that takes place on the Floating Opera. Todd enacts in his daily life what minstrelsy would relegate to the realm of make-believe.

Todd's decision to live in the Dorchester Hotel, which otherwise houses the semi-indigent elderly, signals the odd outsider status he has assigned himself. In the aftermath of his father's suicide, Todd loses his childhood home. But his father does provide him with a legacy, an envelope with five thousand dollars cash that Thomas Andrews held back from his market speculation. When Todd receives this envelope, he hopes for some explanation but only finds a note that "said all the things I certainly didn't want to hear, in just the wrong language" (184). It is what Todd does with this money that allows us to glimpse again his Tambo-like tricksters side, that part of him that revels in exposing the absurdity of white male privilege. He mails the money to the richest man in Cambridge, Col. Henry Morton. In the relationship that develops, Morton plays a stunned Mr. Interlocutor to Todd's trickster Tambo. To Morton, the money can only be a bribe of sorts, and he obsessively tries to find out what Todd wants. Todd's repeated insistence that the money is nothing more than a gift and carries no obligation baffles Morton, and the rich man repeatedly tries to discharge his sense of obligation by offering

Todd increasingly lucrative employment opportunities, each of which Todd refuses. This only confounds Morton further, who senses a kind of threat to his patriarchal authority in Todd's refusal to profit from what to the rich man can only be some sort of business transaction. Morton remains convinced that Todd wants something from him and so is relieved when Todd accepts an invitation to Morton's New Year's Eve party. The octogenarian Morton introduces Todd to his forty-year-old wife and in the excess of the party's conclusion, during which guests take cold showers in the upstairs bathrooms, Todd accidentally finds himself embraced by a soaking Evelyn, who suggestively grinds herself against Todd before passing out at the sight of her husband who has witnessed her performance. Col. Morton, who both by his inherited honorific and wealth represents southern Whiteness, has become a virtual cuckold to trickster Todd. In short, Todd, like Tambo, makes a fool of the white authority figure.

If Todd finds himself as the imagined third in Col. Morton's marriage, he is literally this figure in the marriage of Harrison and Jane Mack. Between 1932 and 1937, Todd has regular sexual relations with Jane that grow out of an experiment the Macks initiated to prove that they were not conventionally jealous. As a result, the paternity of Jane's daughter, Jeanne, is in doubt. Just as Todd gifted Col. Morton with five thousand dollars, Harrison gives Todd the gift of his wife. And while Harrison tells Todd that there is no obligation, Todd senses that Harrison very much wants him to feel obliged. The dynamic of this ménage à trois works in ways that Eve Sedgwick described in *Between Men*. Although Todd brags about his heterosexual exploits ("I have been uncommonly lucky with women" [123]), his heterosexuality is largely passive. Initiated at age seventeen into sexuality by Betty June Gunter, Todd finds, even in this initial encounter, heterosexuality to be ridiculous. Moreover, Jane seduces Todd. Although Todd enjoys the sex with Jane, the far deeper relationship is between Todd and Harrison, so that Jane serves as a displaced consummation of the two men's friendship; Todd and Harrison partake in verbal intercourse, discussing philosophy and legal matters, while Todd and Jane's intercourse is exclusively sexual. Because he always assumes that he is more advanced in his thinking than Harrison, Todd is comfortable in this relationship since, as mentor, he assumes a position of mastery.

It is Jane, however, who asserts control and ends the three-way relationship, in part because Todd has become "such a pansy" (76), as she puts it, since he increasingly fails to perform sexually when they are together. When his relationship with Jane ends in June of 1937, Todd seems actually relieved to retire from heterosexuality. But since it is the

Macks' decision to end their relations with Todd, his sense of mastery in this relationship is shattered, which leads to an existential crisis. It is not his choice that makes the world but the choices of others that are shaping him.

Todd, then, is not in control of his minstrel performance, and his "decision" to blow up the Floating Opera speaks at many levels to the rage that motivates him beneath his apparently affectless persona. Todd's father has committed suicide for reasons he finds inexplicable. The very day that Todd has decided to kill himself, Jane has told him she wishes to end their affair. Todd acts as though he is perfectly in control of his emotions, as though her decision means nothing to him, but how might Todd's unconscious be motivating him in response to this news? And how might one read Todd's decision to commit mass murder as an adjunct to suicide? Contextualized through his supposedly final entry in his *Inquiry*, we see that, although his choosing suicide is couched in existential terms of mastery and choice, Todd's choice of his means (blowing up many of his fellow citizens) takes on a different significance if we see it less in existential terms and more in racialized ones.

His urge toward mastery, in this southern racial context, is an urge toward whiteness. Todd, in other words, is trying to find a way to turn his whitefaced blackness white again. But his efforts to transform himself are less successful than those of his father's mortician, since Todd's attempts to regain whiteness are always undone by his black, trickster unconscious. Who finally is that masked man?

It is in chapter 25, "The Inqury," that Todd is most explicit about his sense of himself as always masked. He makes his discovery of the series of masks he has assumed in life—rake, saint, cynic—only on the eve of the day he decides to kill himself. What unhinges Todd is his sense that these guises were "not the stages of intellectual development," (225) but a series of illogical resolves that he only justified after the fact. Todd's imperiled whiteness must be understood in relation to his heart: "My heart, reader! My heart! You must comprehend quickly, if you are to comprehend at all, that those masks were not assumed to hide my face, but to hide my heart from my mind, and my mind from my heart! Understand it now, because I may not live to end the chapter! To be sure, each mask hid other things as well, as a falseface hides identity and personality as well as nose and mouth" (223).

Throughout *The Floating Opera*, Todd has reminded the reader of a diagnosis he received when he was nineteen that informed him that he was susceptible to heart attacks. The above passage invites us to read "heart" as Todd's heart condition, which means he might drop dead at any moment. Although Todd is acutely aware of his mortality, what he suffers from, of course, is nothing more or less than the human condition, since everyone lives with this death sentence, though, unlike Todd, we are largely forgetful of this fact through the business of our daily lives. But there is a significant equivocation on the word "heart" that becomes clear at this juncture.

Todd's realization that his masks represent no intellectual progress brings on a "black" mood (225), at which point he appears to suffer the heart attack about which he has repeatedly warned us: "And suddenly my heart filled my entire body. It was not my heart that would burst, but my body, so full was it of my heart, and every beat was sick. Surely it would fail! I clapped my hand quickly to my chest, feeling the beat; clutched at the window frame to keep from falling; stared at *nothing*, my mouth open, like a fish on the beach. And this not in pain, but in despair!" (226).

Rather than a heart attack, the emotion of despair overcomes Todd. But in a way, this is merely a heart attack of a different stripe. As a figure, the heart is traditionally imagined as the seat of human emotion. What Todd's double-valanced trope reveals is that his masks are constructed at least as much by his emotional responses to crucial life events as they are by his attempt to escape an awareness of his mortality. His despair, then, is generated as much by the proposition "I am governed by emotions" as it is by "I am going to die." In fact, the two are related, since Todd's emotional responses are often generated by his awareness of his physically fragile heart.

If his father turned himself black by killing himself (and thus figuratively rendering his son an artificial Negro), Todd hopes to restore his whiteness by an assertion of detached logic and will: killing himself is merely an unfortunate consequence of his need to kill off that black trickster, his ungovernable, irresponsible emotions: "There was no mastering the fact with which I lived; but I could master the fact of my living with it by destroying myself, and the result was the same—I was the master" (227). The racial subtext is fairly obvious but to be explicit: to not be the master is to be a slave and to be a slave is to be black.

In a perverse way, even as whiteface Todd is choosing a nihilistic end for himself and his townsmen, black trickster Todd *is* taking responsibility for his actions, and in the very fashion that Ellison's protagonist calls for at the end of *Invisible Man*'s Prologue. By trying to blow up the whole masquerade of southern Whiteness, which of course is the whole point of the showboat's minstrel performance, white Todd is mastered by his "black" self—that unconscious part of himself that knows he is not white. In exploding the white masquerade of blackface minstrelsy, which mythologizes and sentimentalizes southern history, Todd would avenge his black(face) father, who in death was denied whiteness. Todd would do so by putting nearly everyone in Cambridge in blackface; not burnt cork, but the literally burnt bodies would be "black, cracked, smoking" (243), even those of Jane and the child he possibly has fathered.

Had Todd succeeded, his act of mass murder would have been consistent with his earlier trickster acts that consistently work to expose the fraudulence of the performance of south white maleness, whether it is Col. Morton's or the senior Harrison Mack's. Todd's act, even failed as it is, serves as yet another attempt to communicate with his dead father. It is as if by killing himself and 699 others, Todd is showing his father the right way to face up to the loss of whiteness, which is to give the lie to whole show of whiteness itself.

Having survived his planned massacre of his fellow citizens, Todd returns to his room and makes a final addition to his evening's work, perhaps his final gesture of playing in the dark, as he looks out over the "dark graveyard" and the "black expanse of the sky, the blacker as the stars were blotted out by storm clouds" (250). He then adds to his conclusion that "there's no final reason for living" the parenthetical "(or for suicide)" (250). Alone in his room at the end of the novel, with a resolve to carry his *Inquiry* further, Todd again resembles nothing so much as Ellison's invisible man. Both write to us from their marginal spaces, having survived near-apocalyptic violence. Both have learned lessons. The invisible man, of course, learns painful ones about trying to perform black leadership in a white world. Todd has learned that all absolutes, like Hamlet's "to be or not to be," are "absolutely, meaningless" (251). This is key, because in rejecting absolutes, Todd must also question existentialism, for while Sartre might continue along the path mapped out by Neitzsche's notion of the death of God, the French philosopher still insists on an absolute of the human condition—the freedom to choose. In a southern context, if absolute freedom and mastery are untenable, so too is whiteness (particularly the myth of the white master). Like the invisible man in Ellison's Epilogue, Todd in Barth's final chapter is poised for the next step. If the invisible man contemplates what politics might ground effective action based on the full knowledge of his cultural invisibility, Todd also ponders a new ground for living. Though Todd's philosophical meditations are not overtly political, they nevertheless have political implications for his racial identity. Todd, the mass murderer manqué, wonders "whether, in the real absence of absolutes, values less than absolute mightn't be regarded as in no way inferior and even lived by" (252). While he acknowledges that this will have to be "another inquiry, and another story" (252), what Todd begins to map is a way to imagine a contingent whiteness, which may be the way for him to turn his black face white again. To the extent that Todd may be able to make his peace with a contingent value such as whiteness, the more subversive possibilities of *The Floating Opera* are contained. While it might seem that a contingent whiteness would challenge the law and custom of the South that produced the insanity of the "one-drop rule," by which any trace of African genetic material made one Negro, the effect of contingent whiteness in Todd's case means that his "blackness" is, in the last instance, reduced to a rhetorical mask. No one in the white community doubts Todd's whiteness; if he could come to accept whiteness as a contingent value, Todd would not have to doubt his racial identity either. Such growth, of course, can never happen to Todd within the discursive confines of *The Floating Opera*. Barth's characters, however, continue teasing out the problem of whiteness in his next two novels.

IN A SENSE, A BLACK JACOB HORNER

His second novel, *The End of the Road*, John Barth tells us, is the twinned companion piece to *The Floating Opera*: "The *Opera* I regarded as a nihilist comedy, *Road* as a nihilist catastrophe. . . . Their situations have in common that they are narrated by the Other Man in a more or less acknowledged adulterous triangle complicated by an ambiguous pregnancy. The personnel of the two triangles—their ages, social positions, attitudes, and moral voltages—are dissimilar, but the narrators share a radical alienation that fascinated me at that time" (Foreword vii). Both novels play out against a backdrop of Sartrean existentialism, but while Todd Andrews recognizes his fundamental irresponsibility, Jacob (Jake) Horner desperately wants to find some ground for responsible action.[8]

Barth, whose initial failures at novel writing had him on the verge of returning to graduate school, seems to use his first two published novels to come to terms with an authorial identity: the first-person narrators in both are neophyte novelists, each producing their first works. Todd, a lawyer, quite literally is writing his way into a genre of which he happily tells us he has no real understanding. The very nature of Todd's writing—an attempt to communicate perfectly with his dead father—is interminable. *The Floating Opera* is merely a footnote in the unending project of Todd's *Inquiry*. Jake, who completed all his degree requirements (except his thesis) for the MA in English, not surprisingly, is less daunted by the task of novel writing. Jake's writing, moreover, has a clear terminal point, and has been written with some reflective distance of time—the story takes place during the 1953–54 academic year, but he writes in the fall of 1955. Todd also writes about a specific moment from his past, the day he last changed his mind, but seems unable to keep focused on his purpose; digressions lead to more digressions. Jake is a more disciplined writer. The key difference is that Todd's text *is* the wound of trauma, whereas Jake's text is *therapy*, a coming to terms with trauma, ostensibly his implication in the death of Rennie Morgan.

I would extend Barth's characterization of the twinned nature of his first two novels to include figurative racechange: the radical alienation of their narrators is a racialized alienation. As we saw in the previous section, Todd, the son of a black(face) man unconsciously plays a culturally black trickster role. The twinning of Barth's first two novels, I argue, encompasses a complicated authorial performance of whiteface minstrelsy. Jacob Horner is another individual who presents a white face to the world despite his identification with blackness. If Todd has a father who is figuratively black (inasmuch as Thomas Andrews's suicide is a "blackface" performance), Jake has a father figure who is literally black. While Todd struggles in his writing to communicate perfectly with the dead father, Jake seeks to break free of the mastery of the African American Doctor.

Todd Andrews's problem is doubly racialized because, obsessed by controlling things, he seeks to be the master of every situation; however, his goal of being "the master" is undercut in a southern context by his unrecognized "black" identity, which is the deepest source of his trauma. At best, Todd can be a minstrel trickster figure, queerly performing white masculinity. Jake's problem is more fundamental. If Todd must always doubt whether his choices lead toward mastery, Jake simply cannot choose, a condition that sometimes leads to actual physical paralysis. But the very fact of his novel's existence shows that this is a condition from which Jake no longer suffers, at least to the extent that he has exerted an author-ity in making the choices that constitute the text one reads. In other words, Jake's text suggests the possibility of a cure for the trauma from which Todd suffers, namely, the repressed knowledge that he is not fully white. It is precisely through his turn to authorship that Jake learns to choose and by choosing effectively finds the responsibility and mastery that always elude Todd. Todd concludes by acknowledging that "in the absence of real values, values less than absolute mightn't be regarded as in no way inferior and even lived by." As I argued in the previous section, one of the values challenged by the lack of absolutes is whiteness. If Todd claims it will take "another story" to make this clear (*Floating* 252), I believe Jake's is that story.

Readings of *The End of the Road* have certainly articulated its parallels to *The Floating Opera*, but tend to stress the relationship between Jake and Joe Morgan. Charles Harris, for example, sees both novels as about "schismatic identity," (32) but emphasizes the ways that Barth splits Todd's role between Jake and Joe in his second novel. As a result, for Harris, Jake and Joe are doubles, and not just on the basis of their rationality. Harris sees "homosexual" proclivities in both men, both of whom have rather modest appetites for heterosexual contact (34). Patricia Tobin develops her thinking about the triangular relationship by drawing not on Freud's oedipally triangulated sense of desire, but rather on René Girard's revision of Freud in which the mimetic precedes desire, so that "it is identification, rather than desire, that is primary" (45).[9] While not wishing to gainsay the usefulness of seeing the doubling between Jake and Joe (it is, after all, what helps mark Jake's queer performance of southern masculinity), I wish to emphasize a different figure of Jake's identification, his relation to "the Doctor," the novel's crucial African American character.

The criticism of this novel has been remarkably silent on the matter of the Doctor's race.[10] But, in not dwelling on the Doctor's racial identity, critics only follow Barth himself, who allows the reader to assume for the first sixty-nine pages that the Doctor is white simply by not marking his race. This tweaking of the reader's nose, so to speak, puts Jake in relation to the reader rather as Todd is to his friend Harrison. In *The Floating Opera*, Todd jokes that a client, a young black woman, is poor and so pays for his legal services with sexual favors. Harrison believes Todd and is shocked, revealing his prejudice, even as he denies it: "'I'm not prejudiced; I just couldn't have anything to do with a Negro girl,' is what he said, but *'You've been unfaithful to Jane and to me; you've defiled yourself and us in that black hussy"* is what he meant" (41). If Todd exposes racism through the story he tells, Jakes chooses to reveal it through his discursive strategy that forces readers to assume that the Doctor is white.

It is precisely his relation to the Doctor (as yet unmarked by race) that Jake makes the focus of his opening chapter. We learn that Jake has been under the care of this doctor for some time at a rural and oddly named Remobilization Farm near Wicomico, Maryland. Everything about the Doctor and his facilities suggests whiteness. He wears a "white medical-looking jacket" (74) and "white trousers" (1). The Progress and Advice Room, where the Doctor meets his patients, is "about as large as an apartment living room, only high-ceilinged. The walls are flat white, the windows are covered by white venetian blinds, usually closed, and a globed ceiling fixture provides the light. In this room are two straight-backed white wooden chairs, exactly alike, facing each other in the center of the floor, and no other furniture" (1). Because the chairs are placed so closely together the patient has no choice in how to sit facing the Doctor. As Jake explains it, this room is the site of the Doctor's mastery:

> It is not fit that you should be at your ease in the Progress and Advice Room, for after all it is not for relaxation that you come there, but for advice. Were you totally at your ease, you would only be inclined to consider the Doctor's words in a leisurely manner, as one might regard the breakfast brought to one's bed by a liveried servant, hypercritically, selecting this, rejecting that, eating only as much as one chooses. And clearly such a frame of mind would be out of place in the Progress and Advice Room, for there it is you who have placed yourself in the Doctor's hands; your wishes are subservient to his, not vice versa; and his advice is given you not to be questioned or even examined (to question is impertinent; to examine, pointless), but to be followed. (3)

The entire passage is troped in terms of a master/servant relation. The patient is not there to be served, even if the Doctor might appear to be a liveried servant. The Doctor's absolute authority reinforces the notion of his whiteness. The only color that is mentioned other than white in the opening chapter is the Doctor's "pink tongue," which is visible as he moves his cigar from one side of his mouth to the other. Although pink tongues are not race specific, this additional detail seems calculated to mislead the reader, since the color pink is often used to describe "white" skin.

It is only in chapter 6, when Jake tells us how he met the Doctor in the Baltimore train station, that race enters the text. Just before the Doctor rouses Jake from his immobility (brought on by Jake's radical inability to choose a destination, Jake (as narrator) casually mentions that the Doctor is "a Negro" (69). Race clearly matters. This is the Jim Crow South of 1951. The Doctor cannot enter the "whites only" coffee shop. It is Jake's narratorial decision, though, to keep this detail from the readers for nearly half the novel that matters more, since this choice gives the reversal of the traditional southern white-black relations such force, inasmuch as it requires that readers reevaluate their assumptions about the Doctor. Retrospectively, then, the strangeness of the relationship between Jake and the Doctor only grows when the Doctor first takes Jake to the Remobilization Farm. Jake sees that this black doctor's clientele consists exclusively of elderly white people. We have, in other words, a plantation (if you will) on which all the whites are subject to the will of the black master. If this historical reversal were not estranging enough, the Doctor's therapies, such as suggesting homosexual encounters for some of his male patients, are wildly unorthodox and have nothing to do with psychoanalysis of the 1950s. Unlike Freudians, for whom the etiology of the disease is crucial, the Doctor wants "no biography" since he claims that "it doesn't much matter what caused it [the paralysis] anyhow" (72). The Doctor asks Jake to note the fact that his patients like him, but then warns: "But don't think I have an equal love for them. They're just more of less interesting problems of immobility." The Doctor then immediately problematizes his relationship with Jake, telling him: "You've no way of knowing whether anything I've said or will say is the truth, or just a part of my general therapy for you." Truth and lie are both the same to the Doctor since any treatment ultimately is either "therapeutic or antitherapeutic" (74).

As we saw in *The Floating Opera*, Sartrean existentialism creates resonances with Ellison's *Invisible Man*, resonances that continue in *The End of the Road*. The Doctor, though, is invisible in his blackness, not because the reader cannot see an African American as an individual, but rather because for so long Jake refuses to let us see the Doctor's blackness. Just as we never learn the name of Ellison's invisible man, we never learn the name of Barth's Doctor, despite the odd turns both texts at times must make to keep these names secret. Moreover, the Doctor endorses existentialism, but only for its therapeutic potential: "read Sartre and become an existentialist" but only "until we find something more suitable for you" (79). The Doctor's, however, is an existentialism without ethics because the ultimate advice is to "act impulsively: don't let yourself get stuck between alternatives, or you're lost" (79).

The Doctor is a trickster figure who constitutes Jake as his surrogate trickster. If Jake's initial paralysis results from an inability to choose a destination, he finds a destinator, a quest-giver, in the figure of the Doctor. From the moment the Doctor tells Jake that he must "teach prescriptive grammar" (5), Jake becomes the Doctor's (secret black) agent in the white world, despite the fact that, even after his first visit to the Remobilization Farm, Jake is aware that "the Doctor was operating either outside the law or on its very fringes. Sexual Therapy, to name only one thing, could scarcely be sanctioned by the American Medical Association. This doubtless was the reason for the farm's frequent relocation. It was apparent that he was a crank—though perhaps not an ineffective one— and one wondered whether he had any sort of license to practice medicine at all" (80).

Although he senses early on that the Doctor is a fraud, Jake continues his relation with the Doctor for four years. In Jake's Scriptotherapy, his act of writing *The End of the Road*, he chooses to speak emphatically of his "*alliance* with the Doctor" (73). This word might seem strange, since alliances are typically made for mutual benefit. Since, in the story, the

Doctor is all agency and mastery, while Jake has none, one might have expected instead the words "reliance on." In order to chart the distance between the paralyzed Jake who is a character in the story and the Jake who is the more empowered author-narrator of the story, one must consider how his relationship with the Doctor "colors" Jake's other relationships, particularly his one with Joe.

Whatever homoerotic attraction exists between Jake and Joe, it is mediated and triangulated less through Rennie than through the Doctor. There is a doubling of Joe and the Doctor that is signaled by Jake's first visit to the Morgan's apartment, which is an uncanny repetition of the Progress and Advice Room, the Doctor's white space that was "about as large as an apartment living room" (1). What of the Morgan's living room? "Their apartment was very clean; what furniture they owned was the most severely plain modern, tough and functional, but there was very little of it. . . . [N]ot a piece of furniture above the necessary minimum. . . . Because the walls and ceiling were white, the light pouring in through the open venetian blinds made the living room blindingly bright. I squinted; there was too much light in that room for me" (38). But more than the Morgan's white walls, venetian blinds, and minimal furniture suggest the Progress and Advice Room. It is in fact the Morgan's relationship that intrigues Jake inasmuch as Rennie's relation to Joe reproduces many elements of Jake's relation to the Doctor. Jake notices that in the Morgan's relationship, Joe is the master and Rennie submits to his world picture. Noticing that Joe tends to dominate Rennie and to discuss her as a kind of work in progress, Jake says, "You talk about her as if she were a patient of yours" (41).

Both Joe, who is almost a doctor of philosophy (he is writing his dissertation), and the Doctor model mastery for Jake. Jake's two models of mastery embody a central piece of Todd Andrews's philosophy by the end of *The Floating Opera*: the Doctor emphasizes the inevitability of masks and lies, while Joe, who understands that there are no absolute values, emphasizes the reality of "less-than-absolutes" (39). In other words, the Doctor represents poetics ("mask" is a way of naming "character"; "lies," of naming "story"), while Joe advocates ethics ("responsibility"). To the extent that Jake is the text's secret black agent, his attraction to Joe and desire to best him in their verbal wrestling might be read against William Faulkner's repeated examinations of interracial desire. In the relationship between Charles Bon and Henry Sutpen in *Absalom, Absalom!*, for example, Faulkner is aware that miscegenation opens the door to both hetero- and homoerotic possibilities.

In all the multiple identifications of *The End of the Road*, desire is played out among men. Rennie counts for very little, other than a means for Jake to play doctor. On their horseback rides together, Jake notices that, although Rennie is always graceful in athletic situations, when they sit together and smoke, "she was simply without style or grace: she flopped and fidgeted. I think it was her self-consciousness about this inability to handle her body that prompted her to talk more freely and confidentially during our rides than she would have otherwise" (50). In her unease with her body sitting with Jake, Rennie essentially becomes Jake in the Doctor's Progress and Advice Room, a space in which the patient's body is positioned to make it ill at ease. Moreover, the details of the beginning of her relationship with Joe, which Rennie reveals in her conversations with Jake, make her the double for Jake and his position of non-mastery in which he begins the novel.

We learn that Joe and Rennie had been dating for a while in New York, but that Joe decides to break off the relationship because he feels her values are not developed enough to have a relationship of "real exchange" (53), and so walks off and leaves her on a park bench. It is this detail that makes Jake pay particular attention (he asks, "On the bench?") because he sees himself and his condition in Rennie. Like Jake, whom the Doctor finds paralyzed on a train station bench, Rennie experiences a sense of self as "complete blank" (54) on a bench in a public place.

Even though they never meet, Joe and the Doctor struggle over shaping Jake's world picture. This struggle is repeated and complicated by the ways in which Jake and Joe struggle over shaping Rennie's world picture. To the extent that Jake wants to become the Doctor (that is to say, to operate from a position of mastery), he must try to win Joe's "patient," Rennie, away from him. And to win Rennie, Jake must show her that Joe is not quite the fellow he appears to be. Jake becomes the trickster who tempts Rennie to spy on Joe one evening. "*Real* people," she tells him, "aren't any different when they're alone. No masks. What you see of them is authentic." Jake responds, "Nobody's authentic" (65). Looking through the window, they see Joe dancing, mugging in front of a mirror, and finally, picking his nose while masturbating.

But even as he tries to become the Doctor with Rennie, Jake plays Joe with the Doctor. During Jake's first fall visit to the farm, the Doctor immediately recognizes a change in Jake's demeanor and helps Jake recognize "that [he] *was* imitating Joe Morgan" (82). Far from being a problem, the Doctor is pleased that Jake is "assuming a role." It is the first step in understanding Mythotherapy. As the Doctor explains it, Mythotherapy is based on existentialist premises: "that human existence precedes human essence . . . and that a man is free not only to choose his own essence but to change it at will" (82).[11] The Doctor wants Jake to become self-conscious of the fact that "everyone is necessarily the hero of his own life story" and assigns "other people the essences of minor characters" (83). To become aware of this is a therapeutic form of ego protection. The black master reveals to his patient that life is nothing more than narrative poetics. The key to Jake's therapy, the Doctor claims, is to continuously place himself in a narrative, since to do so means assuming a role, a character: "you're too unstable to play any one part all the time—you're also too unimaginative, so for you these crises had better be met by changing scripts as often as necessary." The key is to never "get caught without a script, or with the wrong script in a given situation." The Doctor leaves Jake with a couple of options for thinking about their relationship:

Perhaps—I'm just suggesting an offhand possibility—you could change to thinking of me as The Sagacious Old Mentor, a kind of Machiavellian Nestor, say, and yourself as The Ingenuous But Promising Young Protégé, a young Alexander, who someday will put all these teachings into practice and far outshine the master. Do you get the idea? Or—this is repugnant, but it could be used as a last resort—The Silently Indignant Young Man, who tolerates the ravings of a Senile Crank but who will leave this house unsullied by them. I call this repugnant because if you ever used it you'd cut yourself off from much that you haven't learned yet. (84)

While Jake must assume his masks "wholeheartedly," the Doctor admonishes Jake not to "think there's anything behind them: *ego* means I, and *I* means ego, and the ego by definition is a mask" (84–85). In this regard, the Doctor teaches Jake what that whiteface black, Todd Andrews, had learned in *The Floating Opera*, namely that "identity" or "essence" is nothing but a series of roles one plays; no unveiling of a mask ever reveals anything but another mask.

Following his visit to the Doctor, Jake continues using the "Joe script," so to speak, in an encounter with Peggy Rankin. Jake takes everything Joe holds sacred about his relationship with Rennie and travesties it in seducing Peggy, even convincing her (as Joe did Rennie) that his striking her is a sign of the degree to which he takes her seriously. Convinced by the strength of his apparent convictions, Peggy immediately hops into bed with Jake: "I made a mental salute to Joseph Morgan, *il mio maestro*" (92). But Jake does not serve two masters. He might parody Joe's values by his insincere pastiche of Joe's words, but Jake does so out of his belief in his black master. In other words, Jake believes in the Doctor's treatment of him with Mythotherapy, and he has accepted the script that sees the

Doctor as a Machiavellian Nestor.

Rennie's pregnancy only allows Jake to play Doctor more fully. With the paternity of her fetus uncertain, Rennie decides to commit suicide if Jake is unable to find someone to perform an abortion. This tight spot moves Jake to plot at a manic pace, constructing the role of Mr. Dempsy for himself, who telephones local doctors with the story that he and his wife have recently moved to Wicomico and that his wife, who has been under psychiatric care, needs an abortion because of her mental health. When Jake finds a local doctor who is willing to perform the abortion, contingent on hearing from Mrs. Dempsy's Philadelphia psychiatrist, Jake goes to the library, gets a book on abnormal psychology, and drives to Philadelphia. Having identified with the Doctor, Jake now writes as a doctor, Harry L. Siegrist, explaining in a detailed letter Susan Bates Dempsy's case history and why she must immediately have an abortion. Jake calls from Philadelphia and tells the Wicomico doctor that the letter is on its way and has no trouble having his letter notarized by a Philadelphia notary public. Jake is, discursively and rhetorically, the Doctor, the master of this narrative.

Jake's mastery, however, proves illusory, since Rennie refuses to go along with the script Jake has written. His last resort is to ask the Doctor to perform the abortion. The Doctor is primarily irritated that Jake has set his therapy back by his involvement with the Morgans. The Doctor agrees to perform the abortion only if Jake will turn over his bank account, quit his job, and help the Doctor relocate the Remobilization Farm in Pennsylvania, in part so that the Doctor can monitor Jake's therapy twenty-four hours a day, but also because he will "need a young man to do a great deal of manual labor while the new farm is being set up" (174). The Doctor will own Jake, body and soul (such as it is or is not). Jake will become, in effect, an African Amercan's slave.

It is, curiously, in this discussion between Jake and the Doctor that Jake comes closest to pulling the Doctor's mask off. Rather than physically perform the abortion, Jake first asks the Doctor to write a prescription for Ergotrate to induce miscarriage. The Doctor's response is noteworthy: "Don't be any more naïve than you have to. You could just as well write one yourself" (172). This comment suggests that Jake's earlier perception of the Doctor as a fraud is correct: the Doctor cannot write the prescription because he is not a licensed doctor. His claim that Jake could "write one" himself both points back to Jake's convincing letter that he wrote while pretending to be psychiatrist and toward the mastery he will achieve through Scriptotherapy. By becoming an author, Jake indeed writes the prescription he needs.

It is, in fact, the Doctor's lack of mastery of the abortion procedure (clear instructions that Rennie was not to eat before the procedure—or simply asking "Have you eaten anything this evening?"—would have prevented her death), but Jake, of course, allows the procedure to continue even though he has evidence that the Doctor is no doctor. Joe is disgraced and fired from the college, but Jake sees no alternative other than to continue his treatment with the Doctor. The final word of the novel is the one-word sentence "Terminal" (188), a directive to the cab driver where to go but also, figuratively, a suggestion that Jake is a terminal case.

In following the Doctor, Jake effectively chooses the Doctor's poetics over Joe's ethics, but in following through with Scriptotherapy, Jake may be able to have his cake and eat it too. That is to say, Jake can triumph over the white master (Joe), retain the teachings of the black master (the Doctor), and become the Author who "far outshine[s] the master" (84). Jake outshines the Doctor by transforming the Doctor's advocacy of masks and endlessly scripted self-creation into the very means for claiming responsibility. In other words, if Jake as a character fails to take responsibility for his actions in the story, by telling the story, Jake as narrator claims the experience and takes on a larger responsibility: "To turn experience into speech—that is, to classify, to categorize, to conceptualize, to grammarize, to syntactify it—is always a betrayal of experience, a falsification of it; but only so betrayed can it be dealt with at all" (112). Jake finds mastery through his performance of an invisible racial passing when that performance turns aesthetic. His mastery quite simply derives from his authorship. He may be another black in whiteface, but Jacob, unlike Todd, writes his way to mastery. In other words, through authorship, Jake is mastering Todd Andrews's trauma, which is that he is black but does not know it. In following the African American Doctor's treatment, which has always been "directed toward making [Jake] conscious of [his] existence" (78), Jake is able to use his "black" interiority.

Jake is not terminal, nor is his author. Barth, in effect, has found in Jacob Horner a way to solve what was a literal problem for the undertaker in *The Floating Opera*—how to turn a black face white again. With this newfound ability to address non-white artistic interiority, Barth can now complete his Maryland trilogy with a character, Henry Burlingame, who actually is racially mixed. Barth, like his disavowed master, William Faulkner, has come to terms with the blackness that he senses is the writer's true identity. Unlike Faulkner, who in his major fiction uses his position as a whiteface minstrel to tease out the contradictions of southern racial politics, Barth uses his sense of whiteface mastery to cast his lot with a less-than-absolute, yet still perfectly usable, white identity.

RED MAN, PALE FACE: BURLINGAMING WHITENESS

Barth's third novel, *The Sot-Weed Factor*, a massive comic imitation of the Fieldingesque eighteenth-century novel, completes the Maryland trilogy. In it, the containment of racial difference and the domestication of the dangerous potential of the whiteface minstrel becomes explicit. Barth imagines the adventures of Ebenezer Cooke as he leaves England behind to manage his father's tobacco plantation in a wild and barbaric colonial Maryland. Much of the barbarism, though, is generated by the white English settlers. Once again, an author figure is one of the main characters, for Eben believes he has been appointed by Lord Baltimore as the poet laureate of Maryland. Unlike Barth's first two novels, however, the writer figure is not the first-person narrator. (Jacob Horner's first-person narration, which helps resolve the problematic relation between writing and mastery, might be said to enable Barth to explore other forms of narration.)

By far, the more interesting character is Henry Burlingame III, who is hired to tutor Ebenezer and his twin sister, Anna, but whose mentoring of the twins does not end when he is fired. What Burlingame teaches the would-be poet Eben is similar to what the Doctor teaches Jake about Mythotherapy, namely, that life is and can only be nothing more than a series of roles. Unlike the Doctor, however, who is always "the Doctor," Burlingame's pedagogy is interactive and highly performative. Burlingame is an anachronism, Barth's smiling nihilist well versed in existentialist premises, taken out of time and placed in a plot that occurs at the end of the seventeenth century. Burlingame embraces the aesthetics of Ellison's Rinehart in ways that the invisible man and even Todd Andrews cannot. Todd might theorize his masks, but Burlingame is nothing but masks, disguising himself variously as Lord Baltimore (indeed at the moment when Eben is named poet laureate!), a pirate captain, various Maryland political figures, and even Ebenezer. After awhile, the reader suspects that any and every new character introduced is Burlingame in disguise. He uses his masks to act as a secret agent in the dense and convoluted intrigues of Protestant and Catholic interests in Maryland, but whose side he is really on in this struggle remains a mystery. The only side he is on, ultimately, is that of whiteness.

Burlingame is, in effect, Todd and Jake out of the closet. If Todd is defensive and insistent about his heterosexuality and Jake is unaware that his truest love is for Joe (even as he beds Joes' wife), Burlingame is openly bisexual and admits to Eben that he desires nothing so much as to have sex with both Eben and Anna. Like Todd and Jake, Burlingame is another of Barth's racially inflected trickster figures, but unlike Todd and

Jake, who are only figuratively miscegenated, Burlingame is actually racially mixed, the son of an Indian chief. Although mentored by Burlingame, Eben is not racially transformed by the association as Todd is by his relationship with his blackface father or Jake is through his relation with the African American Doctor, which suggests that Barth has found a way to fully contain the threat of racechange that loomed in his first two novels. The writer might not, after all, have to become racially other in order to write. What, then, is at stake in taking the reader to a moment in history when the whiteness of America is not an established fact but merely a possibility, and having a miscegenated, nihilistic trickster operate in the interest of the English colonists?

While in England, the presumed orphan, Burlingame, has but one clue to his family history—a portion of a manuscript written by a Sir Henry Burlingame, who explored portions of the eastern coast of America with Captain John Smith. The contemporary Burlingame assumes he is related, and one element of the novel's plot is his attempt to discover his genealogy. Late in the novel, Eben is captured by a coalition of Ahatchwhoop Indians and escaped African slaves who live on Bloodsworth Island and plot the extermination of the white settlers. Through translated conversations with the Tayac (or Chief) Chicamee, Eben leans that Sir Henry Burlingame was Chicamee's father and that, in turn, Chicamee (also known as Henry Burlingame Two) is the father of Henry Burlingame III, who was banished for his white skin.

The hatred of whiteness among the Ahatchwoops comically derives from the white man, Sir Henry, who was left in captivity by John Smith and the other white explorers, after Sir Henry is named the Tayac for defeating an Ahatchwhoop champion in an eating contest. Sir Henry's son, Chicamee, takes a young woman who is herself half white and half Indian. Because of his tribe's hatred of whites, Chicamee agrees that if any of his children are white, they will be killed. Of the three sons he fathers, the first is dark, the second is the same copper color as Chicamee, but the third is white. Because he cannot bring himself to drown the child, Chicamee places the baby in a canoe, writes the boy's name on his chest (Henry Burlingame III), and sets him adrift on the Chesapeake with the hope that he may be saved and raised by the English. This Moses-like beginning for Burlingame deploys as it confuses elements of the Exodus narrative. The boy is set adrift to live among the oppressor race by the very king who had decreed that all white babies must die.

Chicamee spares Eban's life but charges him to send Burlingame to him, which Eban does but not without some trepidation:

How slight and qualified were Henry's ties to the cause of Western
Civilization (to say nothing of English colonialism!). . . . Had he not
extolled the virtues of every sort of perversity, and pointed out to Ebenezer
man's perennial fascination with violence, destruction, and rapine? It was
by no means unthinkable that, whatever his present intention, Burlingame
would remain on Bloodsworth Island to ally his wits with those of
Drepacca and Quassapelagh. . . . God help the English colonies in
America! (706–7)

Eban has nothing to worry about, however, for when Burlingame returns
to "his people," it is not, as it was with Moses, to make common cause
with the dispossessed racial other but rather to sow the seeds of discord
among the various factions within the Indian and African coalition. On
the island, then, Burlingame shows us what blood is worth. Not much,
apparently. When, after several months' absence, Burlingame returns to
his English friends, he looks "for all the world an Ahatchwhoop in dress
and coiffure" (746). He is pleased both to have discovered his Indian family and to be successfully undermining the planned uprising against the
colonists. Civilization may be a sham, but it is the sham Henry knows,
and whiteness is the system of privilege he can game. He returns to
Bloodsworth Island to match wits with his copper-skinned brother (who
advocates killing the white settlers), never to be seen again. In summing
up, the narrator simply says, "Whether owing to [Burlingame's] efforts or
not, the great insurrection did not materialize" (748).

Able to pass at will along the racial (as well as sexual) divide,
Burlingame knows full well the contingency of his whiteness, yet ultimately chooses to defend it. The defense of white privilege by a man who
is not fully white serves as a logical outcome of Todd Andrews's ability, in
the end, to let go of absolute value as the ground of action (which means
that absolute whiteness need not ground white identity), and of Jacob
Horner's embrace of a "black," trickster Mythopoetics of infinite becoming as a way toward mastery.

Like Faulkner, Barth used blackness to construct his early authorial identity. But while Faulkner's blackness always threatened to erupt in his major
fiction through the queer performance of white southern masculinity, Barth
puts his early problematizing performances of whiteness behind him.
Whatever promise for developing a critical purchase on southern racial
politics through whiteface minstrelsy that Barth constructs in *The
Floating Opera* is largely played out by the time he finishes his Maryland
trilogy. Had he not contained the problem of race in this fashion, Barth

might have, in his subsequent career, produced a body of fiction that we would today more readily identify as the work of a southern novelist.

DOROTHY ALLISON, "NIGGER TRASH," AND MISCEGENATED IDENTITY

IN CHAPTER 4 OF DOROTHY ALLISON'S *BASTARD OUT OF CAROLINA*, Ruth Anne (Bone) and her sister, Reese, look forward to the wedding of their mother, Anne, to Glen Waddell, but discover the reality falls short of their expectations:

> Reese and I hated the honeymoon. We both thought we would get to go. For weeks before the wedding Mama kept telling us that this was a marriage of all of us, that we were taking Glen as our daddy at the same time she was taking him as her husband. . . . But Mama and Glen left halfway through Aunt Alma's dinner, with only one quick kiss goodbye.
> "Why don't we get to go?" Reese kept demanding while everybody laughed at her. I got so mad I hid in Alma's sewing room and cried myself to sleep in her rocker. (42)

In their grief, these deceived members of the wedding, the central cultural ceremony celebrating heteronormativity, point us to Frankie Addam's grief over her exclusion from the honeymoon that follows her brother's wedding in Carson McCullers's *The Member of the Wedding*. Both the bisexual McCullers and the lesbian Allison produce Künstlerromans that may be read as queer portraits of the artist as a young woman. Both Frankie and Bone cannot help telling stories as a way to cope with their sense of alienation and difference. The threat of heterosexual violence looms over both. Frankie is nearly raped by a drunken soldier, while Bone is horrifically raped by Daddy Glen. In the aftermath of their harrowing experiences with heterosexuality, both young women find support in another female character: a year later, Frankie develops a passionate friendship with another teenage girl, and Bone is taken in by her lesbian aunt.

To the extent that it can be read as one of *Bastard out of Carolina*'s intertexts, McCullers's novel, with its middle-class ethos, becomes an object of implied critique from Allison's grittier working-class perspective. Despite her sense of difference, Frankie lives in a protected and privileged world: her father can afford an African American servant. Her widowed Papa, who seems to have renounced sexual desire, knows when she is too big to sleep with him in his bed. And though Frankie might flirt with danger and criminality, the law is always there to protect her from the kinds of violation Bone experiences. Even Frankie's near rape seems unreal, as the twelve-year-old girl easily escapes her assailant by breaking a glass pitcher over his head (which is quite different from Bone's ineffectual attempt with her broken arm to stop Daddy Glen). But for all of Allison's class-based revision of McCullers's queer story of coming of age in a heteronormative culture, both novelists still invoke the artificial Negro paradigm that I have been exploring in this study. That is, they both deploy figurative blackness as a way of delineating the anxieties of their young protagonists.[1]

In her imagination, Frankie is clearly playing in the dark, attempting to construct an identity that draws on the otherness of African Americans. On the morning she decides to tell the town that she is not returning after her brother's wedding, Frankie exchanges a glance with "an old colored man" and feels "a new unnamable connection" (50). Later that day, the Addams' servant, Berenice, explains what it means to be "caught" by social constraints of heredity: "Everybody is caught one way or another. But they done drawn completely extra bounds around all colored people. They done squeezed us in one corner by yourself. So we caught that firstway I was telling you, as all human beings is caught. And we caught as colored people also. Sometimes a boy like Honey feel like he just can't breathe no more. He feel like he got to break something or break himself. Sometimes it just about more than we can stand" (113–14).

Frankie identifies with the African American Honey Brown, saying, "Sometimes I feel like I want to break something, too. I feel like I wish I could just tear down the whole town" (114). Honey's violent urges are a response to American apartheid, while Frankie's sense of identification with blackness grows out of an adolescent frustration as she begins to sense the gender limitations in her southern community. The community's responses to these two are massively different: Honey's actions land him on a chain gang, while Frankie's "criminality" is subliminal. She steals a pocket knife from the Sears and Roebuck, a moment refigured in *Bastard* when Bone and her cousin Grey break into a Woolworth's and he takes all the knives. Still, in her imagination, Frankie identifies with blackness so thoroughly that she casts herself into roles that suggest she is becoming figuratively black.[2] On the bus ride home after the wedding, humiliated at not being taken on the honeymoon by her brother and his bride, Frankie sits "back with the colored people" (135). Once home, she decides to run away, taking her father's pistol. She ends up in the alley in back of her father's jewelry store, contemplating suicide:

> She pointed the pistol at the side of her head and held it there a minute or two. If she squeezed down on the trigger she would be dead and deadness was blackness, nothing but pure terrible blackness that went on and on and never ended until the end of all the world. . . .
>
> The alley was black, and it smelled of garbage cans, and it was in the alley where Lon Baker had his throat slashed that spring afternoon. . . . If only there was someone with her! If only she could hunt down Honey Brown and they could go away together! (144)

Frankie's unconscious choice of the place for contemplating suicide, a site of black-on-black violence, coupled with her conflation of death with blackness, shows the extent to which she codes her adolescent gender anxiety in racial terms. Frankie's desire to run off with Honey still denies sexuality, so it doesn't really invoke the southern horror of miscegenation as much as it bespeaks her desire to play Huck Finn to Honey's Jim in a fantasy of racial otherness.

For Allison, racial difference is hardly the main matter of her novel, focused as it is on the revaluation of the category "white trash." Allison has spoken frankly about the racism she deplores in her own family and in the culture of poor southern whites more generally:

> One real thing about the working class in the South is that they are not ashamed of being racist. . . .
>
> It's one thing to know that in theory about the working class. And it's another thing to run into it in the people you love. It's hell for me dealing with my sisters. . . .
>
> When one of my sisters was at my house, and a black woman friend of mine was also there for a party, my sister could not deal with her. My sister could deal with her as this black woman who's like—there. But not the fact that she and I were really close friends. That we talked personally. That we

made jokes about our girlfriends. My sister could not handle it. And the
look on her face was this kind of deep disgust. ("Dorothy Allison" 33)

As a lesbian feminist who participated in all sorts of consciousness-raising
groups since the 1970s, Allison positions herself as a social activist and as
avowedly antiracist. Yet, despite a greater degree of self-awareness and
guilt about racism than any of the other authors in this study, Allison still
in a number of curious ways appropriates blackness and black culture in
order to plumb the depths of her semi-autobiographical narrator, Bone.

Told in first-person, Bone's narrative owes a debt to the modern
African American novel. Allison identifies James Baldwin (whose *Nobody
Knows My Name* [1962] provides the epigraph Allison uses in *Bastard*),
Toni Morrison (particularly *The Bluest Eye*), Alice Walker, and especially
Zora Neale Hurston as major influences in the development of her "feminist writing voice": "When I found Zora Neale Hurston, it was like getting kicked in the butt. It was a *voice*—the weird thing was that it was a
voice that I heard in *my* head. That I was familiar with. The speech, the
rhythms of my family, the kind of language that I grew up with
resounded for me in the books written by those women. It didn't read to
me black. It read to me working class" ("Dorothy Allison" 31).

Allison's sense of herself as a working-class novelist, then, performs
and appropriates black cultural expression, a performance doubled by
Bone's narrative. This form of black talk helps illustrate that the space
between the southern concepts of the "Negro" and "white trash" is nar-
row indeed.

At the most literal level, the Boatwright family acknowledges the distinct possibility of racial mixing in their genealogy. Bone's favorite uncle
is known as Black Earle because of his straight, jet-black hair, a physical
feature Bone shares with him. Granny attributes Bone's "black as mid-
night" eyes and hair to Bone's great-great-grandfather, "a black-eyed bastard himself" (26–27), whom she claims was Cherokee. But when
Granny tells Bone "You even got a little of the shine of him" (27),
although referring to Bone's eyes and hair, the description becomes
racially ambiguous, since "shine" is nearly as offensive as "nigger" as a
racial epithet. Bone's Aunt Raylene goes one step further since she tells
people that the Boatwrights "had a little of the tarbrush on" them (53).

Although Granny's and Raylene's comments hint at miscegenation,
the novel veers away from the literal to the figurative, most particularly in
Bone's identification with blackness. In becoming black, Bone learns the
lesson that Ab Snopes tries to teach Sarty in Faulkner's "Barn Burning,"

namely, that the subject position of "white trash" is nearly impossible to distinguish from that of "nigger," save for color.

The film critic Constance Penley, describing her own childhood as a poor white in central Florida, sums up the difficulties in distinguishing differences that strongly resonate with Bone's racialized South Carolina childhood:

> A Southern white child is required to learn that white trash folks are the lowest of the low because socially and economically they have sunk so far that they might as well be black. As such, they are seen to have lost all self-respect. . . .
>
> If you are white trash, then you must engage in the never-ending labor of distinguishing yourself, of codifying your behavior so as to clearly signify a difference from blackness that will, in spite of everything, express some miniscule, if pathetic, measure of your culture's superiority, at least to those above you who use the epithet "white trash" to emphasize just how beyond the pale you are. (90)

One of the things *Bastard* does is to underscore those moments in which it becomes impossible for a poor white to maintain even a minimal distinction from the poor black. As a child, Bone quickly realizes that "people were crazy on the subject of color" and recalls hitting another child who call her a "nigger": "When I started school . . . a skinny rat-faced girl . . . had called me a nigger after I pushed her away from the chair I'd taken for mine. She'd swore I was as dark and wild as any child 'born on the wrong side of the porch,' which I took to be another way of calling me a bastard" (54). Although the incident is trivial, it underscores why the state of South Carolina, at that time, felt it had the right to certify certain children with the stigma of bastard status. More than enforcing moral values regarding female chastity, "bastard" polices racial lines. If the father is unknown or unnamed, the specter of the ultimate southern horror—miscegenation between black men and white women—arises, as Faulkner's bastard out of Mississippi, Joe Christmas, knows only too well. As filtered through the memory of his racist grandfather, who has placed young Joe in an orphanage, the boy learns this racialized lesson quite early when he asks a black man doing yard work "'How come you are a nigger' and the nigger said 'Who told you I am a nigger, you little white trash bastard?' and he says 'I aint a nigger' and the nigger says 'You are worse than that. You dont even know what you are. And more than that, you wont never know. You'll live and you'll die and you wont never know' and he says 'God aint no nigger' and the nigger says 'I reckon you ought to know what God is, because dont nobody but God know what you is'" (383–84).

Given the one-drop rule of southern culture, if one's father is unknown, one's racial identity is to a degree always indeterminate. As Barbara Ladd notes, if a white woman gives birth to a child of an unnamed father, that "child might be the carrier of what the white racist would have understood as social and cultural contagion" (164). Ladd's observation has clear resonances with Bone's situation. Even though Bone's presumptively white biological father is an open secret among many in the Boatwright family, because he could not be named publicly when she was born, indeterminacy circulates in the communal unconscious: Bone is a "white trash"/"nigger" bastard.

Such social stigma surrounding identity is particularly freighted for Bone's stepfather, Daddy Glen, whose family never lets him forget his position as a Waddell who has married into the Boatwrights. Glen's father owns a dairy and his brothers, Daryl and James, are both professionals. To the Waddells, Glen has married beneath himself, so that the now working-class Glen, although he attempts to imitate the masculinity of the Boatwright men, is always conflicted about his relation to this clan. When Bone's Aunt Fay and Uncle Nevil rent a particular house, Glen complains, "It's a goddam nigger shanty! Don't they care how they're living?" (82). Glen's irruption grows out of his anxiety about his loss of class position and his inability to provide middle-class housing for his family.

Glen's desire to differentiate the family he heads from those of other Boatwrights is frustrated whenever this family visits either Glen's father's or brothers' houses. On one such visit, Bone overhears Daryl and James:

"Look at that car. Just like any *nigger trash*, getting something like that."
"What'd you expect? Look what he married."
"Her and her kids sure go with that car." (102, emphasis added)

From their smug middle-class lives, Daryl and James blame their brother's class position on his marriage into a working-class family. More importantly, their epithet, "nigger trash" effectively erases the difference between "white trash" and "nigger" and underscores that, to better-off whites, the desperate efforts of poor whites to distinguish themselves from the racial other is meaningless.

Daryl and James's identification of difference, during which Bone is the hidden observer, serves as a kind of primal scene of race and signals her subsequent movement toward figurative blackness. The process of Bone's becoming black comes into clearer focus in relation to the novel's

uncanny figure of absolute whiteness, the albino Shannon Pearl. If whiteness, as Toni Morrison's *The Bluest Eye* so admirably demonstrates, was
in mid-twentieth-century America the unquestioned standard of beauty,
Allison inverts this by marking Shannon's whiteness as an almost transcendent ugliness that elicits from Bone responses ranging from "awe to
disgust" (155). Shannon's coloring represents the logical extreme of "not
colored" and provides a sharp contrast to Bone's description of her own
skin, which is "as dark as walnut bark" (206).

Through her relation to Shannon's family, Bone develops a love of
gospel music, a music that figures the imbricated relationship between
her spirituality and her becoming black. Shannon's father is a promoter
who scouts new talent for the gospel music circuit. Bone's discovery of
gospel music coincides with her turn to religion. Her response to religion
and gospel music reproduces the dynamic of the unspeakable incest she
suffers at the hands of her stepfather. Bone goes to revival meetings to
come forward as a sinner, yet defers her baptism because she wants to
remain on the border between salvation and damnation, a situation that
doubles her inability to reveal the abuse she knows she ought to speak. As
Bone puts it, "It was that moment of sitting on the line between salvation
and damnation with the preacher and the old women pulling bodily at
my poor darkened soul. I wanted that moment to go on forever" (151).
Bone's "poor darkened soul" points us to the whiteface performance of
identity she enacts; she stages the moment of becoming saved in a way
that doubles her becoming black. But sustaining this liminal position in
which she is the object of the gaze replicates one of her key masturbation
fantasies in which she imagines people watching while Daddy Glen beats
her. The actual beatings are horrific, filled with Bone's screams, but in her
fantasy, power relations are reversed: "In my imagination I was proud and
defiant. I'd stare back at [Glen] with my teeth set, making no sound at all.
Those who watched admired me and hated him. I pictured it that way
and put my hands between my legs. It was scary, but it was thrilling too.
Those who watched me, loved me. It was as if I was being beaten for
them. I was wonderful in their eyes" (112).

In the religious experience, Bone is "wonderful" in the eyes of those
who see a sinner coming to salvation, an element that is repeated in the
sexual fantasy. This fantasy, which revises as it recalls Freud's 1919 paper
"'A Child is Being Beaten': A Contribution to the Study of Sexual
Perversion"; for Freud, the female child's masochistic masturbation fantasy of being beaten is always only a fantasy produced by someone not
subject to actual beatings by the father. Bone's fantasy, which does grow
out of real beatings, reminds us of Freud's denial of women's reports of

sexual abuse by their fathers. At the same time, the parallels between Bone's sexualized beating fantasy and the scenes of her conversion brinkmanship suggest how the unconscious produces repetition. By constantly staging the moment of her near baptism, Bone is able in public to experience the thrill of being desired, of becoming the love object of all who watch her, particularly those already "saved."

With religion, she is able to substitute God, the transcendent Good Father, for the violating Daddy Glen. Once her mother forces Bone to be baptized, religion loses much of its appeal, but her passion for gospel music and its surrounding culture remains. At one level, that is because the unseen, backstage world of the singers quite literally reproduces Bone's molestation: "Both of us [Shannon and Bone] had learned to walk carefully backstage, with all those hands reaching out to stroke our thighs and pinch the nipples we barely had" (163). At a more subliminal level, though, the gospel lyrics that Bone recalls evoke her abuse: "*While I was sleeping somebody touched me, while I was sleeping, Oh! Somebody touched me . . . musta been the hand of the Lord*" (141). The pleasure Bone takes from these lyrics is that they both speak to her violation and mask the guilt she feels regarding Glen and the way he touches her with his large, powerful hands.

Bone's "odd but acceptable lust" (158) for gospel music is symptomatic of her larger movement toward blackness. From African American spirituals to the Fisk Jubilee Singers first tour in 1871, gospel has been a black cultural form, albeit with a hybrid origin. Gospel grows out of slave owners desire to Christianize their slaves. Slaves often appropriated traditional hymn melodies but modified the lyrics and added African rhythms (Cusic 48). Until the 1950s, it would almost be redundant to say "black gospel music," but since then, various white gospel traditions, derived from black gospel, have emerged. The one Allison represents is southern gospel, featuring the quartets and family groups resembling those in country music. White gospel emerged more from the marketing end of the music industry as a way to overcome the problem of how to sell black music to white audiences (Cusic 59–60), a reality that *Bastard* thematizes at a crucial moment in Bone's becoming black.

Bone unconsciously is drawn to the appropriation of black culture before she ever associates this music with African Americans; however, the racial implications of performing blackness become all the more significant when she experiences what to her is the most authentic gospel experience that she has ever had. This moment of identifying authenticity serves simultaneously as an unreflexive claim to identity. On a trip with the Pearls, Bone and Shannon wander off from a gas station break and hear arresting music: "Gut-shaking, deep-bellied, powerful voices rolled through the dried leaves and hot air. This was the real stuff. I could feel the whiskey edge, the grief and holding on, the dark night of terror and determination of real gospel. 'My God,' I breathed, and it was the best 'My God' I'd ever put out, a long, sacred whisper that meant I just might start to believe He hid in cottonwoods" (169).

The music comes from a country church, and Bone wants to hurry back to tell Mr. Pearl, convinced that he will want to put these singers under contract. Shannon, however, degrades the moment by racing it: "'It's colored. It's niggers.' Shannon's voice was as loud as I'd ever heard it, and shrill with indignation. 'My daddy don't handle niggers.'" Bone reacts to this racial epithet in a deeply personal way; responding to Shannon, Bone realizes that her "voice was shaking": "The way Shannon said 'nigger' tore at me, the tone pitched exactly like the echoing sound of Aunt Madeline sneering 'trash' when she thought I wasn't close enough to hear." In her anger, Shannon characterizes Bone's relatives as "drunks and thieves and bastards," ending with and elliptical claim: "Everybody knows who you are . . . " But what is Bone? It is in this elliptical space that the southern political unconscious resides, one in which the distinction between "trash" and "nigger" once again implodes. Bone's subsequent enraged outburst serves as a racially transforming moment: "You bitch, you white-assed bitch" (170). Responding with black talk, Bone proclaims her distance from whiteness.

This rupture in Bone and Shannon's friendship helps underscore a larger context in which Shannon functions as Bone's double. If Bone is a scapegoated figure within her own nuclear family, Shannon, because of her hyperwhiteness, is a pariah in a broader social context. Both girls are nascent novelists. Bone's popularity as a babysitter derives from her storytelling, which "featured bloodsuckers who consumed only the freshly butchered bodies of newborn babies, green-faced dwarfs promising untold riches to children who would bring them the hearts of four and forty grown men" (119). Shannon also tells "horrible stories, most of which were about the gruesome deaths of innocent children" (157). While Bone tells her stories to her cousins, Shannon has only Bone as an audience for her narratives. Bone exhibits the same fascination with Shannon's stories that Bone's cousins have for hers. There is a difference, however: what fascinates Bone is the verisimilitude of Shannon's stories, which were "not fantasies," as Bone realizes her own stories are, but "had the aura of the real—newspaper headlines and autopsy reports—and she loved best little children who had fallen in the way of a large machine" (157).

In their choice of violent, shocking subject matter, both of these girls point to Allison's own aesthetics in her storytelling. In her essay "Believing in Literature," Allison says, "I thought of my stories, my characters, the albino child I murdered in 'Gospel Song' [an earlier version of Shannon's death], the gay man who kills his lover in 'Interesting Death,' the little girl who tries to seduce her uncle in 'Private Rituals.' Bad characters, bad acts, bad thoughts—as well-written as I can make them because I want my people to be believable, my stories to haunt and obsess my readers. I want, in fact, to startle my readers, shock and terrify sometimes, to fascinate and surprise" (*Skin* 172).

In wanting to write believable characters, yet ones that will "haunt and obsess," Allison suggests the ways in which her two storytellers in *Bastard* figure her own writerly inclinations in relation to realism and the fantastic. The difference between Bone's and Shannon's storytelling makes Shannon's death all the more critical to how Allison tells her story because, at the moment of Shannon's death, we see Bone learning how to wed her narrative strategy to Shannon's. The depiction of Shannon's death almost seems to figure Allison's movement away from a Shannon-like reportage that one sees in her essay collection, *Skin*, toward an incorporation of Bone's use of fantasy.[3] If Allison's essays tend toward the journalistic, autobiographical reflection, her first novel illustrates fiction's ability to transfigure the autobiographical through a nonlinear symbolic logic.

Shannon's death, at first glance, seems like a story Shannon herself would relish telling since it involves the gruesome death of a child, but it is Bone who describe what happens after the lighter fluid can that Shannon had been squirting on the grill explodes: "Shannon didn't even scream. Her mouth was wide open, and she just breathed the flames in. Her glasses went opaque, her eyes vanished, and all around her skull her fine hair stood up in a crown of burning glory. Her dress whooshed and billowed into orange-yellow smoky flames. . . . I saw Shannon stagger and stumble from side to side, then fall into a heap. Her dress was gone. I saw the smoke turn black and oily. I saw Shannon Pearl disappear from this world" (201).

Although realistically rendered (again, as Shannon would), Shannon's death, within the symbolic logic of the larger narrative, instantiates an element of Bone's fantasy life that links blackness and queer desire. It matters, in short, that the ultrawhite girl dies "black."

As in Bone's second masturbation fantasy of being watched while she is beaten, Shannon does not cry out in agony as the flames consume her but takes the pain in silence. Strikingly, Shannon dies in a fashion that recalls Bone's earlier masturbation fantasy: "I would imagine being tied up and put in a haystack while someone set the dry straw ablaze. I would picture it perfectly while rocking on my hand. The daydream was about struggling to get free while the fire burned hotter and closer. I am not sure if I came when the fire reached me or after I had imagined escaping it. But I came. I orgasmed on my hand to the dream of fire" (63). Fire, in fact, was always part of Bone's attraction to Shannon. She sees in Shannon's interiority the rage that doubles her own: "Shannon Pearl simply and completely hated everyone who had ever hurt her, and spent most of her time brooding on punishments either she or God would visit on them. The fire that burned in her eyes was the fire of outrage" (157–58).

One of the people who hurts Shannon is a gospel singer who, startled at meeting her, calls her ugly. Mrs. Pearl enters the tent the next moment and starts fawning over the singer. Mrs. Pearl's inability to see how people mistreat her daughter (or register Shannon's response to this mistreatment) mirrors the novel's larger maternal blindness, notably Anne's denial of Glen's abuse of Bone. Reading the hatred in Shannon's face, Bone realizes that she "loved [Shannon] with all [her] heart":

> I reached for Shannon's hand. She slapped mine away. Her face was blazing. I felt as if a great fire was burning close to me, using up all the oxygen, making me pant to catch my breath. I laced the fingers of my hands together and tilted by head back to look up at the stars. If there was a God, then there would be justice. If there was justice, then Shannon and I would make them all burn . . .
> "Someday," Shannon whispered.
> "Yeah," I whispered back. "Someday." (166–67)

Without ever touching, theirs is a sexualized relationship. Once again, the details surrounding the fire imagery implicitly recall Bone's masturbation fantasy. In particular, her panting recalls her breathing as she approaches sexual climax. Although in her mother's presence Shannon slaps Bone's hand away, the girls' whispered word—"someday"—seems to promise a future consummation. Shannon's being consumed by fire thus serves as a coded consummation of queer desire.

In the immediate aftermath of Shannon's death, Mrs. Pearl's sense of Bone's implication in Shannon's death speaks a figurative truth: Mrs. Pearl "kept screaming '*You!*' over and over like I had done something, but all I had done was watch. I was sure of that" (200). But, in fact, Bone does more; she transforms watching into telling by narrating the fiery death of her friend/enemy/double. To the extent that Allison is a "black" author (recall that all of the novelists in her usable tradition are African American), what might it mean that she kills the hyperwhite girl? The scene of Shannon's death recalls nothing so much as one from Toni Morrison's *Sula*, in which Sula's mother, Hannah Peace, burns to death. Sula's grandmother is left with the suspicion that "Sula had watched Hannah burn not because she was paralyzed, but because she was interested" (78). This is the interest of aesthetic contemplation. Sula, who has an artistic consciousness but no artistic form, stands as one of Morrison's clearest examples of the way that watching is never "just" watching but always implicates the watcher in the act watched, particularly if the one who watches is then able to use what is seen to create art.

A storytelling narrator who enacts Allison's own sense of authority, "black" Bone effectively kills her white double in this act of more than watching. Seeing Shannon die in the fire, Bone witnesses her masturbation fantasy made real; Shannon's death is another guilty pleasure inasmuch as it allows Bone to produce the very kind of narrative that Allison describes as her desired aesthetic effect. In Shannon Pearl's death, Allison gives us a queer story of a grotesque white girl whom fire blackens, which is, of course, a fantastic version of Bone's own narrative arc as the white girl whose fire-figured sexuality constantly moves her toward blackness. We might say, then, that killing Shannon allows Allison to disavow a part of her storytelling self that might prevent her from becoming a complete novelist.

Allison's colorization of whiteness goes hand in glove with her transvaluation of "white trash," a project that is most overtly thematized by Bone's lesbian aunt, Raylene. Aunt Raylene lives at a bend in the river where refuse collects, which she retrieves and sells; quite literally, she recovers trash. Yet even joining her aunt in recovering trash implicates Bone in a process of becoming black, a becoming that once again is linked to nonheteronormative sexual identity. Bone quickly proves adept at her aunt's recovery work. Bone's most significant find is a four-pronged dredging hook, an object that immediately fascinates her. From its moment of discovery, the hook links up to Bone's figurative black identity. Although she is the one who wades into the water to retrieve the hook, it is one of her cousins who initially sees the object and calls out "Lookit the shine!" (183). While most literally denoting the metal's reflection of light, a racial connotation once again lurks in the word "shine," which was used in the first half of the twentieth century to identify African Americans, since they were associated with the operation of shoeshine stands. Earlier her grandmother notes that Bone shares the "shine" of her Cherokee great-great-grandfather.

While spending the night at Raylene's, Bone takes the hook and chain into her room. After removing the chain and polishing it, she incorporates it into another masturbation fantasy. Placing the chain between her legs, Bone thinks about the women in Daddy Glen's pornography:

> I held the chain and . . . rubbed it against my skin and hummed to myself. I wasn't like the women in those books, but it felt good to hold that metal, to let those links slip back and forth until they were slippery. I used the lock I had found on the river bank to fasten the chain around my hips. . . . It was mine. It was safe. Every link on that chain was magic in my hand.
> I put my head back and smiled. The chain moved under the sheet. I was locked away and safe. What I really was could not be touched. (193)

Mary Wiles argues for the importance of the hook as a lesbian fetish, noting that Bone "projects the phallus onto her own body, disavowing the lack of the female body and the prohibition of access to it. Yet the fetish not only serves the passive function of protection but also takes on an active role in establishing human agency" (156). While it is not precisely the hook in this instance but rather the chain that attaches to the hook, this found "trash" object is crucial to an identity formation that links blackness and sexuality. As protection, the chain—a kind of homemade chastity belt—makes Bone feel safe from the violating hands of Daddy Glen, but when the hook emerges from its closeted role in the bedroom, its coming out is black.

Bone devises a plan to break into the Woolworth's where she and her mother had been humiliated when Anne had tried to teach Bone the importance of honesty by making her daughter return an item she had stolen. The lesson backfires, since what Bone learns is class difference: the store manager bans her from the store. Bone's plan, then, refigures the manager's assumption that trash always steals by embracing the criminality of this prejudice. Far beyond the criminality of a minor incident of shoplifting, Bone's new crime exhibits a design and daring that exceeds the presumptive abilities of poor whites. She asks her older cousin Grey to help her and, because she thinks a boy will attract less attention carrying the sack with the hook and chain, she lets him take the prized hook home with him. On the night of the break-in, Bone discovers that Grey has painted the hook and chain black to camouflage it. It is with this blackened hook, then, that Bone is able to climb to the roof of Woolworth's and enter through an airshaft. Once inside, she swings the blackened hook, smashing the nuts case in a kind of symbolic castration of the store manager. Significantly, Bone steals nothing. She does allow

Grey (who is oblivious to the symbolic significance of Bone's restraint) to take all the jackknives he can carry, then leaves the front door unlocked and tells a group of poor men she sees that the door is open, ensuring that store will be completely emptied by morning. To cast the matter in terms of McCullers's *Member of the Wedding,* Bone is much closer than Frankie to the African American Honey Brown who "got to break something or break himself" (McCullers 114).

However much Bone is figuratively blackened by this scene itself, historical context provides an additional measure of her enactment of a whiteface minstrelsy. Bone's action against the Greensville, South Carolina Woolworth's occurs in 1960 and results from her understanding that she "was barred from the Woolworth's counters" (97). Although Bone makes no mention of it, Allison, who, like her protagonist, was eleven in 1960, surely was aware of another protest against Woolworth's that made national headlines that year.[4] In Greensboro, North Carolina, four African Americans male students from North Carolina A&T College were refused service at Woolworth's lunch counter. This resulted in a six-month-long sit-in that spread to other Woolworth's stores in the South and that eventually led to desegregating the Woolworth's lunch counter. Allison, in effect, creates a signifying "Green" space (whether "sville" or "sboro") in which Bone performs as another one of the protesters against Woolworth's exclusionary practices. If the African American protesters sought equal access based on race, Bone, in a sense, provides open access for those poor whites too economically disadvantaged to be welcome by this discount merchandiser. Historical context helps link the subject positions of African Americans and poor whites, underscoring the ways in which the poor white performs cultural blackness in whiteface.

Ultimately, Allison's playing with blackness cannot help but allude to the color-coding of southern racial politics, even when race is not an issue of representation. In Allison's second novel, *Cavedweller,* the relation between blackness and identity becomes even more figurative. In this novel, Cissy escapes the entanglements of her mother's poor white background by literally going underground. The first time she is immersed in the total darkness of a cave, Cissy's experience resonates with Bone's relation to the black lesbian fetish:

> Cissy titled her head back slightly. . . . She wanted to hum but was too self-conscious. It would have been good, though, to hum deep in her chest . . . to let that sound come up out of her to assume color and shape in the dark. . . . A tear ran down Cissy's cheek from one burning eye to her chin.

She wiped it away. The words in her head were white on white: I am safe
here. Nothing can find me that I do not want to find me. If I do not move,
the dark will fill me up, make me another creature, fearless and whole.
(243–44)

Bone's humming and Cissy's urge to hum, coupled with their mutual
sense of safety, constitute key similarities between the two passages. In
particular, Cissy and Bone both see their safety in relation to a blackness
that speaks to these two white girls' experience of authenticity. They
might appear white to the world, but their interiority is filled with blackness. Subsequently, Cissy leads two college women into repeated explorations of a local cave, and once again, blackness becomes linked with
nonheteronormative sexuality. Cissy's two sisters are conventionally
straight, but Cissy never expresses an interest in boys. Eventually, after
the revelation that her two caving partners (with whom she has been playing with in the dark) are lesbians, Cissy asserts, "Maybe I'm a lesbian too"
(400).

Allison's figurative appropriation of blackness in her portrayal of
Bone's becoming black certainly helps create what E. Patrick Johnson has
identified as "new epistemologies of self and Other" (6). *Bastard* force-
fully underscores the futility of poor whites to ever successfully differentiate themselves from African Americans in the eyes of the white middle
class. But Allison stops short of Irish novelist Roddy Doyle. Doyle's
working-class northern Dublin lover of soul music, Jimmy Rabbitte, recognizes his marginality as a subject position akin to "niggers," which leads
him to proclaim (in a direct appropriation of a James Brown song), "Say
it loud, I'm black an' I'm proud" (9). Perhaps Allison's characters cannot
openly proclaim a black identity because blackness remains linked to
criminality and unchecked libidinal energy. While these two forces are
marked as liberating, Bone's property crime exemplifies the contradictions of color-coded raecechange: she is a white girl who, because of her
bastard status and class background, is not fully white; she asserts her
agency and strikes her most literal blow against white patriarchy in a
criminal act performed in whiteface, wherein the blackened hook signifies the interiority of her already "black" sexuality.

The blackness of boundary-crossing libidinality is complicated further
by the fact that Bone is not the only character who figuratively goes dark.
If Bone, the victim of incest, in some sense becomes black, so too is the
perpetrator of the crime, Daddy Glen. His darkened eyes are repeatedly
linked to his rages. One morning after Daddy Glen has sat up all night
nursing his private anger, Bone notices that "his blue eyes were so dark

they looked black" (68). After the first time he molests her, Bone notices that "his eyes had gone dark" (47). Glen's black eyes, then, are simultaneously a mark of his primitivism, his being before civilization, and the primal taboo against incest. Inasmuch as Allison claims she learned about voice from Morrison's novel about the father's violation of his daughter, *The Bluest Eye*, one might be tempted to re-title Allison's first novel *The Blackest Eye*. Unlike Pecola Breedlove, who is violated by her father and desires white beauty, as signified by blue eyes, Bone takes pride in her black eyes that suggest racial ambiguity. But when Daddy Glen's eyes go black, they mark his loss of caste and, by implication, his claim to whiteness.

More disturbingly, Bone's much-loved yet equally black-eyed uncle, Black Earle, progressively ages while the barely legal waifs he seduces remain the same age. Earle, in a sense, is Glen's kinder (though hardly gentler) double. What *Bastard* leaves us with, then, is a very mixed view of white performances of blackness: if all forms of illicit sexuality enacted by poor whites—from adultery and incest to guilty masturbation and nascent lesbian eroticism—perform "black" libidinality, then the performance can always stop and white identity still has plausible deniability vis-à-vis blackness. In other words, the black hook might bespeak a lesbian identification, but if Bone chooses when to strap it on as a form of empowerment, she also decides when to take it off. "Black" sexual perversity, one might argue, remains the abject other of whiteness. Blackness might well figure authenticity, but if blackness may be set aside, then Allison cannot help reinstituting the urge of poor whites to maintain a minimal separation between themselves and blacks that her critical writing at times so cogently critiques.

In this regard, the novel's ending is pertinent to understanding Allison's conflicting impulses. After Daddy Glen's violent rape of Bone, Anne must choose between husband and daughter, and to Bone's (and most readers') horror, she chooses Glen. Before leaving permanently, however, Anne visits Bone at Raylene's to leave a piece of paper in an envelope. Despite her sense of abandonment, Bone experiences the envelope's contents as a legacy of love, one that, in the closing words of the novel, creates the ground for her future identity and, ultimately, a way to forgive her mother. The envelope contains a copy of Bone's birth certificate, but when she opens the bottom third of the document she discovers "It was blank, unmarked, unstamped" (309).

Anne's parting gift to her daughter is whiteness. This copy of the birth certificate, unmarked with the block letters "ILLEGITIMATE" that all previous copies had proclaimed, erases the social uncertainty that wants to hail Bone as black. With an unmarked birth certificate, she may now enter into the equally unmarked, deracialized state of whiteness, a situation that endows Bone with an empathy for the abandoning mother and her hard life. At the same time, the gift solidifies identity: "I tucked the envelope inside my pocket. . . . I was who I was going to be, someone like her, like Mama, a Boatwright woman" (309).

What her embracing of her clan identity means is that Bone may now present a white face to the world, even though she knows her sexuality to be "black." In this regard, Allison can be seen as another writer working in the tradition of William Faulkner and his whiteface minstrels. The question Patricia Robyn asks Faulkner's artist figure, Gordon, in *Mosquitoes* may be one that could be similarly asked of Allison's artist figure, Bone: Why are you so black? But although Allison, unlike Faulkner, does not explicitly ask this question, her attempt to perform black culture through her writing underscores the persistence of the artificial Negro as a problematizing and problematic guise of the white southern novelist.

CHAPTER 6

BLACK WRITING AND WHITEFACE

TO THIS POINT, MY FOCUS HAS BEEN EXCLUSIVELY ON THE WAYS IN WHICH white southern writers have inverted the conventions of blackface minstrelsy through a recurring whiteface figure—the sometimes minstrel, sometimes trickster character who is racially white, but who, in some sense, is always only passing as southern White. We have seen how, for example, Faulkner's Uncle Ike McCaslin, O'Connor's Hazel Motes, and Barth's Todd Andrews end up, without their conscious recognition, performing cultural blackness. These characters, whose enactments of white masculinity are decidedly at odds with social expectations, serve as sites of multiple misrecognitions within their white communities. They are, after all, a strange kind of artificial Negro. Blinded by the white, no one can actually identify these characters' difference as racially inflected. As I have argued, these whiteface characters, no matter how well or poorly their authors imagine cultural blackness, have a subversive potential inasmuch as they problematize the assumption that whiteness transcends race and serve as the universal norm against which all darker difference may be measured. What I wish to do in this concluding chapter is to consider how the whiteface figure might also operate in twentieth-century African American fiction. I turn specifically to Zora Neale Hurston's *Moses, Man of the Mountain* and Ishmael Reed's *Mumbo Jumbo*. There are several reasons for taking up these two texts. It allows me, in abbreviated form, to retrace the historical terrain I covered with twentieth-century white southern fiction, which ran from modernism to the contemporary. If Hurston was an iconoclast of the Harlem Renaissance, often challenging the status quo on the matter of the appropriate representation of race, Ishmael Reed is a postmodern gadfly who challenges contemporary racial and gender pieties. Moreover, both of Hurston's and Reed's texts engage the biblical story of Moses, which invites us to revisit (and to some extent rethink) what is at stake in *Go Down, Moses*, a move that is particularly useful inasmuch as I have cast William Faulkner as the generative southern practitioner of whiteface minstrelsy in the twentieth century. But finally, what makes *Moses, Man of the Mountain* and *Mumbo Jumbo* so important to my study is the way that both thematize the appropriation of blackness, even as these texts work in part as parodic appropriations of whiteness.

In order to fully appreciate Hurston's and Reed's re-visioning of Moses, it is crucial to consider yet another writer who used Moses to think about how he might be differentially raced. I constellate Sigmund Freud's *Moses and Monotheism* with Hurston's and Reed's novel since Freud's study looms as an intertext for both these African American writers. While there is no reason to suppose that Hurston read Freud, the historical conjunction of their thinking about Moses is striking; for Reed, however, Freud is a figure to be appropriated and radically reshaped.

ZORA NEALE HURSTON'S MOSES, THE ARTIFICIAL HEBREW

There is a curious modernist moment during the rise of European fascism in which three very different authors revisit the story of Moses, the lawgiver and liberator. What does it mean that Sigmund Freud, Zora Neale Hurston, and William Faulkner each imagines a version of the Moses story that hinges on an explicit racial transformation, where Moses (or the figure of Moses) comes to leave behind his original racial identity to such a degree that he comes not merely to embody but to epitomize the racial other?[1]

Pursuing this question, I believe, helps us reconceive southern modernism by more fully linking the Southern Renascence and the Harlem Renaissance and allow us to see how Faulkner's and Hurston's narratives function in both transnational and regionalist contexts. The ambivalence of racial identity in Hurston's *Moses, Man of the Mountain* (1939) and Faulkner's *Go Down, Moses* (1942), moreover, may be underscored in relation to Freud's *Moses and Monotheism* (1939). Both Freud and Hurston conceive of Moses as an Egyptian. The Jews, therefore, are not God's chosen people but, rather, the people chosen by Moses. In Faulkner's novel, as we saw in Chapter 2, the Moses figure, Issac McCaslin, repudiates his patrimony, which turns out to include his white identity. African Americans, whether he knows it or not, become his chosen people, which results in his becoming figuratively black. While Freud and Hurston (as well as Faulkner to a lesser extent) use the Moses story to reflect on German fascism, Hurston and Faulkner deploy Moses to show that there is more to southern racial politics than the one-drop rule since in their narratives, biology matters less than performance in the shaping of racial identity. Moreover, both Hurston and Faulkner focus on the issue of racialized masculinity and manhood in a patriarchal culture.

From the perspective of African American literature, one can identify the story of Moses from Exodus as a kind of passing narrative. Moses is really a Hebrew who was only unwittingly passing as an Egyptian until his true racial identity is revealed and he embraces his Hebrew origin. In this regard, Exodus depicts the matter of authenticity in terms of racial essence, much as the traditional novel of passing ostensibly does. For example, at the conclusion of James Weldon Johnson's *The Autobiography of an Ex-Coloured Man*, first published in 1912 and reissued with an introduction by the white patron of the black arts, Carl Van Vechten, in 1927, the light-skinned narrator makes it clear that he lives out his life feeling spiritually empty by his decision to pass as white. After attending a meeting at Carnegie Hall at which Booker T. Washington and other black leaders speak, the narrator confesses, "Beside them I feel small and selfish. I am an ordinarily successful white man who has made a little money. They are men who are making history and a race. I, too, might have taken part in a work so glorious." Having aspired to make a significant contribution to African American music, the narrator ultimately chooses the personal safety and security of whiteness instead. Left with "a vanished dream, a dead ambition, a sacrificed talent," he concludes that he has "sold [his] birthright for a mess of pottage" (211). Although his conclusion articulates his belief that he has denied his authentic racial identity as an African American, thus killing his spirit for material gain, the whole of his narrative works against this claim. His ability to cross and recross the color line at will throughout the novel, far from stabilizing identity, underscores instead the performativity of all racial identity. However, what is common in the African American novel of passing, whether in the hands of Johnson or later in the subtler work of Nella Larsen, is that the passer always crosses the racial divide from the position of the racial other in order to enjoy the privileges of being racially unmarked. What Freud, Hurston, and Faulkner do is rework the simple narrative of passing from Exodus and make the racechanges vertiginous by inverting the convention; their passers move in the wrong direction—from the position of literal or figurative whiteness to that of otherness.

In his final book, Freud reads the biblical story with the same hermeneutics of suspicion that he read all myth. Aware of parallels between Moses's miraculous rescue from the Nile and similar narratives in other myths and cultures, Freud sees the story of Moses as an inverted form of Otto Rank's monomyth of the hero, one suited to the needs of enslaved people. In arguing for an Egyptian origin of Judaism, Freud points out that, against the polytheism that characterized ancient Egypt, at one particular moment in the fourteenth century BCE, a Pharaoh (Amenhotep IV) arose who advocated a monotheism based on Aton, the sun god, that emphasized ethics over "all myth, magic, and sorcery" (26). Freud sees uncanny parallels between Atonist monotheism and Judaism, particularly their denial of magic and emphasis on ethics. Freud's alternative story tells of an Egyptian priest or nobleman who could not give up his Atonist faith after Egypt returned to its polytheism, but who found in the Hebrews a people "to whom he could give the religion that Egypt [now] distained" (32). Freud's story of a Moses who gives up his racial and class privilege to align himself with otherness is precisely one that Huston and Faulkner revisit.

Freud's initial reasoning has a certain rhetorical force. As Jan Assmann has noted, Freud in a number of instances drew on evidence and assumptions well known to Egyptologists of his day, such as the Egyptian etymology of the name "Mose," which means "child" (Assmann 150). Freud's argument, however, becomes indistinguishable from the novelistic form he had originally planned for his Moses book when he uses the Moses story to confirm, by way of repetition, his sense of the liminal moment in the transition from nature to culture in *Totem and Taboo*, and the construction of the incest taboo out of the primal horde's killing of the primal father. Freud posits two Moses—an Egyptian Moses (who led the Hebrews out of Egypt and was subsequently murdered by them for his strictness) and a Midianite Moses—the prophet of the demon god, Yahweh. Over time, the repressed guilt resulting from the murder of Egyptian Moses caused the Jewish people to embrace his ethics-based monotheism over the more supernatural religion of Midianite Moses.[2]

Although Freud's notion of Judaism as the result of the return of the repressed has been thoroughly questioned by Yosef Hayim Yerushalmi, what makes a consideration of Freud germane to my study is the way that it contextualizes modernist racial masquerade.[3] Freud writes from the impossible identity of "Jew/not a Jew." The book of a dying man, *Moses and Monotheism* attempts to understand the basis for anti-Semitism and forces Freud to confront the Jewishness that he often closeted in his effort to establish the legitimacy of psychoanalysis. The opening sentence of Freud's study emphasizes his own precarious position vis-à-vis the material he will examine: "To deny a people the man whom it praises as the greatest of his sons is not a deed to be undertaken lightheartedly—especially by one belonging to that people" (3).[4] His initial gesture of claiming his own Jewish identity, however much it may be removed from Judaism as a faith, is nothing short of astounding in Freud, the largely assimilated Jew who tried so hard to deflect the perception that psychoanalysis was a Jewish science.

Although largely assimilated in the Viennese social circles, Freud is forced, during the rise to power of the National Socialists in Germany, to acknowledge, if only pragmatically, his Jewishness as a race. Nazism impacted Freud directly, as the two introductions to Part III reveal: the first is written in Vienna, as threats to his safety are becoming clearer; the second, from London where he shortly thereafter dies in exile. In the London preface, Freud notes, "In the certainty of persecution—now not only because of my work, but also because of my 'race'—I left, with many friends, the city which from earliest childhood, through seventy-eight years, had been a home to me" (69–70). It is in Part III that Freud seeks the grounds of anti-Semitism. Freud finds part of the reason in what he sees as Jewish superiority—the Jewish belief that they really are a chosen people whose culture and practices are superior to those of other people. In this, it is "one man, the man Moses" (136) who is responsible both for the Jews' greatest strength and for their greatest weakness. That is, Moses, for Freud, explains both Jewish resilience and one basis for anti-Semitism.

But the deepest roots of anti-Semitism Freud discovers in the relationship between Judaism and Christianity, both of which have at their origins a crime. If the murder of Moses instantiates Judaism, the death of Jesus instantiates Christianity. Anti-Semitism arises from what Freud sees as the "tragic guilt" of the Jewish people, which he tropes in terms of father-son rivalry. Christianity's solution to their monotheistic problem of the guilt over killing the primal father is the death of the Son, an act that in a sense serves as the expiation of the death of God the Father. For Freud, Moses's Atonism, the unacknowledged foundation of Judaism, suppressed the polytheism of the Egyptian pantheon. Christianity, however, under the guise of being monotheistic, is in fact, with its notion of the Trinity, the "return of the repressed" of polytheism (112). Therefore, Christianity is, on the one hand, a historical regression but, on the other hand, an "advance in the history of religion" (113). We should be careful here not to suppose that Freud thinks that Christianity is superior to Judaism in any absolute terms. Freud sees all religion as mystification and error; an advance in the history of religion is merely an advance in the history of mystification. What, then, is the nature of the advance? Freud attempts to speak the unconscious of Christianity vis-à-vis Judiasm:

"'You won't *admit* that you murdered God' (the archetype of God, the primeval Father, and his reincarnations). . . . 'It is true, we did the same thing, but we *admitted* it, and since then we have been purified'"(115).

Since for Freud the sacrament of the Eucharist is but an unacknowledged ritualized cannibalism of the murdered god, the only good of Christianity is that it is a step toward escaping religion more generally, which is ever and always implicated in the oedipal violence of fathers and sons. Christianity, then, is merely a stage in the historical development leading toward the end of religion, a period when the post-theological, cultural Jew will no longer have to worry about anti-Semitism, which was always religiously based. Freud's reading of the relation between Judaism and Christianity helps explain the way he indirectly circles back to his own Jewishness in the penultimate paragraph of his study: "Only a part of the Jewish people accepted the new doctrine [Christianity]. Those who refused to do so are still called Jews" (176). As Freud makes clear, he does not accept Christianity and is still called a Jew, and thus is still constructed by Nazism as the racial other.

After making his claim that Moses created the Jews, Freud inserts a section in his third essay titled "The Great Man" that opens with a question: "How is it possible that one single man can develop such extraordinary effectiveness, that he can create out of indifferent individuals and families *one* people?" This short section almost seems like a précis for the work Theodor Adorno would do after World War II on the authoritarian personality. For Freud, the "great man" arises precisely because "people have a strong need for authority which they can admire, to which they can submit, and which dominates and sometimes even ill-treats them." This collective urge for an authority figure derives from "the longing for the father that lives in each of us from his childhood days. . . . [A]ll of the features with which we furnish the great man are traits of the father, that in this similarity lies the essence . . . of the great man. The decisiveness of thought, the strength of will, the forcefulness of his deeds, belong to the picture of the father; above all other things, however, the self-reliance and independence of the great man, his divine conviction of doing the right thing, which may pass into ruthlessness. He must be admired, he may be trusted, but one cannot help also being afraid of him" (140). It is hard not to draw parallels between the strong father figure Moses and the Führer, Adolph Hitler, who tells the German people that, as members of the Aryan race, they are superior, chosen by this destiny to rule darker skinned peoples. In this regard, Hitler serves as the unconscious of Freud's interpretation of Moses.

If Freud's text raises the question of Moses's relation to fascism through the concept to the great man, Hurston teases out the matter further. As Deborah McDowell notes in her introduction to *Moses, Man of the Mountain*, Hurston's "concern with questions of racial purity . . . gains significance when we consider that this is the year Hitler ordered the attack on Poland and led Germany into a world war" based on his theory of eugenics (xiv) and that "the shadow of Nazism is cast from the beginning" of the novel, "which opens on the process of marking Hebrew male babies for extinction" (xv).[5] Hurston writes (as do Freud and Faulkner) at a period of history when science was challenging biological theories of racial difference. But even as modern science was questioning race as a category, Western cultures were taking their stand for an absolutist understanding of race. If the Nazi's enacted laws of racial purity, the Jim Crow South had laws against miscegenation. The purity of the master/master's race was central to both sides of the Atlantic.

While Hurston's novel speaks to broad international concerns about European fascism, it also, like Faulkner's, is specific to the Jim Crow South and to homegrown fascist tendencies.[6] Both Huston and Faulkner play on the longstanding tradition of African American appropriations of the biblical story of Exodus. One can scarcely overstate the importance of the Exodus narrative in African American political discourse from the early nineteenth-century through the Civil Rights movement.[7] In turning to Moses and appropriating the African American appropriation, both novelists address a crisis of masculinity in the South—for Faulkner, as we saw in Chapter 2, it is white southern masculinity; for Hurston, it is African American masculinity. To address racialized southern masculinity, both novelists use the Moses story to stage a kind of whiteface minstrelsy; that is, Hurston's Moses, like Faulkner's Moses-figure Ike, presents the master's face to the world, even as he performs cultural blackness.

As the author's introduction makes clear, Hurston is lifting Moses out of white Christian conceptions of him and placing him instead in a pan-Africanist tradition. Far from Moses and monotheism, Hurston's Moses signifies within the polytheism of Haitian vodun. Moses is a man of god-like powers and ultimately serves as Hurston's curious solution to the problem of black manhood. If, in a transnational context, Hurston can use Pharaoh's treatment of the Hebrews to comment on Hitler's contemporary treatment of the Jews, in a southern regionalist context, Hurston's Hebrews, who speak a signifying black English, represent contemporary rural southern African Americans. One of the key problems in Hurston's novel, then, is the emasculation or erasure of black manhood. Pharaoh's decree, announced at the outset, that all Hebrew male children will be

killed underscores the way in which the Jim Crow South denied manhood to the black male. As Amram, the father of the baby whom the
Israelites believe has been taken into the Egyptian palace and raised as
Moses, says prior to his son's birth that he does not want another son:
"Even if the soldier's don't find him and kill him, I don't want him feeling like I feel. I want him to be a man" (7). Amram's claim not to want
another son speaks directly to the sense of emasculation he feels. Having
to hide the very birth of his child, Amram can only say, "I don't feel like
no man at all" (8). Yet, he tells his first son, Aaron, who is afraid to go
outside to watch for Egyptian secret police while his mother is in labor,
"Go on! It's got so that Israelite boys can't wait to be grown to be men.
You will have to be a man right now" (11). The contradiction is that social
conditions force the Hebrew/black male to take on, very early, the responsibilities of manhood without ever feeling like a man. As is the case with
Richard Wright's Dave Sanders in "The Man Who Was Almost a Man"
(which I discussed in Chapter 1), Amram realizes he works like a man but
is never accorded the respect of a man. In the South of the 1930s, an
African American male was never granted the honorific "mister," a minimal sign of respect automatically granted to any white man.

    In Hurston's novel, Moses's Hebrew identity results from the fabrica-
tion of the nine-year-old Miriam, who falls asleep while she is supposed
to be watching the river where her baby brother had been left floating in
a basket. While it is just barely possible that she unintentionally gets
things right, Miriam invents the story of the baby's rescue from the Nile
to avoid punishment when questioned by her mother.[8] Amram's skepti-
cism ("Humph! Pharaoh's killing every Hebrew boy child he can get his
hands on and his daughter taking one home for a son. Ridiculous!" [32])
recalls Freud's; however, the story Miriam tells meets a need of the
oppressed Hebrews (much as Freud imagined such a narrative would)
and becomes a widely held belief. Here, after all, is "something for the
men to dream about" (35), since Miriam's story is one that grants manhood to a Hebrew/black men. The boy Moses, however, is almost certainly not Hebrew but a member of the master class, a Prince of Egypt.
But what does it mean to be Egyptian? Hurston's Moses is not pure
Egyptian but is the son of a royal princess and an Assyrian prince who has
died. Even the princess may have Hebrew blood. Hebrews, as the slaves
well know, had been close to the royal family since the time of Joseph.
Hearing Miriam's story about how Moses has been taken into the palace,
one of the Hebrew men says, "There is plenty of Hebrew blood in that
family already. That is why that Pharaoh wants to kill us all off. He is
scared somebody will come along and tell who his real folks are" (33). Just

as the mixing of the races was an open secret in the South, Hurston portrays race mixing in an Egypt where the only thing that is unspeakable is
admitting kinship to the racial other.

To be Egyptian is also to be African. As the case of Moses's Ethiopian
treaty wife reveals, skin color is not what determines the unmarked ethnic
status of the Egyptian.[9] Had this marriage produced a child, it would
have been a member of the Egyptian royalty. An Egyptian of the master
class, then, is likely to be racially mixed, but the enabling social fiction is
that, so long as no Hebrew blood is acknowledged, the Egyptian is
untainted. This is how Hurston instantiates her complexly conceived
whiteface minstrelsy: racial blackness (from the perspective of the southern one-drop rule) performs figurative southern Whiteness; however, her
"white" (read "racially unmarked") Moses ultimately chooses cultural
blackness. In other words, the literal, figurative, and the cultural meanings of race and color are crossed and recrossed by Hurston's novel.

If Faulkner's Ike McCaslin loses his ability to be called "Mister" in the
South, Hurston's Moses ultimately chooses against his honorific as
"Suten-Rech" (literally, "cousin to Pharaoh" but a broader term of class
position). Beginning with a figuratively white identity, Moses finds a
number of surrogate father figures who lead him to the adult performance
of what is a Hebrew/culturally black identity.

Mentu, one of the stable hands, although not a Hebrew, also speaks a
kind of black English and leads young Moses to a respect for the dispossessed. Mentu, who appears as an almost Uncles Remus-like figure, tells
the boy stories about animals and claims to "understand the language of
the birds and the animals and the plants" (41). As another figurative
black, Mentu "blackens up," that is, he wears a kind of minstrel mask, to
prompt young Moses to act in the old man's interest. For example,
Mentu's story about the hungry old lizard causes Moses to realize that
Mentu must be hungry, too, and to bring the aging servant food from the
royal table. Moses proclaims his love for the servant, but Mentu gently
reminds the boy that "all love is tempered with something" (43).

Mentu, the name of the Egyptian god of war, teaches Moses about
horses. Moses uses this knowledge to defeat his Uncle Ta-Phar in the war
games that Pharaoh stages to impress foreign kings. Moses's tactical use of
his cavalry overwhelms Ta-Phar's less maneuverable war chariots. While
Moses's martial skill earns him Pharaoh's favor, it also earns him the
hatred of his uncle. After Moses is named commander in chief of the
Egyptian army, Ta-Phar threatens to whip Moses, but Moses erupts with
his first instance of black talk, the influence of Mentu's martial tutelage:

"You don't want no parts of me, and I know it; and you know it, and you know that I know you know it" (57).

Even as Mentu teaches Moses things that make him a great military tactician, the old man also leads Moses toward matters of spirituality and magic: "It was the talk of Mentu which stirred the inquisitive Moses to stealing into the enclosure of the priests" (43). Moreover, Mentu is the first to tell Moses about the book of Thoth, and inspires Moses's quest to find this sacred text. Mentu's teaching may have enabled Moses to rise to the head of Pharaoh's armies, but it is also Mentu's spiritual influence that leads Moses to question Egypt's colonial aggression. Because Moses criticizes Egyptian supremacy, Ta-Phar is able to use the Hebrew story about the baby saved from the river to circulate rumors that Moses has Hebrew blood. Moses is, after all, "a Suten-Rech who takes sides with Hebrews and hangs around the stables with grooms" (51).

It is precisely in these and other suggestions of Hebrew miscegenation that we see the minstrel impulse in *Moses, Man of the Mountain.* Hurston's subversive play with racial difference turns stereotypes inside out, even as it deploys them. Even though Moses's marriage to an Ethiopian princess is merely political, interracial marriage, per se, is not a problem. In fact, Moses's black wife's racial identity is not an issue because it is unmarked. The ironies abound. To be of the master class (no matter what one's skin color) is to be white in the novel's southern regionalist context. In other words, Moses's wife is racially black, but culturally white. The only subject position that is racially other is that of the Hebrew.[10] Believing the rumors spread by Ta-Phar that Moses is really Hebrew, the black princess plays the role of the southern white woman threatened by the Negro. When Moses enters her bedroom to tell her that he has to leave on another military campaign, she upbraids him for having kissed her as part of their marriage ceremony:

> "You Hebrew! Putting your hands on *me!*"
> "Hebrew? I a Hebrew? What ever put that notion in your head?"
> "Get out of my room. The very idea of me being married to a Hebrew makes me sick at the stomach. Don't you dare to come near me. That gang of rapists and slaves." (63–64)

Here, the dark-skinned "white" woman "knows" that all Hebrew/ black men want to rape Egyptian/"white" women, a scene that exemplifies Hurston's comic subversion of racial stereotypes.

In the context of these rumors, once Moses kills the Egyptian overseer who was abusing a slave, Moses has no choice but to flee. His escape across the Red Sea literalizes a crossing of social categories, which Huston makes clear in the concluding paragraph of chapter 10:

> Moses had crossed over. He was not in Egypt. He had crossed over and now he was not an Egyptian. He had crossed over. The short sword at his thigh had a jeweled hilt but he had crossed over and so it was no longer the sign of high birth and power. He had crossed over, so he sat down on a rock near the seashore to rest himself. He had crossed over so he was not of the house of Pharaoh. . . . He was subject to no law except the laws of tooth and talon. He had crossed over. The sun who was his friend and ancestor in Egypt was arrogant and bitter in Asia. He had crossed over. . . . He was a man sitting on a rock. He had crossed over. (78)

For Barbara Johnson, this passage implies that "Moses undergoes the cancellation of all he signifies. The crossing over is also a crossing out" (24). But this crossing out entails the simultaneous possibility of a filling in. What Moses figuratively is crossing is the color line. He leaves behind his proper identity as a "Suten-Rech," much as Isaac McCaslin denies his proper white identity as a "Mister." The racial transformation that Moses undergoes is both cultural and spiritual.

In crossing over, Moses may have left behind his whiteness, but he has not yet become Hebrew/black. Mentu initiates this transformation, but the completed racial reassignment depends on Moses's next mentor, Jethro, the Midianite prince and priest who becomes Moses's father-in-law. Jethro speaks not the formal language of the Egyptian court but a relaxed dialect, again suggesting black English. Moses quickly comes to a decision: "I want to talk the dialect of your people," he tells Jethro. "It's no use of talking unless people understand what you say" (92), and within months "he was mastering the language of the Midianites as if he had been born to it" (98). More importantly, for the next twenty years, Jethro takes over Moses's education in matters of nature and magic. Jethro is a mind reader and a conjure man who is happy to see his son-in-law exceed him in achievement. Jethro encourages Moses to complete his quest to find the book of Thoth. This is a particularly interesting detail in light of Jethro's subsequent insistence on a monotheistic perspective.

While Moses is gone for a year seeking the book of Thoth, Jethro recalls all of Moses's supernatural achievement. Long before being charged by God to deliver the slaves from bondage, Moses has turned water into blood so that "the rivulets and springs and wells and streams ran blood all that day"; has stricken a "malicious gossip" with leprosy; and has even "found out how to make the excrescence that he called Manna appear on a certain plant" (116–17). In other words, when Moses later performs these miracles in Egypt and during the exodus, God's agency is not in any way necessary.

When Moses returns, he tells Jethro how he summoned magical workman to pull the box containing the book of Thoth from the river and wrestled for three days with the deathless snake guarding the book. Thoth, the god of writing and language, was the tongue of the Egyptian god Ra. Again, long before he brings the Hebrews the word of God on stone tables, he has already learned the word of the Egyptian gods. After Moses has read the book of Thoth "he was able to command the heavens and the earth, the abyss and the mountain, and the sea. He knew the language of the birds of the air, the creatures that people the deep and what the beasts of the wilds all said. He saw the sun and the moon and the stars of the sky as no man had ever seen them before, for a divine power was with him" (119–20). It is then a Moses who is the master of all polytheism's magic who is charged first by Jethro to go to Egypt to free the Hebrews. But Moses is not interested in this mission. What is interesting here is that while Jethro wants Moses to go to Egypt in the name of "the one true God" (121), Jethro selects an individual whose powers he knows are already godlike precisely because of that individual's knowledge of polytheism's sacred text. And while Moses refuses Jethro's request, chapter 16 concludes with Jethro's determination to make Moses perform this task: "Well, he might think I'm through with the thing, but first and last he's going to find out different. I ain't been to Koptos, it is true, and had no fight with no never-dying snake, but maybe there is still something about snakes that he can learn. The backside of that mountain may get too hot to hold him yet" (124).

At the beginning of chapter 17, Moses supposedly hears the voice of God. But does he, or is it Jethro, who, rather like the Wizard of Oz, manufactures the burning bush, the voice, and the poisonous snake that becomes Moses's rod of power? Read retrospectively, Jethro's words at the end of chapter 16 seem to be his formulation of the plan that he will execute on Mount Sinai in order to make Moses accept the challenge. The evidence is not definitive, but after Jethro dies, Moses does not hear the voice of God again.

For Hurston, Egyptian Moses's path is to give up racial privilege and choose cultural blackness by identifying with the Hebrews. It is important to note that Hurston's Moses has a moment where he is tempted to return to his "white" identity. After parting the Red Sea and subsequently killing Pharaoh and his army by closing the sea over them, Moses realizes that all who had opposed him and had identified him as a Hebrew are dead. He could go back to Egypt and become the new pharaoh. Sitting in the same spot where he had earlier realized that he had crossed over (again, a figurative crossing of the color line), Moses now chooses not white kingship, but black leadership.

In *Moses, Man of the Mountain*, blackness is not a racial essence but a cultural performance. Moses is not Hebrew/black by birth but, through a series of choices, comes to model the possibility of claiming a black manhood that the dominant culture would disallow. He ultimately chooses his successor—Joshua, one of the former Hebrew slaves. Joshua may speak black English naturally, but he learns black manhood from Moses. In this regard, Jethro is like his mentor, Moses, who learned his performance of blackness from mentors (Mentu, Jethro) who were not themselves Hebrew.

Uncannily carrying forward Freud's project of reimagining Moses as a racechanged figure, both Hurston and Faulkner draw characters that unhinge the racial thinking of southern modernity. But both projects have limitations. While Hurston's Moses triumphs and imagines the possibility of an empowered black manhood, her portrayal of an Egyptian/African member of the master class who chooses to perform culturally as the abject racial other must, I think, be read as a moment of utopian thinking in the context of racial violence in the 1930s South. Hurston's Moses may be the "best hoodoo man around," as his father-in-law Jethro proclaims, but any man (whatever his racial mix) in the Jim Crow South who claimed authoritative black identity risked violent death at the hands of white mob authority.

The tragic Moses figure in *Go Down, Moses*, Uncle Ike, maps the limit of Faulkner's ability to think through racial difference. Ike fundamentally does not understand that to be Moses is to give up being a member of the master class. Ike hopes to lead the next generation of white southern males to a more ethical enactment of white masculine identity. This cannot happen, however, because he cannot recognize the ways in which he has ceased to be white. Hurston's Moses, however, embraces his racial transformation and chooses to lead her novel's coded African Americans, who come to accept "white" Moses's performance as authentically "black."

PSYCHOANALYTIC *MUMBO JUMBO*: ISHMAEL REED AND THE LIMITS OF WHITEFACE

I want to conclude by turning to Ishmael Reed, who sounds a cautionary note to what has been, at times, my celebration of the artificial Negro as a trope in white southern fiction. Reed, of course, is not typically considered a southern author, yet his presence in this book has a kind of diasporic logic that is of a piece with the thinking that sometimes places Toni Morrison in the context of southern literature. After all, so the argument goes, since her parents migrated from the South, Morrison was raised with southern structures of feeling, and her fiction sometimes has southern settings. On such grounds, Reed's claim to be linked to southern literature is even better than Morrison's because he was actually born in the South. Although raised in Buffalo, New York, Reed was born in Chattanooga, Tennessee, where he spent his early childhood. His Neo-Hoodooist aesthetic is culturally tied to New Orleans (not to mention Haiti), a city that serves as the setting for the opening of his 1972 novel, *Mumbo Jumbo*. Even the main setting of this novel, the New York of the Harlem Renaissance, is linked to the South, inasmuch as it is a site where African American writers who had migrated from the South often struggled with their southern legacy.

Still, Reed seems strange to consider in a southern literary context because of his style. Oprah Winfrey will never make a movie based on a Reed novel. Morrison, with her interests in community and intergenerational family conflict, can be read beside a modernist such as Faulkner. Reed, however, is not a representational writer interested in psychological depth or affect. Writing out of the black militancy and broader countercultural movements of the 1960s, *Mumbo Jumbo* is a postmodern novel that is easier to understand in relation to Thomas Pynchon's *The Crying of Lot 49* (1967). Both episodic satires of American culture are full of flat characters (many of whom appear only briefly) and conspiracy theories; both play with the form of the detective novel.

In this romp through Western history, Reed questions whether a white man can ever stop being white. (I use the male pronoun in the previous sentence because in Reed's novel, men's actions and ideas alone make history.) *Mumbo Jumbo* suggests that any white attempt to perform cultural blackness inevitably is inauthentic, a form of blackface minstrelsy. The novel tells the story of an outbreak of Jes Grew in America that is causing odd behavior in people of all races. Jes Grew is a life-affirming anti-plague that causes people to become possessed by black cultural expressive forms, such as jazz, and that in turn causes them to lose their inhibitions and dance. This pandemic creates panic among the Wallflower Order, a conspiracy of white power brokers in government, industry, academia, and entertainment. As Henry Lewis Gates, Jr. explains, the Wallflower Order is pun on the Ivy League (225).

The novel's central conflict is between Papa LeBas, who runs the Mumbo Jumbo Cathedral where the Hatian loas are honored and fed, and Hinkle Von Vampton, who is charged by the Wallflower Order to stop the outbreak of Jes Grew. Von Vampton knows how to do this because he is aware that Jes Grew is seeking its liturgy, the Book of Thoth, a text that Von Vampton has been controlling. Von Vampton turns out to be the last member of the Knights Templar who discovered the Book of Thoth that Moses had hidden in Solomon's Temple. He has kept himself alive since the end of the Crusades with the power contained in the Book of Thoth. As part of his strategy to combat Jes Grew, Von Vampton creates a literary magazine ostensibly to publish Harlem Renaissance writers, but which in fact subverts black expression.

With the help of some Haitians, Papa LeBas uncovers Von Vampton's plot and arrests him at a party of Harlem Renaissance artists and critics. The guests at the party want to know why Von Vampton is being arrested. Playing with the form detective story, Reed takes what is typically the detective's brief summing up of how the crime was committed and turns it into LeBas's retelling of a history of the West that comes out of Egypt (which for Reed also means out of Africa). Part of this history is a version of the story of Moses, his relation to Jethro, and his successful attempt to recover the Book of Thoth. Reed's Moses is neither a liberator nor a lawgiver, but merely a charlatan whose interest in the Book of Thoth is linked neither to any spiritual quest (certainly not the Hebrew's) nor to a social good, but is only a power grab, an appropriation of blackness.

While Reed parodies a number of black and white writers in *Mumbo Jumbo*, what I find of particular interest in the context of this study's focus on racechange is the way that Reed appropriates and parodies both Freud and Hurston, who themselves wrote iconoclastic versions of the Moses story. Even in my brief characterization of Reed's novel, one can clearly see pieces of Freud's and Hurston's Moses that Reed engages. The story that Papa LeBas tells as the solution to Von Hampton's crime is essentially familiar in its broadest outline to the one Freud tells in *Moses and Monotheism*—a centuries old struggle between polytheism and monotheism. Reed names the ideological force against which LeBas struggles "Atonism," which denotes any religion or system of thought that believes in one god or privileges one master narrative. The religions Reed names are Christianity and Islam (but not Judaism): however, psychoanalysis and Marxism are Atonistic for their respective insistence on Oedipus and class conflict. For Freud, the origins of Judaic monotheism derive from Amenhotep IV/IIkhnaton's endorsement of the monotheistic Aton religion. For Hurston, the book of Thoth is the sacred text that her Moses heroically recovers and reads, giving him godlike powers that allow him to become the liberator of the Hebrews.

Reed is playful regarding his appropriation of Freud and Hurston, clearly foregrounding it but, at the same time, hiding the Freud and Hurston texts that are most significant to *Mumbo Jumbo*. Hurston's description of the process of the formation of a vodun loa serves as one of the epigraphs to Reed's novel, and Freud actually appears as a minor character, though it is a Freud who has been remade as a Christian.[11] Yet, despite the clear presence of these two modernists, Reed hides their truest presence in his 104-item "Partial Bibliography," a send-up of scholarship that simultaneously functions as a truth claim for his fantastic history.[12] Reed lists two books each for Freud and Hurston (as well as a biography of Freud), but not their books on Moses. For me, then, the interesting question is why Reed feels he must travesty two of modernism's most iconoclastic renditions of the Moses narrative in his allegorical narrative of black culture and racial identity.

In part, Reed's appropriation of Hurston derives from what he sees as her complicity with the white power structure. Hinkle Von Vampton is clearly Reed's satiric portrayal of the famous white patron of the black arts, Carl Van Vechten, and Reed implies that those African American authors who affiliated themselves with Van Vechten were, like the African American's Von Vampton manipulates, merely unwitting agents in blackface. This would, of course, include Hurston, whose 1938 study of Jamaica and vodun practices in Haiti, *Tell My Horse*, was dedicated to Van Vechten, who she calls "God's image of a friend."[13]

But what precisely makes these earlier versions of Moses so problematic for Reed that he must conceal his critical engagement with them? Reed's larger problem seems to be that both Freud and Hurston present a "white" Moses who can give up his position of racial privilege and ultimately lead the racial other. Freud's case is particularly freighted, since Freud, like Reed, attempts to unpack a specific history of racism, though Freud explores anti-Semitism rather than anti-blackness. For Reed to admit the history of Judaism as a cultural force would deeply complicate his narrative of the white conspiracy against people of color. If Freud strips Moses of his Hebrew identity, Reed goes one step further, stripping Freud of his Jewishness. Reed needed a Freud who was unproblematically white in order to portray the white conspiracy repressing the African origins of Western civilization. The notion of the Jew as (another) racial other would have unhinged Reed's narrative, which is, at heart, a mythological rendering of the argument Martin Bernal would later make in *Black Athena*. In other words, replacing Africa for Greece as the ultimate source for Western culture leaves no room for Hebrew Jerusalem.

Unlike Huston, who takes the longstanding African American appropriation of Moses and the Exodus narrative from the biblical tradition
and reimagines it from a pan-Africanist persceptive, Reed finds nothing
in either the biblical Moses or Hurston's Moses that sustains black culture. Hurston's Moses, a racial passer, becomes a true hoodoo man;
Reed's Moses is a racial poser, a charlatan who is only trying to use black
culture (stripped of its spiritual roots) for personal profit and power. If
Hurston's Moses suggests that someone who begins life racially privileged
might embrace black culture in such a way that they can effectively "cross
over" (that is, cross the color line) and make common cause with the
racial other, Reed's Moses indicates the author's suspicion that the racial
divide can ever be bridged or that whites can ever escape what George
Lipsitz calls "the possessive investment in whiteness."[14]
   One episode in *Mumbo Jumbo* emphasizes that whites can never truly
be trusted to give up their white privilege. Papa LeBas's protégé,
Berbelang, makes the mistake of trusting Thor Wintergreen, the son of a
wealthy white capitalist, and pays for it with his life. Berbelang leads a
group that raids art museums in order to return art and sacred objects that
European colonizers had taken to their countries of origin. Convinced
that Thor truly believes in this cause, Berbelang includes Wintergreen in
his plans. Having captured Biff Musclewhite, the Curator of the Center
for Art Detention, Berbelang leaves Thor to guard Musclewhite. As soon
as they are alone, Musclewhite appeals to Wintergreen precisely on the
basis of a continuously constructed whiteness. Musclewhite explains that
as an Eastern European, his people were not always white: "We were your
niggers; you colonized us and made us dirt under your heels. But in
America it's different. . . . We've learned to bullshit the way you do,
build up an aura of sacredness about the meanest achievement"
(111–12). In telling the story of how Eastern Europeans became white
in America, Musclewhite (who has muscled his way to whiteness) speaks
of the superiority of the cultural traditions of white people and ultimately convinces Thor to free him with this claim: "They are lagging
behind us, son, and you know in your heart this is true. Son, these niggers writing. Profaning our sacred words. Taking them from us and
beating them on the anvil of BoogieWoogie, putting their black hands
on them so that they shine like burnished amulets. Taking our words,
son,.these filthy niggers and using them like they were their god-given
pussy" (114).
   Casting the matter in the racist and sexist way that he does,
Musclewhite's view of African Americans profaning white sacred words
points directly to what is at stake in Papa LeBas's telling of the Moses

story, which reveals that the real sexualized profanation was of the black word. To fully see this point, however, requires a moderately long excursion through the history of the world according to Reed, one ultimately leading both to Moses's sexualized conquest of the Book of Thoth and to a better understanding of Reed's satiric poetics of appropriation.

According to Papa LeBas, contemporary America must be read in terms of ancient Egyptian mythology, particularly the conflict between Osiris and Set. In Reed's telling, Osiris, after studying from black masters in Ethiopia, returns to Egypt, bringing agricultural civilization. Egypt, under Set, had practiced cannibalism. Osiris can perform magic through music (the Black Mud sound) and dance. All was good until people spontaneously burst into Osiris's dances, which interrupted farm labor. Thoth offers to record and illustrate Osiris's dances so that "Osirian priests could determine what god or spirit possessed them as well as learn how to make these gods and spirits depart" (164). After Set betrays and murders Osiris, Thoth takes his sacred book to Isis, Osiris's sister/wife. Sets attempts to establish Atonistic monotheism largely fail because the people prefer to continue the Osirian mysteries underground. At this point, Reed's borrowing from Freud's study becomes clear: "That [the attempt to establish monotheism] was until Amenhotep 4 (about 1500 BC). He was a frail tall and weakling interior-decorator type who became an Atonist and changed his name to Akhnaton (devoted to Aton) while he spent sometime in Heliopolis hanging out on the beach the Atonists made popular, now a decadent, Joe Atlas scene" (174). Against the heteronormative manliness of Osiris and all the polytheists, Reed casts Freud's originator of monotheism as gay.

Reed introduces Moses as the adopted son of Thermuthis, an Egyptian princess with monotheistic leanings. Moses, a prince of Egypt, however, becomes an Osirian initiate. The Osirians are troped as bluesmen, and Moses wants to learn "the heaviest sound they had ever heard" (176). The consensus is that Jethro the Midianite plays the most authentic of the old songs. Moses goes to Jethro and, on hearing the Midianite play his twenty-five string guitar, thinks he could become the head of the Egyptian Osirians if he could learn to play like Jethro. Light-skinned Moses even marries dark-skinned Zipporah, since Jethro will only teach his art to a son-in-law.

At this point, Reed's fanciful reworking of Hurston is obvious. Moses learns from Jethro and prepares to return to Egypt when Jethro tells Moses about the Book of Thoth in Koptos at the temple of Isis. Moses climbs Mount Horeb to contemplate. On the twelfth night, he is visited by the ghost of Set, who will tell him "how to circumvent the deathless snake who guards the temple at Koptos" (a creature that Hurston's Moses learns about from Mentu) if Moses promises "to restore the cult of Aton to Egypt" (178). Set's key to unlock the secrets of the Book of Thoth is to talk "trash" to Isis.

Isis reveals the Book of Thoth to Moses, but unlike in Hurston's version, where his learning the sacred text results from his magical labors, for Reed, it is Moses's sexual conquest. Jethro warns Moses that the time is wrong to go to the temple of Isis and that if he does, he will learn "only a few things about converting rods to snakes; simple *bokor* tricks, the rest will be so awful that you will wish you had never known The Work" (179). Ignoring Jethro's warning, Moses seduces the dangerous goddess by "talk[ing] to her the way the Osirians talked to her in their rites. He told her how much he loved her and that he would die for her. Cut his throat swim in a river of thrashing crocodiles fight lions for her pussy." As Isis moans and whimpers: "Moses's hand moved down and touched her Seal. He fished her temple good. She showed him all her rooms. And led him into the depths of her deathless snake where he fought that part of her until it was limp on the ground. He got good into her Book tongued her every passage thumbing her leaf and rubbing his hand all through her binding" (182).

What is clear from LeBas's "history" is that Musclewhite's fear of black appropriation of white culture (black writers using sacred white words "like they were their god-given pussy") is a kind of reaction formation. The real exploitation/rape of sacred words has always been the white appropriation of black culture. And in Reed's masculinist world, taking a man's words is the symbolic equivalent to taking a man's woman.

Jethro was right, though. When he returns to Egypt, Moses fails to become the next Osiris, despite his knowledge of the Book of Thoth. Moses's music does not sound right to the people and he becomes an object of derision, just as Set had. Moses becomes so angry that he takes a page from the Book of Thoth and creates a nuclear explosion. Far from learning the life-affirming spirit of the right-handed practice of vodun, Moses has only become a death-dealing left-handed practitioner. If Hurston tells us that Moses has been worshiped as a god in a pan-Africanist context, Reed insists that Moses is a false god. Reed's Moses can hardly be said to even be a part of the Mosaic tradition, for he is a Moses without Hebrews. In this regard, Reed follows Freud and Hurston, both of whom imagine a Moses who is not a Hebrew. And like Freud's Moses, Reed's tries to install Atonism as a monotheism, albeit for the Egyptians, rather than the Hebrews.

As I have suggested, Reed travesties Freud in part because he is unwilling to admit the degree to which he used *Moses and Monotheism*. Papa LeBas's, though, has a certain sympathy for the Freud who appears as a character in *Mumbo Jumbo*. If Christianity for centuries persecuted people for their association with Osirian rites, LeBas sees Freud as one of the Atonist compromises inasmuch as Freud "refined the rhetoric of the Church and eased the methods of dealing with the problem. Freud saved many lives which would ordinarily have been dealt with by the Church in an inhumane manner" (172). As Reed tells it, Freud was sent to America in 1909 to stem the tide of Jes Grew that would come to its full flowering in the 1920s. Papa LeBas tries to meet Freud in order to "*teach him the Work*" (45). LeBas is prevented by Freud's followers, "*much to Freud's and Western Civilization's loss*" (46). The reason LeBas thinks that Freud might be teachable is that, like vodun, psychoanalysis recognizes the central importance of sexuality to human well-being. Freud's problem, as an Atonist, is that he always naturalizes manifestations of the spiritual world (such as possession) by explaining them as psychological problems (neuroses and complexes). In the face of all the unrepressed libidinality of Jes Grew in America, Freud faints: "What did this man see? What did this clear-headed, rational, 'prudish' and 'chaste' man see? 'The Black Tide of Mud,' he was to call it. 'We must make a dogma . . . an unshakable bulwark against the Black Tide of Mud,' uttered this man who as a child returned from church and imitated the minister and repeated his sermons in a 'self-righteous manner'" (209).

Reed here draws directly on Carl Jung's memory of a conversation he had with Freud in 1910: "I can still recall vividly how Freud said to me, 'My dear Jung, promise me never to abandon the sexual theory. That is the most essential thing of all. You see, we must make a dogma of it, an unshakeable bulwark. . . . In some astonishment I asked him, 'A bulwark—against what?' to which he replied, 'Against the black tide of mud'—and here he hesitated a moment, then added—'of occultism'" (Jung 150). Reed implies that the "black tide of mud" is Freud's fear of primitive black sexuality, an expression of Freud's unconscious, as Reed makes clear in an imagined news conference with Jung:

Q. What did the Doctor mean by "The Black Tide of Mud?"
A. He meant occultism.

Q. Why, then, did he employ the language of the Churchman: "Dogma"?
A. It was merely a figure of speech.

Q. But according to his theories, don't figures of speech have latent significance? (209)

But the historical Jung, far from papering over Freud's language as merely figurative, has already asked the reporter's question: "First of all, it was the words 'bulwark' and 'dogma' that alarmed me; for a dogma, that is to say, an undisputable confession of faith is set up only when the aim is to suppress doubts once and for all. But that no longer has anything to do with scientific judgment; only with a personal power drive" (Jung 150). For Jung, far from warning him about overvaluing primitive sexual instincts, Freud is cautioning Jung about his interest in religion and parapsychology as a way to understand the human psyche. Reed's intentional misreading of Freud is hard not to read in Freudian terms. In order to clear the ground for his idealization of vodun fertility rituals, Reed must use his satire to metaphorically kill Freud, who wants to read primitive sexuality scientifically.

If Freud is chief figure of satire, Jung's presence in *Mumbo Jumbo* also seems to encode something very personal about Reed that helps us better see him as a southern author. Following the above imagined news conference, Reed continues to modify history: "Later Jung travels to Buffalo New York and at a dinner table discovers what Freud saw. Europeans living in America have undergone a transformation. Jung called the process 'going Black'" (209). Jung did utter these words, but not in an American context, and certainly not in Buffalo, where Reed grew up. In 1925 Jung traveled in East Africa to study "primitive psychology." Jung notes that during his stay in Africa, he did not dream about Africa subjects but rather "scenes from home," which he takes as evidence that for his unconscious his trip was less real than symbolic: "Only once during the entire expedition did I dream of a Negro. His face appeared curiously familiar to me, but I had to reflect along time before I could determine where I had met him before. Finally it came to me: he had been my barber in Chatanooga, Tennessee! An American Negro. In the dream he was holding a tremendous, red-hot curling iron to my head, intending to make my hair kinky—that is, to give me Negro hair" (272).

Awaking in terror, Jung takes this dream to be a warning from his unconscious about the primitive: "At that time I was obviously all to close to 'going black'" (272). What is key here is the origin of the "American Negro" who haunts Jung. This black man is from Chattanooga, Tennessee, Reed's birthplace. Reed, in other words, is slyly avowing his southern heritage even as his text covertly acknowledges his northern migration—Buffalo as a home away from home. By linking himself to

Jung's barber, Reed becomes the black man who is always already haunting the unconscious of psychoanalysis. At the same time, in the logic of sexist trope that we saw earlier, Reed (through his poetics of appropriation) is precisely the black man Musclewhite fears. Reed takes Freud's and Jung's words and turns them every which way, using them as if they were his "god-given pussy."

But as we have seen, in his phallically conceived aesthetic, where appropriation is figured as rape, Reed is equally willing to violate the black woman, Hurston, because of her perceived collaboration with white culture. Although he uses her words from chapter 10 of *Tell My Horse* as one of his epigraphs, he deliberately misquotes her in a way that almost completely changes her meaning. Here is the epigraph as it appears in *Mumbo Jumbo*: "Some *unknown natural phenomenon* occurs which cannot be explained, and a new local demigod is named" (11, Reed's emphasis). Reed makes Hurston appear to endorse his concept of Jes Grew. In fact, Hurston is trying to demystify (and to an extent, debunk) the apparent existence of an enormous number of vodun gods and goddesses: "It is easy to see the unlettered meeting some unknown natural phenomenon and not knowing how to explain it, and a new local demigod is named" (*Tell My Horse*, 138–39).[15] Hurston, far from ascribing the proliferation of loas to the force Reed names Jew Grew, actually attributes it to a superstitious people. Reed's willingness to radically (mis)appropriate both white and black texts makes problematic the exact nature of the culture work he is performing.

Mumbo Jumbo has been characterized as a text that "works out of a critical matrix akin to the philosophical project of deconstruction" (Hogue 93); however, the novel itself creates a series of binary oppositions that are themselves open to deconstruction:

Atonism	Jes Grew
one	many
monotheism	polytheism
Christianity, Islam	Voodoo
whiteness	people of Color
being	becoming
death drive	pleasure principle
technology	spirituality
Apollonian	Dionysian

These oppositions recur throughout history in a series of battles that are strictly between men:

bokor	houngan
Set	Osiris
Moses	Jethro
Hinkle Von Hampton	Papa LeBas

What is crucial to notice in these pairs of men is that, although the ones on the left appear to be monotheistic Atonists, they, in fact, know that the spirit world is polytheistic. They advocate monotheism to the world, even while covertly practicing vodun magic. They are bad vodun priests (bokors) who use their skills to profit only themselves, unlike the men in the right column, who use their magic to advance the greater good. What we see in the left-handed practice of vodun is a whiteface ministrelsy—a white face masking a black interiority—gone terribly wrong. Since these men know, and secretly identify with, the power of Africa's cultural and spiritual legacy, their whiteness, like that of the racial passer, is perversely staged in order to claim the privileges of being racially unmarked. Hinkle Von Vampton, then, is merely the latest instantiation of Set and Moses. Although the designated defender of the Wallflower Order, we learn that, when he is alone, he first dresses in his Templar outfit and then worships and kisses "some ugly nigger doll," as his landlady puts it (55). Von Vampton's particular worship of a black idol seems to encode both Carl Van Vechten's homosexuality and Negrophilia, and to call into question once again Van Vechten's role as a patron of the black arts.

The mixed message of Reed's Jes Grew is finally problematic. It is as if Reed were saying that, during the Roaring Twenties, masses of whites were acting black but did not know it. In this regard, these white people's relation to Jes Grew is analogous to Erline's possession by the loa Erzulie, which causes her to behave promiscuously. No one at Mumbo Jumbo Cathedral blames Erline for her actions while possessed. In effect, when whites are infected with Jes Grew, they too become possessed—they lose their inhibitions—they get rhythm, laugh loudly, and fornicate heartily. They become blacks in whiteface. The problem, of course, is that these whiteface blacks enact gross racial stereotypes that even the African Americans characters in *Mumbo Jumbo* would be embarrassed to claim as central to their black identity. Things become more problematic still. The minute a white becomes conscious of embodying cultural blackness, the relation to blackness shifts from innocent possession to corrupt performance. The white performer, then, instead of being possessed by blackness, attempts to appropriate and possess blackness, a gesture that immediately turns the whiteface minstrel performance into a blackface one.

Despite having authored a novel attacking Atonism, Reed himself cannot escape implication in Atonism to the extent that he has a master narrative, namely, that all culture comes out of Africa (Osiris, the Egyptian/African, studies under "the long-bearded Black men in the university at Nysa" [162]) and that vodun is the truest religion. After all, Papa LeBas is a vodun priest, not a Unitarian Universalist. The very notion of Jes Grew itself cannot stand overmuch scrutiny since it can only function as an oppositional aesthetic—a kind of countercultural moment of aesthetic possibility that enables a critical purchase on white hegemony. If Jes Grew ever managed to become the order of things, it would just stop growing. In fact, if we grant Reed's history when Osiris reigned in Egypt, there were problems when an ostensibly black culture was the hegemony. Fertility rituals eventually went out of control. The result? Atonism itself "jes grew" as a counterhegemonic possibility to the Osirian order of things.[16]

Despite the logical limitations of Reed's fictional world, *Mumbo Jumbo* nevertheless remains an important text for the way that it challenges the whiteness of Western culture by telling an alternative story of the shaping influences of Africa. Moreover, Reed's opposition between those whites who become possessed by blackness (people infected with Jes Grew) and those whites who try to possess blackness (such as Hinkle Von Vampton) resonates broadly with the white southern writing that this study has examined. By unconsciously becoming black, Faulkner's Uncle Ike McCaslin, O'Connor's Hazel Motes, Barth's Todd Andrews, and Allison's Bone, in Reed's terms, are each infected with "Jes Grew," and so, in a sense, are carriers of cultural blackness even though they do not realize it. As for their authors—Faulkner, O'Connor, Barth, Allison—they cannot avoid implication in the attempt to possess blackness, if only as a construct of authorial mastery. But to acknowledge that implication is not to deny the power of these white authors' subtle figurations of racial transformation since these racial masquerades repeatedly work to unhinge southern racial absolutism. If my study of whiteface minstrelsy has brought anything into clearer focus, it is, I hope, that each act of appropriating blackness needs nuanced examination, since to fail to do so is to see southern fiction simply in terms of black and white.

NOTES

PREFACE

1. The extent to which Clinton's induction into the Arkansas Black Hall of Fame signals his cultural blackness can be found in the ABHF's mission statement: "Throughout its history, the annual induction ceremony has sought to correct the omissions of history and to remind the world that Black history is a signification part of American history. The foundation seeks to further the impact of the annual induction ceremony by providing an environment in which a future generation of African American achievers with Arkansas roots will thrive and succeed" (ABHF Web site).
2. Robert Rebein argues that there has been a return to various forms of realism since 1980 in American fiction after the metafictional experiments of the 1960s and 1970s. Although he does not address Allison's fiction, see Rebein's chapter 4, "Hick Chic, or 'The White Trash Aesthetic'" (66–81).

CHAPTER 1

1. As Thadious Davis notes, "Faulkner . . . never knew or wrote about 'black' people. . . . He wrote about 'the Negro,' the white man's own creation" (*Faulkner's* 2). Following Davis, I wish to use the term "Negro" to name African American characters when the context is what Faulkner, O'Connor, and Barth imaged as they wrote about blacks.
2. For example, Morrison sees Willa Cather's inability to appropriately imagine an African American mother in *Sapphira and the Slave Girl*, causing "a breakdown in the logic and machinery of plot construction" (*Playing* 25). Elsewhere, Morrison finds Hemingway using "improbable . . . syntax . . . to avoid a speaking black" (*Playing* 72). In her various close readings of racial figuration, Morrison never finds a moment of a white writer doing anything other than diminishing African Americans or propping up white identity, which is curious given her positive interpretation of Bill Clinton's blackness.
3. Gubar briefly discusses three of the authors I take up—Faulkner, O'Connor, and Barth. Faulkner and Barth figure in her discussion of white modernists' appropriation of black linguistics as part of their formal experiments with

language. Her two-page treatment of Faulkner's "Go Down, Moses" focuses on the newspaper editor who parodies Mollie Beauchamp's speech in order to make fun of her desire to have the story of her dead grandson, executed in Chicago for killing a policeman, appear in the Jefferson, Mississippi, paper. Granting that "Faulkner examines racial impersonation as an act of violence comparable to that at work in the dynamics of black-face," Gubar asks the reader to wonder whether Faulkner's African American characters are' not simply "his guilty awareness that he is not the Other and, indeed, that his linguistic transgressions have helped to Other black people." While leaving this question open, she allows that Faulkner's "presentation of the ethical complication" behind representing black language "cast[s] suspicion on the art of racial ventriloquism that served as the basis of his own artistry" (162). Treating Barth's *Floating Opera* with thirteen lines of commentary, Gubar identifies the novel with its representation of a minstrel show as an acknowledgement of "white guilt about linguistic racechange," in which his use of "black talk" is an "indefensible but enthralling trope of condescension" (167). Gubar even more briefly treats O'Connor's "The Artificial Nigger," noting that the story "dramatizes the community/communal solidarity effected by [Eric Lott's] dynamic [of love and theft] when a feuding white grandfather and his grandson are reunited through their discovery of" a racist plaster statue (85).

4. O'Connor called herself an "integrationist," but qualified that commitment to the "legal but not the aesthetic sense" (Wood 96). O'Connor's aesthetic sense, however, apparently extended to her criticism of Eudora Welty's protest following the murder of Medgar Evers and her refusal to meet James Baldwin when he visited Georgia.

5. Although I draw attention to queer white performance, I do not mean to "hinge antiracist struggle on the question of the white subject" (Wiegman, 296). The study of whiteness can be but one front on which to challenge forms of American racism.

6. Johnson, writing from the recognition that his own declared homosexuality may problematize his authority to write about blackness, much as certain African American critics from the 1960s marginalized James Baldwin, nevertheless takes on a number on striking instances of black performance, including a white, largely atheistic Australian choir that sings only gospel music.

7. The most notable exception was the limited success of Arkansas's Southern Tenant Farmers Union in the 1930s. For a brief history of this union, see Egerton, 154–58. For a reading that historicizes "Barn Burning" through the work of the STFU, see Lessig, 82–96.

8. In his desire to own a gun, Dave's sense of the politics of racial identity is better than he knows. As Theodore W. Allen argues (177–200), gun ownership has been one of the constitutive structures of whiteness. Instantiated by a series of skin-privileging laws during the colonial period, gun ownership became one of the key guarantors of white identity. Every bit as much

as voting rights, gun ownership was denied African Americans. Dave's urge to own a gun (very like gun ownership among poor whites) is an urge to put on whiteface inasmuch as it challenges one of the defining material privileges of whiteness, a privilege that poor whites still call on to shore up their marginal whiteness. My thanks to Jay Watson for pointing out Allen's legal research and suggesting its implications to Wright's story.

9. Lessig largely concurs with Godden regarding Ab Snope's relation to blackness, though challenges Godden's claim that Ab's racism means that he fails to achieve full class consciousness (92).

10. For Lessig, the story "undermines the racial identity of the Snopes while asserting de Spain's claim to true 'whiteness'" (93). My reading of figurative blackness surrounding Ab and Sarty complements Lessig's claim, which he develops from historical context.

CHAPTER 2

1. For Frann Michel, Faulkner is a lesbian author, who, terrified of cultural emasculation, ultimately uses lesbian sexuality to avoid representing male-male desire; for Minrose Gwin ("Did Ernest"), Michel misses instances of homoerotic possibility between male characters; for Lisa Rado, Gwin, and Michel overlook the fundamental androgyny of Faulkner's artistic imagination. And Meryl Altman argues for the unhinging of "'homosexuality' or 'lesbianism' from 'effeminacy,' 'inversion,' even 'gender dysphoria,' in order to observe the conjunctions and disjunctions that occur historically between the two sets of ideas" (51).

2. In this regard, my claim complicates Davis's useful historical point about racial naming, namely, that Faulkner wrote about "the Negro" rather than "blacks" (*Faulkner's* 2). While her point is certainly valid regarding African Americans, Faulkner did write about black people—those Caucasians who turn out to be only passing as southern whites.

3. Judith Sensibar's *The Origins of Faulkner's Art* remains the most thorough examination of Faulkner's relation to the Pierrot mask, which she sees, in part, as a way for Faulkner to work out various possibilities of poetic and narrative voice. For Sensibar, in a move anticipated in *Vision in Spring*, Faulkner renounces Pierrot when he turns to fiction, substituting instead unreliable narrators (*Origins* 197–98). Besides Sensibar, only Michael Kreyling has argued at length for the importance of Pierrot as a foundational literary figure for Faulkner's. For Kreyling, however, Pierrot allowed Faulkner to blend "the *fin-de-siècle* Pierrot with the southern heroic, and that strange hybrid enabled the difficult continuity in Faulkner's work from apprenticeship through *Go Down, Moses*" (*Figures of the Hero* 126). Although Kreyling does not address the implications of racial masking, I agree with his long view of Faulkner's investment in Pierrot.

4. See James G. Watson (46–47).

5. For the Irish use of blackface, see Lott (*Love* 94–96); for the Jewish use, see Rogin (73–119).

6. My thinking derives in part from chapter 6 ("Psychopathologies of Black Envy: Queer Colors") of Gubar's *Racechanges*, in which she argues for a reflexive relationship between racial and sexual crossings such that "the blurring of normative categories of eroticism contributes to the permeable boundaries of racial borderlines" (176).

7. For a full account of the deletions, see Gwin's "*Mosquitoes*' Missing Bite."

8. As Karl notes, in the early 1920s, Faulkner, who read widely in the library of his mentor, Phil Stone, would have had found access to Havelock Ellis there (186).

9. Appendix A of *Sexual Inversion*, "Homosexuality among Tramps," posits that an unusually high percentage of American tramps engage in homosexuality. As a particular instance of the lower class, this obviously fits Ellis's scheme, but casts a curious light on Faulkner's self-fashioning posture as the tramp.

10. James Watson briefly notes the way Faulkner encodes pieces of himself in Gordon and other artist figures in *Mosquitoes* (157).

11. Of the major Yoknapatawpha a fiction, only *As I Lay Dying* disregards the social reality of race more thoroughly than *Sanctuary*.

12. As Noel Polk has pointed out, this opening scene, in which the two characters merge, constitutes Popeye as Horace's double: "he is at once Horaces' twin, his alter ego, at the same time his id and his superego; he is at once the reductio ad absurdum of Horace's darker sexual impulses" (23).

13. Polchin catches the irony of Horace's claim that he would be scared of Popeye's shadow if it were his (20) since "Popeye is [Horace's] shadow, the darker side of his sexual self—the feminized, unnatural man" (152).

14. Michel Gresset also notes that "Popeye shares exactly the same characteristics as Faulkner in *Mosquitoes*: he is little, and he is black—at least from the suit he wears" (5). Gresset, however, does not pursue the sexual connotations (beyond impotence and voyeurism), suggesting, instead, that there seems to be "a double evil potential in undersize linked with blackness" (5). Gresset does go on to raise a question to which my work responds: "Could it be that there was no way Faulkner could dissociate his consciousness of himself from a nagging awareness of his being forever 'juxtaposed,' as he often writes in *Go Down, Moses*, with the black race? This would go a long way toward explaining why and how Faulkner's *fiction* about the racial issue in America was always so characteristically metaphysical rather than social" (8).

15. Faulkner's occasional use of a corncob pipe must surely have been his wry acknowledgment that to some of his critics he would only ever be "Mr. Corncob" (Karl 811).

16. In addition to Popeye's homosexuality, Polchin sees Temple's account to Horace of her imagined moment of sex change "as a psychological case of psychosexual inversion that grounded so many discussions in the popular psychology texts and confession magazines of the time" (153), and reads

Horace's erotic projection of himself into the scene of Temple's rape as his fantasy of anal intercourse (154). For Polchin, what Horace represses is not incestuous desire but in fact homosexual desire.

17. Ellis's engagement with Freud's work on narcissism helps reveal the linkage between incest and inversion in *Sanctuary*. If the male children have an early incestuous desire for the mother or the sister, they overcome it by "taking refuge in Narcissism, the self becoming the sexual object." Thus, "their pursuit of men is determined by their flight from women" (Ellis 304). Horace's narrative begins with a flight from one woman, Belle, which returns him to another, Narcissa, the sister. Figuratively, this might be read as Horace's regression to the state of narcissism, the condition that mediates between incest and homosexuality.

18. Towner reads this scene as Temple's way to maintain her whiteness even as it establishes her "belief that violating presences are black and male" (18).

19. Although less explicit that Polchin, Polk was one of the earliest readers to register the sexchanging nature of Horace's nightmare experience (20).

20. One of the stories Faulkner knew was the 1908 lynching of the African American bootlegger, Nelse Patton, who was lynched for raping and killing a white woman. An excellent account of this history is in Williamson (157–61).

21. For Lacan, the *object petit a* "is something from which the subject, in order to constitute itself, has separated itself off as organ. This serves as a symbol of the lack, that is to say, of the phallus, not as such, but in so far as it is lacking. It must, therefore, be an object that is, firstly, separable and, secondly, that has some relation to the lack" (*Four Fundamental Concepts* 103).

22. For Fowler, who also clearly sees the racial implications of the lynching, the punishment ultimately signifies an instance of the Freudian primal scene wherein "miscegenation replaces the prohibition against incest" (421).

23. In *Was Huck Black?* Fishkin argues that *Huckleberry Finn* derives from Twain's unacknowledged appropriation of African American culture inasmuch as Huck's linguistic performance was actually based on a real black child.

24. In this section, I hope to respond to a question that Thadious Davis asks in her magisterial study of *Go Down, Moses*: "Was Faulkner finally using 'race' as a game of self-identification and self-aggrandizement? Was he playfully or painfully inscribing himself into the text of *Go Down, Moses* as 'nigger,' the wished-for, irresponsible, manipulative presence?" (*Games* 194). Davis suggests that Faulkner's black encoding may be found in Tomey's Turl. Alternatively, one could look, as Judith Sensibar does, for Faulkner's figurative relation to blackness in "the black/white *commedia* trickster figure which Faulkner adopted as his first narrative persona and which he resurrects in 'Pataloon in Black'" ("Who Wears the Mask?" 112). Sensibar argues, through a series of deft psychoanalytic readings of several of the author's nonfictional texts, that Faulkner (rider/writer) is the pantaloon in black(face), mourning his Mannie/Mammie (111). While Rider may well

serve as yet another instance of Faulkner's coded self-representation, the author's relation to blackness is, as it were, hidden in plain sight, in Isaac McCaslin.

25. As Ross and Polk explain, no gifts were usually exchanged, though white adults might give black children money (58). One might note in passing that Quentin's enactment of the game is forced: it is not Christmas day, he (rather than a black child) cries "Christmas gift," and he gives money to an old man (rather than to a child). The way Quentin bends the rules of the game suggest just how desperate he is for anyone to acknowledge his whiteness.

26. For another instance of Faulkner's awareness of the significance of "mister" as an honorific in relation to Boon Hogganbeck, see Towner (39–40).

27. The most thorough consideration of homosexual possibility in *Go Down, Moses* appears in Richard Godden and Noel Polk's detailed examination of the novel's representation of the plantation ledgers. Godden and Polk not only question the nature of the relationship between Ike's father and uncle (Buck and Buddy), but also suggest that Ike may misread the ledges (constructing his grandfather's incestuous miscegenation as the reason for repudiating his patrimony) as a way to deny the larger transgression—Buck's purchase of a male slave, Percival Brownlee, for homosexual purposes (302–14).

28. Sedgwick's notion of "homosexual panic" as a way to name a male definitional crisis grows out of the homosexual panic legal defense, which attempts to explain acts of violence against homosexuals by unstably positioned heterosexuals (*Epistemology*, 185–87). What is crucial about homosexual panic is its reflexivity. The very act of identifying another as gay initiates an identify crisis in the identifier, whose own sense of sexual identity is called into question.

29. Although not a literal representation of what Lacan terms the mirror stage, I use the word "mirroring" here with a purpose, since the transformation of identity that occurs in Ike's moment of identification is arguably "a particular case of the function of the *imago*, which is to establish a relation between the organism and its reality" (*Écrits* 4).

30. For a sense of the financial pressure Faulkner felt from mid-1940 through the beginning of 1941, see Blotner (*Faulkner* 1043–69).

31. Race remains central in much of Faulkner after *Go Down, Moses*, but as Towner has suggested, "Faulkner's later fiction admitted with greater and more compelling frequency that there were places his public and private voices could not and perhaps should not try to go" (144).

32. For a full account of the circumstances surrounding Faulkner's letter, as well as the full text of the letter, see McMillen and Polk.

CHAPTER 3

1. Laurel Nesbitt (145–53) demonstrates that O'Connor's assertions about the primacy of Catholicism to her fiction have often led critics to devalue social contexts (particularly race) in favor of theological ones. Michael

Kreyling has also noted, more briefly, the tendency of O'Connor critics to accept "her own testimony as to [her fiction's] Christian meaning" ("Introduction" 3) and goes on to summarize a number of studies of O'Connor that do just that ("Introduction" 10–13).

2. Susan Edmunds challenges those who would dismiss O'Connor's work for failing to take a more progressive stand on issues of civil rights for African Americans, precisely by deferring earthly community for a heavenly one. By underscoring the resonances between O'Connor's fiction and Martin Luther King Jr.'s theologically informed rhetoric, Edmonds convincingly argues that O'Connor's fiction complexly meditates on "the historical struggle for racial (and gender) integration" (564). My work on figurative blackness seconds Edmunds's sense of the complexity of O'Connor's relation to historical struggle of race in the 1950s; I am, however, less concerned with locating whether O'Connor's views were ultimately racist or progressive than in charting the way her fiction often subliminally engages the trauma of Jim Crow and the migration of African Americans from the South.

3. Toni Morrison complains of critics who fail to see a "connection between God's grace and Africanist 'othering' in Flannery O'Connor" (14). A related connection I wish to develop is the linkage, in O'Connor, between grace and the othering of whiteness.

4. A similar coup de grace occurs in O'Connor's later story, "Everything That Rises Must Converge." When her gesture of noblesse oblige is violently rebuffed by her black double, Julian's mother suffers a stroke that rearranges her face. The loss of whiteness here, as in "The Displaced Person," leads to a literal change of appearance prior to death.

5. Morrison briefly cites "The Artifical Nigger" as an example of the strategy of white writers to use "dehistoricizing allegory" to engage the "serious consequences of blacks" (68, 67). As I see it, O'Connor's story allegorizes a historically locatable moment of crisis concerning whiteness. For a call for using of Morrison's strand of whiteness studies to read O'Connor's relation to race, see Julie Armstrong.

6. Lucinda MacKethan notes Mr. Head's belief in his goodness and Nelson's innocence is figured by the absence of African Americans in their community (30).

7. Perreault has carefully teased out the recurring excremental figuration in the story and notes the irony of the slop jar bathed in white light that seems to serve as Nelson's guardian angel, concluding that the boy "must accept the most basic function of the body if he is to be saved from the tyranny of Mr. Head's ideology" (398).

8. See Perreault's useful survey of critical responses to the black woman (402–7); Perreault concludes that "to attribute to the black woman the properties that will humanize Nelson (and by extension whites) and to provide the black woman to represent the embodiment that Nelson needs" means that O'Connor ultimately fails to provide "wholeness in Nelson, Mr. Head, and the black character as well" (407).

9. Nesbitt challenges O'Connor's claim about "the redemptive quality of the Negro's suffering for us all" (*Habit* 78) as an instance of the author's willingness to "appropriate black suffering for white redemption." For Nesbitt, the theological distracts readers from the issue of race, which is not a question of the white character's attitudes toward blacks, but rather the way in which Mr. Head and Nelson "perhaps have come to recognize their own essential and shared 'blackness'" (168).

10. MacKethan has noted some of the parallels between grandfather, grandson, and the statuary (31).

11. Though not interested in its racial implications, James Mellard has analyzed Haze in relation to Lacan's notion of the gaze; see particularly 52–54.

12. Edmunds, in fact, traces a whole series of instances in which yellow is linked to mirroring, which she suggests indicates the threat of miscegenation.

13. My reading of the gaze is indebted to Edmunds (573–74) and Mellard's essay.

14. Edmunds notes that "Taulkinham's all-white population is a . . . grotesquely exaggerated tribute to the effects of the great migration" (566), an exaggeration, one might add, that O'Connor elsewhere reproduces in certain of her rural settings.

CHAPTER 4

1. Barth has noted that his second unpublished apprentice work, *The Dorchester Tales*, was also an attempt to represent his "Eastern Shore Yoknapatawpha at all periods of its human history" ("My Faulkner" 195).

2. William Solomon has noticed the ways in which this scene "offer[s] us a glimpse of the way racialized acts of impersonation can help facilitate the construction of heterosexual identities" (486). What I would add is that those same acts can simultaneously problematize the construction of homosexual identities.

3. I discuss Quentin's relation to minstrelsy more fully in Chapter 2.

4. Eustacia's letter reads as follows: "*Mr. Andrew. Mrs. Mack, has put pickle jars in greenhouse. R. J. Coler, has put on zinas. Eustacia M. Callader. R. J. Coler, has put 72 bottles on zinas. Eustacia M. Callader*" (107). Barth might suggest her limited literacy by the spelling and punctuation errors, but he curiously does not have her inscribe the articles before nouns. This is not a telegraph message, so she does not need to limit her word count. Barth seems to have realized that if he included the articles, he would have to represent them graphically as "the," not "de," which would have created a completely different voice for the character.

5. Theron Britt argues that Barth parodies existentialism. For Britt, Todd's obsession for control ironizes Sartre's insistence on an absolute freedom to choose, since, as Todd's case makes clear, there is never "any clear criteria for judgment" (218). To Britt's argument, I wish to add that, in the context of the South, Todd's urge for mastery cannot avoid a racialized connotation.

6. As Michel Fabre points out, Ellison was urging Richard Wright to read Sartre as early as 1945 (184–85).

7. While I hesitate to go as far as Patricia Tobin to claim that Todd "can be wholly comprehended through concepts developed within traditional psychoanalysis," she is surely correct to note the "effects of the death of a parent upon the surviving child" (22).

8. While the general Sartrean principle that existence precedes essence is accepted in both novels, Charles Harris correctly notes that "Barth is not an existentialist" (48), certainly not in an unironized fashion.

9. Tobin, whose study is informed by Harold Bloom's theory of the anxiety of influence, sees *The End of the Road* as the "antithetical completion" of *The Floating Opera* (42).

10. Harris acknowledges the Doctor's race only to the extent that he quotes Barth's brief physical description of the character that names him as a Negro (41). Tobin discusses the Doctor but never mentions race. It is here that Toni Morrison's perception of a problem in literary criticism may be quite apt: "The habit of ignoring race is understood to be a graceful, even generous, liberal gesture. To notice is to recognize an already discredited difference. To enforce its invisibility through silence is to allow the black body a shadowless participation in the dominant cultural body. According to this logic, every well-bred instinct argues *against noticing* and forecloses adult discourse" (9-10).

11. Thomas Schaub is aware that Barth both appropriates, yet ironizes, Sartre. In presenting Mythotherapy, Schaub notes that the "black doctor's expostulation neatly reproduces the conflict in Sartre's though between the structure of consciousness and the idea of sincerity" (185); at the same time, Schaub is aware that this apparently straightforward use of Sartre turns to comic critique through Jake, who "enacts, to a farcial extreme, the dialectical contradictions of Sartre's thought" (186).

CHAPTER 5

1. Laura Fine argues that Allison represents a progression away from such writers as McCullers and Harper Lee; for Fine, McCullers and Lee are, in Toni Morrison's terms, playing in the dark by "projecting gender alienation onto African Americans," while Allison is seen as "consciously deciding to refuse such presumptions" (121). I am less certain that Allison escapes implication in using racial otherness to plumb white sexual identity. Allison is, unarguably, more outspoken about fighting racism than McCullers and Lee, but careful attention to the figurative blackness in *Bastard out of Carolina* suggests that Allison still deploys blackness as a symbolic resource that does not transcend racialized thinking, even as she problematizes whiteness.

2. Fine argues that Frankie's "most extreme feelings are projected onto the African American characters"; Frankie does internalize and appropriate

blackness as a way of comprehending her gender alienation, but it is not clear how Frankie's appropriation "result[s] in [African American characters'] suffering irrevocable consequences" (123).

3. Although *Skin* appeared two years after *Bastard*, the collection reprints a number of journalistic pieces Allison had previously published, dating back to the early 1980s.

4. Because Bone serves, to a degree, as a fictionalized version of Allison, one might assume that the character, like the author, was born in 1949 and that, since Bone is eleven when she breaks into Woolworth's, the act occurs in 1960. The text, in fact, confirms this timeframe. The only date, 1955, appears in the beginning of chapter 2. By adding up the number of years that pass in chapter 1 from the time Anne gives birth to Bone at age fifteen, one can determine that Anne is twenty-one in 1955, which thus makes Bone's birth in 1949.

CHAPTER 6

1. Barbara Johnson has posed a similar question regarding Freud and Hurston (15). Her answer, in part, is that "whereas Freud's Egyptian Moses ultimately represents the psychoanalytic dead father, or even the unconscious. . . . Hurston's Egyptian Moses stands for the cultural dead father and mother: Africa, the source of the repressed traditions carried to the Americas by the slaves" (20).

2. For a fuller discussion of the way the two Moses characters relate to Jewish dualism, see Assmann (155–59).

3. Given the tradition of Midrash, Yerushalmi suggests that "if Moses had actually been killed by our forefathers, not only would the murder not have been repressed but—on the contrary—it would have been remembered and recorded, eagerly and implacably, in the most vivid detail, the quintessential and ultimate exemplum of the sin of Israel's disobedience" (85).

4. Yerushalmi notes how significant this gesture is, inasmuch as Freud's manuscript draft from 1934 makes no reference to his Jewishness (7). Yerushalmi's study is crucial for anyone considering Freud's relation to racial identity, inasmuch as it details the ways in which Freud maintained a kind of position as a psychological Jew, even as he attempted to assimilate in Viennese culture.

5. Mark Christian Thompson takes this point much further, arguing that "through not only the figure of Pharaoh, but of Moses himself, Huston critiques the ideological premises of National Socialism while at the same time conceding the value of generic European fascism for a program of African American uplift via black cultural nationalism" (395). For Thompson, Hurston's portrayal of Moses, an instance of Freud's righteous and ruthless great man, "implicates Hurston's text in the very fascist model she critiques" (408). While Thompson's argument usefully highlights the methods Moses is forced to use in dealing with the former slaves, it seems to

overlook the fact that Hurston's Moses is never interested in the leadership role that has been thrust on him and that he always seeks to lead the Hebrews to freedom and self-governance. In fact, his political murder of Aaron near the end of the novel is not to sustain Moses's own power, but is part of an endgame to relinquish power. At the end, he wants nothing but his own freedom from leadership and hopes that "the Voice wouldn't trouble him again" (285).

6. Faulkner's novel also engages German fascism, if more obliquely than Hurston's. "Delta Autumn" particularly draws a line from the fascism that Ike imagines to be a part of his legacy as a southern man to that of Adolph Hitler. Set in November 1941, just weeks before America's entry into World War II, the hunters ponder the fate of American in light of a decade of a depressed economy and Hitler's will to power (322–23).

7. As Eddie S. Glaude, Jr., notes in the introduction to his historical study of African American appropriations of Exodus, "Most efforts toward liberation in African American history have been articulated as reenactments of Israel's exodus from Egypt. In the context of slavery, the story empowered Christian slaves and free persons to look beyond their conditions and envision a future in which they were truly free. The events of the Civil War and the mass migrations of the late 1870s and 1880s were also described as reenactments of the Exodus story. . . . This biblical figuralism—always grounded in the urtext of the slave experience—articulated a sense of common history and a shared future" (4)

8. While one of the Princess's servants pulls a basket from the water, the text strongly suggests that it is not the same one that Jochebed places in the river. When she sees it pulled from the water, Miriam assumes the casket contains bathing supplies. The Princess does not examine the retrieved casket, nor does anyone in her party betray the slightest sign that anything unusual is in the casket.

9. In their final conversation, Miriam tells Moses that she thought he might be "an Ethiopian" (263).

10. The Hebrew is the racial other, that is, until Moses leads the Hebrews out of Egypt and to Mt. Sinai. When he is joined there by his Midian wife, Zipporah, Miriam and Aaron try to stir up dissent among the Hebrews by complaining about Zipporah's dark skin, referring to her as "black Mrs. Pharaoh" (242, 245). More than being another way in which Hurston destabilizes racial categories, Aaron and Miriam's complaint introduces the issue of colorism. Here, the lighter-skinned Semitic people (the Hebrews) claim their superiority over a darker-skinned Semitic people (the Midianites). Both the Hebrews and the Midianites are linked to cultural blackness through their shared linguistic patterns, and Moses's relation to Jethro and his family creates a crucial step for Moses in his becoming Hebrew.

11. Reed once briefly acknowledges that Freud was "a big fan of Moses" (169), another clue to the Freudian study not included in Reed's bibliography.

12. Gates is correct to see Reed's bibliography as a parody of "the scholar's appeal to authority and all studied attempts to conceal literary antecedents and influence" (224), but the novel's antecedent texts go beyond Ralph Ellison and Harlem Renaissance novelists.

13. This Hurston book does appear in Reed's bibliography, though his citation is to the 1939 British edition titled *Voodoo Gods*. Moreover, as another apparent gesture that disguises, even as it ostensibly acknowledges, Reed attributes this book to "Hurston, Zoran [*sic*]" (221).

14. I draw here on the title of Lipsitz's 1998 study, which examines "how social and cultural forces encourage white people to spend time and energy on the creation and re-creation of whiteness" (vii–viii). "Possession" here means both an asset (the economic advantage create by being white) and a loss of control (the inability to recognize that being racially unmarked creates privilege).

15. It is worth noting that Reed was reading Hurston prior to the Hurston revival begun by Alice Walker in the mid-1970s. Reed was not, however, interested in Hurston's now hypercanonical novel *Their Eyes Were Watching God* but rather her anthropological work that that dovetailed with his interests in vodun.

16. My thanks to Sandor Goodhart for pointing out the "jes grew" nature of Atonism.

WORKS CITED

Allen, Theodore W. *Inventing the White Race: The Origins of Racial Oppression in Anglo-America.* London: Verso, 1997.

Allison, Dorothy. *Bastard out of Carolina.* 1992. New York: Plume, 1993.

———. *Cavedweller.* New York: Dutton, 1998.

———. "Dorothy Allison." Interview with Minnie Bruce Pratt. *Progressive* July 1995: 30–34.

———. *Skin: Talking about Sex, Class, and Literature.* Ithaca: Firebrand, 1994.

Altman, Meryl. "The Bug That Dare Not Speak Its Name: Sex, Art, Faulkner's Worst Novel, and the Critics." *Faulkner Journal* 9.1–2 (1993–94): 43–68.

The Arkansas Black Hall of Fame. 2005. Arkansas Black Hall of Fame Foundation. 7 Oct. 2006 http://www.arblackhalloffame.org/foundation/

Armstrong, Julie. "Blinded by Whiteness: Revisiting Flannery O'Connor and Race." *Flannery O'Connor Review* 1 (2001–2): 77–86.

Arnold, Edwin. *Annotations to Faulkner's* Mosquitoes. Garland Faulkner Annotation Series 1. New York: Garland, 1989.

Assmann, Jan. *Moses the Egyptian: The Memory of Egypt in Western Monotheism.* Cambridge: Harvard UP, 1997.

Barth, John. *The Floating Opera* and *The End of the Road.* 1956 and 1958. New York: Anchor, 1988.

———. "Foreword to Doubleday Anchor Edition." *The Floating Opera* and *The End of the Road.* New York: Anchor, 1988. v–vii.

———. *Lost in the Funhouse.* 1968. New York: Anchor, 1988.

———. "My Faulkner." *Faulkner and Postmodernism.* Ed. John N. Duvall and Ann J. Abadie. Jackson: UP of Mississippi, 2002. 192–95.

———. *The Sot-Weed Factor.* 1960. New York: Anchor, 1987.

Bernal, Martin. *Black Athena: The Afroasiatic Roots of Clasical Civilization.* New Brunswick: Rutgers UP, 1987.

Blotner, Joseph. *Faulkner: A Biography.* Two Volumes. New York: Random, 1974.

———. "Notes." *Uncollected Stories of William Faulkner.* Ed. Joseph Blotner. New York: Vintage, 1981. 681–712.

Brinkmeyer, Robert H., Jr., "'Jesus, Stab Me in the Heart!': *Wise Blood,* Wounding, and Sacramental Aesthetics." Kreyling 71–90.

Britt, Theron. "Before the Law, after the Judgment: Schizophrenia in John Barth's *The Floating Opera*." *Cohesion and Dissent in America*. Ed. Carol Colatrella and Joseph Alkana. Albany: State U of New York P, 1994. 210–28.

Carroll, Rachel. "Foreign Bodies: History and Trauma in Flannery O'Connor's 'The Displaced Person.'" *Textual Practice* 14.1 (2000): 97–114.

Caruth, Cathy. *Unclaimed Experience: Trauma, Narrative, and History*. Baltimore: Johns Hopkins UP, 1996.

Chauncey, George. *Gay New York: Gender, Urban Culture, and the Making of the Gay Male World, 1890–1940*. New York: Basic, 1995.

Cohen, Philip, and Doreen Fowler. "Faulkner's Introduction to *The Sound and the Fury*." *American Literature* 62 (1990): 262–83.

Cusic, Don. "The Development of Gospel Music." *The Cambridge Companion to Blues and Gospel Music*. Ed. Allan Moore. Cambridge: Cambridge UP, 2002. 44–60.

Davis, Thadious M. *Faulkner's "Negro": Art and the Southern Context*. Baton Rogue: Louisiana State UP, 1984.

———. *Games of Property: Law, Race, Gender, and Faulkner's Go Down, Moses*. Durham: Duke UP, 2003.

Doyle, Don. *Faulkner's County: The Historical Roots of Yoknapatwpha*. Chapel Hill: U of North Carolina P, 2001.

Doyle, Roddy. *The Commitments*. 1987. New York: Vintage, 1989.

Duvall, John N. "Faulkner's Crying Game: Male Homosexual Panic." Kartiganer and Abadie 48–72.

Edmunds, Susan. "Through a Glass Darkly: Visions of Integrated Community in Flannery O'Connor's *Wise Blood*." *Contemporary Literature* 37 (1996): 559–85.

Egerton, John. *Speak Now Against the Day: The Generation before the Civil Rights Movement in the South*. Chapel Hill: U of North Carolina P, 1994.

Ellis, Havelock. 1903. *Sexual Inversion*. Vol. 2, Studies in the Psychology of Sex. 3rd edition, revised. Philadelphia: F. A. Davis, 1924.

Ellison, Ralph. 1952. *Invisible Man*. New York: Vintage International, 1995.

Fabre, Michel. "Richard Wright, French Existentialism, and The Outsider." *Critical Essays on Richard Wright*. Ed. Yoshinobu Hakutani. Boston: Hall, 1982. 182–98.

Fanon, Frantz. *Black Skin, White Masks*. 1952. Trans. Charles Lam Markmann. New York: Grove, 1967.

Faulkner, William. *Absalom, Absalom!* 1936. New York: Vintage International, 1990.

———. "Afternoon of a Cow." 1943. *Uncollected Stories of William Faulkner*. Ed. Joseph Blotner. New York: Random, 1979. 424–34.

———. "Barn Burning." *Collected Stories of William Faulkner*. Ed. Joseph Blotner. New York: Vintage International, 1995. 3–25.

———. *Flags in the Dust*. New York: Random, 1973.

———. *Go Down, Moses*. 1942. New York: Vintage International, 1990.

———. *Light in August*. 1932. New York: Vintage International, 1990.

————. *The Marionettes*. 1920. Introduction and Textual Apparatus by Noel Polk. Charlottesville: UP of Virginia, 1977.

————. *Mosquitoes*. 1927. New York: Liveright, 1955.

————. *Sanctuary*. 1931. New York: Vintage International, 1993.

————. *The Sound and the Fury*. 1929. New York: Vintage International, 1990.

Fetterley, Judith, and Marjorie Pryse. *Writing out of Place: Regionalism, Women, and American Literary Culture*. Urbana: U of Illinois P, 2003.

Fine, Laura. "Gender Conflicts and Their 'Dark' Projections in Coming of Age White Female Southern Novels." *Southern Quarterly* 36.4 (1998): 121–29.

Fishkin, Shelley Fisher. *Was Huck Black? Mark Twain and African-American Voices*. New York: Oxford UP, 1993.

Fowler, Doreen. "Faulkner's Return to the Freudian Father: *Sanctuary* Reconsidered." *Modern Fiction Studies* 50 (2004): 411–34.

Freud, Sigmund. *Moses and Monotheism*. Trans. Katherine Jones. New York: Knopf, 1939.

————. "'A Child is Being Beaten': A Contribution to the Study of the Origin of Sexual Perversions." *The Standard Edition of the Complete Psychological Works of Sigmund Freud*. Vol. 17. Ed and trans. James Strachey. London: Hogarth, 1953. 175–204.

————. *Totem and Taboo*. Trans. James Strachey. New York: Norton, 1950.

————. "The Uncanny." *The Standard Edition of the Complete Psychological Works of Sigmund Freud*. Vol 17. Ed and trans. James Strachey. London: Hogarth, 1953. 219–52.

Gates, Henry Lewis, Jr. *The Signifying Monkey: A Theory of Afro-American Literary Criticism*. New York: Oxford UP, 1988.

Gilroy, Paul. *Against Race: Imagining Political Culture beyond the Color Line*. Cambridge: Harvard UP, 2000.

Glaude, Eddie S., Jr. *Exodus! Religion, Race, and Nation in Early Nineteenth-Century Black America*. Chicago: U of Chicago P, 2000.

Godden, Richard. *Fictions of Labor: William Faulkner and the South's Long Revolution*. Cambridge: Cambridge UP, 1997.

Godden, Richard, and Noel Polk. "Reading the Ledgers." *Mississippi Quarterly* 55 (2002): 301–59.

Green, Martin, and John Swan. *The Triumph of Pierrot: The Commedia dell'Arte and the Modern Imagination*. New York: Macmillan, 1986.

Gresset, Michel. "Faulkner's Self-Portraits." *Faulkner Journal* 2.1 (1986): 2–13.

Griffin, John Howard. *Black Like Me*. New York: New American Library, 1961.

Gubar, Susan. *Racechanges: White Skin, Black Faces in American Culture*. New York: Oxford UP, 1997.

Gwin, Minrose C. "Did Ernest Like Gordon? Faulkner's *Mosquitoes* and the Bite of 'Gender Trouble.'" Kartiganer and Abadie 120–44.

————. "*Mosquitoes* Missing Bite: The Four Deletions." *Faulkner Journal* 9.1–2 (1993–94): 31–42.

Harris, Charles B. *Passionate Virtuosity: The Fiction of John Barth*. Urbana: U of Illinois P, 1983.

Hawkes, John. "Flannery O'Connor's Devil." *Sewanee Review* 70 (1962): 395–407.

Hogue, W. Lawrence. "Historiographic Metafiction and the Celebration of Differences: Ishmael Reed's *Mumbo Jumbo*. *Productive Postmodernism: Consuming Histories and Cultural Studies*. Ed. John N. Duvall. Albany: State U of New York P, 2002. 93–110.

Hurston, Zora Neale. *Moses, Man of the Mountain*. 1939. New York: HarperPerennial, 1991.

———. *Tell My Horse*. Philadelphia: Lippincott, 1938.

Irwin, John T. *Doubling and Incest/Repetition and Revenge*. Baltimore: Johns Hopkins UP, 1975.

Johnson, Barbara. "Moses and Intertextuality: Sigmund Freud, Zora Neale Hurston, and the Bible." *Poetics of the Americas: Race, Founding, and Textuality*. Ed. Bainard Cowan and Jefferson Humphries. Baton Rouge: Louisiana State UP, 1997. 15–29.

Johnson, E. Patrick. *Appropriating Blackness: Performance and the Politics of Authenticity*. Durham: Duke UP, 2003.

Johnson, James Weldon. 1912. *The Autobiography of the Ex-Coloured Man*. New York: Vintage, 1989.

Jung, C. G., *Memories, Dreams, Reflections*. 1963. Ed. Aniela Jaffé. Trans. Richard and Clara Winston. Rev. ed. New York: Vintage, 1989.

Kahane, Claire. "The Artificial Niggers." *Massachusetts Review* 19 (1978): 183–98.

Karl, Fredrick. *William Faulkner: American Writer*. New York: Weidenfeld, 1989.

Kartiganer, Donald M. and Ann J. Abadie, eds. *Faulkner and Gender*. Jackson: UP of Mississippi, 1996.

Kreyling, Michael. *Figures of the Hero in Southern Narrative*. Baton Rouge: Louisiana State UP, 1987.

———. Introduction. Kreyling 1–24.

Kreyling, Michael, ed. *New Essays on* Wise Blood. Cambridge: Cambridge UP, 1995.

Lacan, Jacques. *Écrits: A Selection*. Trans. Alan Sheridan. New York: Norton, 1977.

———. *The Four Fundamental Concepts of Psycho-Analysis*. Ed. Jacques-Alain Miller. Trans. Alan Sheridan. New York: Norton, 1978.

Ladd, Barbara. *Nationalism and the Color Line in George W. Cable, Mark Twain, and William Faulkner*. Baton Rouge: Louisiana State UP, 1996.

Lee, Harper. *To Kill a Mockingbird*. Philadelpia: Lippincott, 1960.

Lessig, Matthew. "Class, Character, and 'Croppers Faulkner's Snopes and the Plight of the Sharecropper." *Arizona Quarterly* 55 (1999): 79–113.

Lipsitz, George. *The Possessive Investment in Whiteness: How White People Profit from Identity Politics*. Philadelphia: Temple UP, 1998.

Lott, Eric. *Love and Theft: Blackface Minstrelsy and the American Working Class*. New York: Oxford UP, 1993.

————. "White Like Me: Racial Cross-Dressing and the Construction of American Whiteness." *Cultures of United States Imperialism.* Ed. Amy Kaplan and Donald Pease. Durham: Duke UP, 1993. 474–95.

MacKethan, Lucinda. "Redeeming Blackness: Urban Allegories of O'Connor, Percy, and Toole." *Studies in the Literary Imagination* 27.2 (1994): 29–39.

Matthews, John T. "Whose America? Faulkner, Modernism, and National Identity." *Faulkner at 100: Retrospect and Prospect.* Ed. Donald M. Kartiganer and Ann J. Abadie. Jackson: UP of Mississippi, 2000. 70–92.

McCullers, Carson. *The Member of the Wedding.* 1946. New York: Bantam, 1962.

McDowell, Deborah E. "Foreword." Zora Neale Hurston, *Moses, Man of the Mountain.* vii–xxii.

McMillen, Neil R., and Noel Polk. "Faulkner on Lynching." *Faulkner Journal* 8.1 (1992): 3–14.

Mellard, James. "Framed in the Gaze: Haze, *Wise Blood,* and Lacanian Reading." Kreyling 51–70.

Michaels, Walter Benn. "Autobiographies of the Ex-White Men." Pease and Wiegman 231–47.

Michel, Frann. "William Faulkner as a Lesbian Author." *Faulkner Journal* 4.1–2 (1988–89): 5–20.

Morrison, Toni. "The Art of Fiction CXXXIV." Interview with Elissa Schappell. *Paris Review* 129 (1993): 83–125.

————. *The Bluest Eye.* New York: Holt, 1970.

————. *Playing in the Dark: Whiteness and the Literary Imagination.* Cambridge: Harvard UP, 1992.

————. *Sula.* New York: Knopf, 1973.

————. "The Talk of the Town." *New Yorker* 5 Oct. 1998: 31–32.

Nesbitt, Laurel. "Reading Place in and around Flannery O'Connor's Texts." *Post Identity* 1.1 (1997): 145–97.

O'Connor, Flannery. *The Complete Stories.* New York: Farrar, 1971.

————. *The Habit of Being: The Letters of Flannery O'Connor.* Ed. Sally Fitzgerald. New York: Farrar, 1979.

————. *Mystery and Manners: Occasional Prose.* Ed. Sally Fitzgerald and Robert Fitzgerald. New York: Farrar, 1969.

————. *Wise Blood.* New York: Harcourt, 1952.

Pease, Donald E., and Robyn Wiegman, eds. *The Futures of American Studies.* Durham: Duke UP, 2002.

Penley, Constance. "Crackers and Whackers: The White Trashing of Porn." *White Trash: Race and Class in America.* Ed. Matt Wray and Annalee Newitz. New York: Routledge, 1997. 89–112.

Perreault, Jeanne. "The Body, the Critics, and 'The Artificial Nigger.'" *Mississippi Quarterly* 56 (2003): 389–410.

Polk, Noel. "The Space between *Sanctuary.*" *Intertextuality in Faulkner.* Ed. Michel Gresser and Noel Polk. Jackson: UP of Mississippi, 1985. 16–35.

Polchin, James. "Faulkner's *Sanctuary* as Psychosexual Text." Kartiganer and Abadie. 145–59.

Rado, Lisa. "'A Perversion That Builds Chartres and Invents Lear Is a Pretty Good Thing': *Mosquitoes* and Faulkner's Androgynous Imagination." *Faulkner Journal* 9.1–2 (1993–94): 13–30.

Rebein, Robert. *Hicks, Tribes, and Dirty Realists: American Fiction after Postmodernism.* Lexington: U of Kentucky P, 2001.

Reed, Ishmael. *Mumbo Jumbo.* 1972. New York: Scribner Paperback, 1996.

Rock, Chris. Saturday Night Live: *The Best of Chris Rock.* Videocassette. Vidmark/Trimark, 2000.

Rogin, Michael. *Blackface, White Noise: Jewish Immigrants in the Hollywood Melting Pot.* Berkeley: U of California P, 1996.

Ross, Stephen M., and Noel Polk. *Reading Faulkner:* The Sound and the Fury. Jackson: UP of Mississippi, 1996.

Sartre, Jean-Paul. *Being and Nothingness: An Essay on Phenomenological Ontology.* Trans. Hazel E. Barnes. New York: Philosophical Library, 1956.

———. *Existentialism.* Trans. Bernard Frechtman. New York: Philosophical Library, 1947.

Schaub, Thomas. "Allusion and Intertext: History in *The End of the Road.*" *Influence and Intertextuality in Literary History.* Ed. Jay Clayton and Eric Rothstein. Madison: U of Wisconsin P, 1991. 181–203.

Sedgwick, Eve Kosofsky. *Between Men: English Literature and Male Homosexual Desire.* New York: Columbia UP, 1986.

———. *Epistemology of the Closet.* Berkeley: U of California P, 1990.

Sensibar, Judith. Introduction. *Vision in Spring.* William Faulkner. Austin: U of Texas P, 1984. ix–xxviii.

———. *The Origins of Faulkner's Art.* Austin: U of Texas P, 1984.

———. "Who Wears the Mask? Memory, Desire, and Race in *Go Down, Moses.*" Ed. Linda Wagner-Martin. *New Essays on* Go Down, Moses. Cambridge: Cambridge UP, 1996. 101–28.

Solomon, William. "Secret Integrations: Black Humor and the Critique of Whiteness." *Modern Fiction Studies* 49 (2003): 469–95.

Stokes, Mason. *The Color of Sex: Whiteness, Heterosexuality, and the Fictions of White Supremacy.* Durham: Duke UP, 2001.

Sundquist, Eric. *Faulkner: The House Divided.* Baltimore: Johns Hopkins UP, 1978.

———. "Mark Twain and Homer Plessy." *Mark Twain's* Pudd'nhead Wilson: *Race, Conflict, and Culture,* ed. Susan Gillman and Forrest G. Robinson. Durham: Duke UP, 1990. 46–72.

Thompson, Mark Christian. "National Socialism and Blood-Sacrifice in Zora Neale Hurston's *Moses, Man of the Mountain.*" *African American Review* 38 (2004): 395–415.

Tobin, Patricia. *John Barth and the Anxiety of Continuance.* Philadelphia: U of Pennsylvania P, 1992.

Torgovnick, Marianna. *Gone Primitive: Savage Intellects, Modern Lives.* Chicago: U of Chicago P, 1990.

Towner, Theresa. *Faulkner on the Color Line: The Later Novels.* Jackson: UP of Mississippi, 2000.

Twain, Mark. *Adventures of Huckleberry Finn.* 1884. Ed. Victor Fischer and Lin Salamo. Berkeley: U of Califorinia P, 2001.

———. *Pudd'nhead Wilson and Those Extraordinary Twins.* 1894. Ed. Sidney E. Berger. New York: Norton, 2005.

Watson, James G. *William Faulkner: Self-Presentation and Performance.* Austin: U of Texas P, 2000.

Weinstein, Philip. *Faulkner's Subject: A Cosmos No One Owns.* New York: Cambridge UP, 1992.

———. *What Else But Love? The Ordeal of Race in Faulkner and Morrison.* New York: Columbia UP, 1996.

Wiegman, Robyn. "Whiteness Studies and the Paradox of Particularity." Pease and Wiegman 269–304.

Wiles, Mary M. "The Fascination of the Lesbian Fetish: A Perverse Possibility across the Body of Dorothy Allison's *Bastard Out of Carolina. Straight with a Twist: Queer Theory and the Subject of Heterosexuality.*" Ed. Calvin Thomas. Urbana: U of Illinois P, 2000. 146–62.

Williamson, Joel. *William Faulkner and Southern History.* New York: Oxford UP, 1993.

Wood, Ralph C. "Where is the Voice Coming From? Flannery O'Connor on Race." *Flannery O'Connor Bulletin* 22 (1993–94): 90–118.

Wright, Richard. "The Man Who Was Almost a Man." 1940. *Eight Men.* Cleveland: World, 1961. 11–26.

Yerushalmi, Yosef Hayim. *Freud's Moses: Judaism Terminable and Interminable.* New Haven: Yale UP, 1991.

INDEX

The letter *n* following a page number indicates a note on that page.

Abner Snopes (Faulkner's "Barn
    Burning"), 11–15, 21, 130
Allen, Theodore W., 170n8
Allison, Dorothy, xviii, 1, 2, 15,
    127–43, 168
    influence of African American writ-
        ers on, 130
    Works: *Bastard out of Carolina*,
        xviii, 1–2, 127–40, 142–43;
        Cavedweller, 140–41
Altman, Meryl, 36, 171n1
Andrews, Todd. *See* Todd Andrews
Armstrong, Julie, 175n5
Arnold, Edwin, 35
Asa Hawks (O'Connor's *Wise Blood*),
    83–86, 88
Assmann, Jan, 148, 178n2

Baldwin, James, 130
Barth, John, xvii–xviii, 64, 91,
    93–125, 145, 168
    Faulkner's influence on, 93–94
    Works: *The End of the Road*, xviii,
        94, 112–21; *The Floating Opera*,
        xvii, 4, 94, 96–112, 113; *Lost in
        the Funhouse*, 94–96; *The Sot-
        Weed Factor*, xviii, 94, 122–25
Benbow, Horace. *See* Horace Benbow
Bernal, Martin, 160

bisexuality. *See* sexuality,
    nonheteronormative
blackface. *See* blackface under
    minstrely
black humor, 64, 97
blackness, xii, xvi, xix, 2–4, 5–7, 17,
    25, 27–28, 36–37, 50, 52, 59–60,
    63–65, 74, 76, 81–87, 90, 99,
    112, 113, 116, 170n6, 172n14,
    173n24
    and artistic production, 30–32, 35,
        49, 121, 124
    as class marker, ix–x, 5, 10–15, 75,
        78, 131–32
    difference from race, xi, 23, 26
    and white sexual identity, xv, 5, 24,
        32, 37, 38, 44–45, 48, 97, 134,
        136, 138–39, 141–42
Blotner, Joseph, 18, 40, 49, 174n30
Brinkmeyer, Robert H., Jr., 65
Britt, Theron, 176n5
Burlingame, Henry. *See* Henry
    Burlingame

Caddy Compson (Faulkner's *The
    Sound and the Fury*), 37, 49
Carroll, Rachel, 67
Caruth, Cathy, 106
Chauncey, George, 32

class, x, xiv, xviii, 2, 4, 8, 10–11, 12, 15, 27, 29–30, 44, 60, 65, 67, 74, 75–76, 77, 98, 107, 128, 129–30, 132, 139, 141, 148, 152–53, 157. *See also* white, poor

Clinton, William Jefferson, ix–x, 169n1

Cohen, Philip, 48

Colonel Sartoris (Sarty) Snopes (Faulkner's "Barn Burning"), 12, 14–15, 21, 130

Compson, Caddy. *See* Caddy Compson

Compson, Quentin. *See* Quentin Compson

Christmas, Joe. *See* Joe Christmas

Davis, Thadious M., 169n1, 171n3, 173n24

Doctor, the (Barth's *The End of the Road*), xviii, 113–22, 123

diaspora, xiv, 8–9, 15, 66–67, 70, 72, 157

and whiteness, 12, 15–16, 73, 79, 91

Doyle, Don, 10

Doyle, Roddy, 141

Drake, Temple. *See* Temple Drake

Edmunds, Susan, 86, 175n2, 176n12, 176n13, 176n14

Egerton, John, 9

Ellis, Havelock, 28–30

Ellison, Ralph, 12, 101, 102–3, 110, 111, 116, 122.
    Work: *Invisible Man*, 12, 101, 102–3, 110, 111, 116, 122

Enoch Emory (O'Connor's *Wise Blood*), 83, 85–88, 90

Ernest Talliaferro (William Faulkner's *Mosquitoes*), 35–36

existentialism, 97, 101–3, 109, 111, 112, 116, 118

Fabre, Michel, 177n6

Fanon, Frantz, 44–45, 46

Fathers, Sam. *See* Sam Fathers

Faulkner (William Faulkner's *Mosquitoes*), xv, 21, 23, 25–26, 27, 30, 33, 35, 37, 39–40, 52, 59, 61

Faulkner, William, x–xi, xiii, xiv–xvi, 1, 2, 4, 5, 8–9, 10–16, 17–61, 63, 71, 80, 81, 82, 83, 91, 93–94, 95–96, 97, 101, 117, 121, 124, 130, 131, 143, 145, 146–48, 151, 153, 157, 168
    Works: *Absalom, Absalom!* xiv, xv, 10–11, 13; "Afternoon of a Cow," 36; "Barn Burning," xiv, 11–15, 83, 130; *Flags in the Dust, 41; Go Down, Moses,* xvi–xvii, 4, 17, 26, 47–60, 146, 151, 157; *Light in August,* xv–xvi, 131; *The Marionettes, 20–22, 26, 38, 40; Mosquitoes, xiv–xv, 18–20, 21, 23–37, 143; Sanctuary,* xv, 37, 38–47; *The Sound and the Fury,* xv, 26, 48–49, 59, 80

Fetterley, Judith, 93, 94

Fine, Laura, 177n1, 177n2

Fishkin, Shelley Fisher, xiii, 48, 173n23

Fowler, Doreen, 38, 173n22

Freud, Sigmund, 29, 40, 47, 53–54, 66, 114, 133, 146, 147–51, 157, 159–60, 162, 163–65
    and race, Work: "A Child is Being Beaten," 133; *Moses and Monotheism,* 47, 53–54, 146, 147–51, 159, 164

Gates, Henry Lewis, Jr., 158, 180n12

Gilroy, Paul, 8, 9, 16

Glaude, Eddie S., Jr., 179n7

Godden, Richard, 12, 13, 171n9, 174n27

Goodwin, Lee. *See* Lee Goodwin

Gordon (William Faulkner's *Mosquitoes*),

Gresset, Michel, 172n14
Griffin, John Howard, 3–4.
    Work: *Black Like Me*, 3
Gubar, Susan, 3–4, 6
Gwin, Minrose C., 35, 171n1, 172n7

Harris, Charles B., 114, 177n8,
    177n10
Hawkes, John, 64, 65
Hawks, Asa. *See* Asa Hawks
Hazel (Haze) Motes (O'Connor's
    Wise Blood), xvii, 1, 67, 75, 79–91,
    145, 168
Head, Mr. *See* Mr. Head
Heller, Joseph, 64
Henry Burlingame (Barth's *The Sot-
    Weed Factor*), xviii, 96, 121–24
Hogue, W. Lawrence, 166
homosexuality, 24, 27, 106, 114, 115
    as inversion, 28–29, 39, 42, 49 (*see
    also* lesbianism)
Horace Benbow (Faulkner's
    Sanctuary), 37, 38–41, 43, 45–47
Horner, Jacob. *See* Jacob (Jake)
    Horner
Hurston, Zora Neale, xviii–xix, 130,
    145–47, 151–57, 159–60,
    161–63, 166
    Work: *Moses, Man of the Mountain*,
    xviii, 145–46, 151, 154, 157;
    Tell My Horse, 160, 166

inversion. *See* homosexuality
Irwin, John T., 28, 29
Isaac (Ike) McCaslin (Faulkner's *Go
    Down, Moses*), xvi, 1, 27, 47,
    49–50, 52–60

Jacob (Jake) Horner (Barth's *The End
    of the Road*), xviii, 96, 112–21,
    122–23
Joe Christmas (Faulkner's *Light in
    August*), xv–xvi, xviii, 26, 95–96,
    131

Joe Morgan (Barth's *The End of the
    Road*), 114, 117–19, 121, 122
Johnson, Barbara, 155
Johnson, E. Patrick, 5–6
Johnson, James Weldon, 7, 147
    Work: *The Autobiography of an Ex-
    Coloured Man*, 147
Jung, Carl, 164–66

Kahane, Claire, 64
Karl, Fredrick, 24, 172n8, 172n15
Kesey, Ken, 64
Kreyling, Michael, 171n3, 174–75n1

Lacan, Jacques, 44–45
Ladd, Barbara, 132
Larsen, Nella, 7, 147
Layfield, Solace. *See* Solace Layfield
Lebas, Papa. *See* Papa Lebas
Lee, Harper, 6
    Work: *To Kill a Mockingbird*, 6–7
Lee Goodwin (Faulkner's *Go Down,
    Moses*), 40, 43–44, 45–46
lesbianism, 28, 127, 130, 171n1
    and blackness, 138–40
Lessig, Matthew, 12, 170n7, 171n9,
    171n10
Lipsitz, George, 161, 180n14
Lott, Eric, 2, 14, 172n5

MacKethan, Lucinda, 175n6, 176n10
masculinity:
    southern black, xix, 11–12, 13, 39,
    151–57
    southern white, xi, xvi, 15, 19, 24,
    36–37, 47–49, 55, 59–60, 75,
    86, 94–96, 113–14, 124, 145,
    151, 157
Matthews, John T., 20
McCaslin, Isaac. *See* Isaac (Ike)
    McCaslin
McCullers, Carson, xviii, 127–28,
    140
    Work: *The Member of the Wedding*,
    xviii, 127–29, 140

192   **INDEX**

McDowell, Deborah E., 151
McIntyre, Mrs. *See* Mrs. McIntyre
McMillen, Neil R., 174n32
Mellard, James, 176n11, 176n13
Michaels, Walter Benn, 7–8
Michel, Frann, 28, 171n1
minstrelsy:
  blackface, x, xi–xii, xvii, 2–3, 4, 7,
    14–15, 17, 20, 25, 68, 83–84,
    86–88, 91, 97–100, 104, 110,
    145, 158
  whiteface, xi, xvi, 3, 6–7, 11, 15,
    17–18, 20–21, 26–27, 36–37,
    38, 40, 45, 49, 60–61, 69, 71,
    77, 91, 93, 96, 107, 113, 122,
    124, 140, 143, 145, 146, 151,
    153, 167–68. (*see also*, Pierrot)
miscegenation, 33, 54, 72, 86, 117,
    129, 151
  as figure, 14, 20, 69, 87, 153–54
Morgan, Joe. *See* Joe Morgan
Morgan, Renée. *See* Renée (Rennie)
  Morgan
Morrison, Toni, ix–xi, 2–5, 130, 133,
    138, 142, 158, 169n1, 175n3,
    175n5, 177n10
  Works: *The Bluest Eye*, 130, 133, 142;
    Playing in the Dark, 2, 169n2;
    Sula, 138
Moses, biblical, 53, 54, 56, 123–24,
    146, 151
  and Freud, 53–54, 146, 148–50,
    160, 163
  Hurston's character in *Moses, Man
    of the Mountain*, 146, 147,
    151–57, 160, 163
  Reed's character in *Mumbo Jumbo*,
    146, 159, 161–63, 167
Motes, Hazel. *See* Hazel (Haze)
  Motes
Mr. Head (O'Connor, "The Artificial
  Nigger"), xvii, 67, 75–79, 86
Mrs. McIntyre (O'Connor's "The
  Displaced Person"), 67–74

Mrs. Shortley (O'Connor's "The
  Displaced Person"), 67–69, 70–71
Mrs. Turpin (O'Connor's
  "Revelation"), 65, 68

Nabakov, Vladimir, 64
Nelson (O'Connor's "The Artificial
  Nigger"), 75–79
Nesbitt, Laurel, 73, 174n1, 176n9

O'Connor, Flannery, xvii, 1–2, 4, 5,
  7, 15, 16, 63–91, 93, 145, 168.
  Works: "The Artificial Nigger," xvii,
    4, 7, 67, 75–79; "The Displaced
    Person," 67–74; "Good Country
    People," 74; "Revelation,"
    65–66; *Wise Blood*, xvii, 67,
    79–91

Papa Lebas (Reed's *Mumbo Jumbo*),
  158–59, 161–62, 164, 167, 168
passing, xii, xv, xviii, 7, 80, 98, 121,
  145, 147
  and class, 11, 66
Penley, Constance, 131
Percy, Walker, 1
Perreault, Jeanne, 75, 175n7, 175n8
Pierrot, 19–22. *See also* minstrelsy
Polchin, James, 40, 43, 46, 172n13,
  172n16, 173n19
Polk, Noel, 172n12, 173n19,
  174n25, 174n27, 174n32
Popeye (Faulkner's *Sanctuary*), xv, 37,
  38–45, 46–47, 52
primitivism, 24–25, 34, 47, 63, 165
  and blackness, xv, 21, 31, 32, 35,
    36, 39, 42–43, 45–46, 85,
    87–88, 107, 164
  and homosexuality, 29–30, 32
Pryse, Marjorie, 93, 94
Pynchon, Thomas, 64, 158
  Work: *The Crying of Lot*, 49, 158

Quentin Compson (Faulkner's
  Absalom, Absalom!), 50

(Faulkner's *The Sound and the Fury*), xvi, 1, 17, 26, 37, 48–50, 51, 59, 96, 97

race, xi–xii, xiv, xvii, xviii, 1–8, 10, 25–26, 29–30, 39–40, 49, 65, 69, 75, 94, 107, 114–15, 125, 140, 149, 151
 and class, 11, 14, 77–79, 132
 as performance, 17, 21, 46, 95
 and sexuality, 95–96, 100 (*see also* minstrelsy)
Rado, Lisa, 171n1
Rebein, Robert, 169n2
Reed, Ishmael, xviii, xix, 145–46, 157–68.
 Work: *Mumbo Jumbo*, xviii, 145–46, 157–68
Renée (Rennie) Morgan (Barth's *The End of the Road*), 113, 117–18, 119–20, 121
Rock, Chris, ix
Rogin, Michael, 2–3, 172n5
Ross, Stephen M., 174n25

Sam Fathers (Faulkner's *Go Down, Moses*), 49, 52–53, 54, 55, 57
Sartre, Jean-Paul, 101–3, 111, 176n5, 177n6, 177n8, 177n11
Sarty Snopes. *See* Colonel Sartoris (Sarty) Snopes
Sartoris, Colonel. *See* Colonel Sartoris
Schaub, Thomas, 177n11
Sedgwick, Eve Kosofsky, 29, 58, 108
Sensibar, Judith, 19–20, 21, 171n3, 173n24
sexual inversion. *See* homosexuality
sexuality, nonheteronormative, 27, 36, 39, 42, 138, 141. *See also* homosexuality; lesbianism
Shortley, Mrs. *See* Mrs. Shortley
Snopes, Abner. *See* Abner Snopes
Snopes, Sarty. *See* Colonel Sartoris (Sarty) Snopes

Solace Layfield (O'Connor's *Wise Blood*), 83, 88–89
Solomon, William, 64, 176n2
Stokes, Mason, 5
Sundquist, Eric, xii, xv
Sutpen, Thomas. *See* Thomas Sutpen

Talliaferro, Ernest. *See* Ernest Talliaferro
Temple Drake (Faulkner's *Sanctuary*), 38–39, 40, 42–44, 45
Thomas Sutpen (Faulkner's *Absalom, Absalom!*), 10–11, 13
Thompson, Mark Christian, 178n5
Tobin, Patricia, 114, 177n7, 177n9, 177n10
Todd Andrews (Barth's *The Floating Opera*), xviii, 96–101, 103–12, 113–14, 119, 121, 122–23
Torgovnick, Marianna, 24–25
Towner, Theresa, 173n18, 174n26
Turpin, Mrs. *See* Mrs. Turpin
Twain, Mark, xi–xiv. Works: *Adventures of Huckleberry Finn*, xiii–xiv; *Pudd'nhead Wilson* xi–xiii

Watson, James G., 171n4, 172n10
Weinstein, Philip, 19, 50
white, poor, ix–x, xiii–xiv, 8–11, 12, 15, 27, 44, 65, 67, 73, 81, 129, 131–32, 139–40, 141–42
 as "artificial Negroes," xvii, 70–71, 75, 77–79, 88, 91, 140 (*see also* class)
whiteface. *See* minstrelsy
whiteness, xii–xviii, 2–11, 15–16, 17, 19, 23, 25–27, 30, 31, 36–37, 39, 44–46, 60–61, 64–67, 68–69, 71–91, 96, 98–99, 101, 107–12, 114–15, 122–24, 133, 135, 138, 142–43, 145–47, 153, 155, 161, 166–68
white "trash". *See* white, poor
Wiegman, Robyn, 170n5
Wiles, Mary M., 139

Williamson, Joel, 173n20
Wolfe, Thomas, 2
Wood, Ralph C., 170n4
Wright, Richard, 11, 15, 177n6

Work: "The Man Who Was Almost
    a Man," 11–12
Yerushalmi, Yosef Hayim, 148,
    178n3, 178n4